Respectable Folly

RESPECTABLE FOLLY

Millenarians
and the French
Revolution in
France and
England

✣

Clarke Garrett

The Johns Hopkins
University Press
BALTIMORE
& LONDON

This book has been brought
to publication with the
generous assistance of
the Andrew W. Mellon
Foundation.

The Johns Hopkins University Press, Baltimore, Maryland 21218
The Johns Hopkins University Press Ltd., London

Library of Congress Catalog Card Number 74-24378
ISBN 0-8018-1618-1

Library of Congress Cataloging in Publication data will be found on the last printed
page of this book.

To Peg

Contents

Preface

FOR OVER a decade, I had intended to make a study of millenarianism and the French Revolution. It was not until 1969-70, while serving as director of Dickinson College's Center for International Studies in Bologna, Italy, that I was able to launch the project in earnest and work in a number of European libraries and archives.

I am grateful to Dickinson for that opportunity and for several research grants. Earlier, a grant from Wake Forest University had enabled me to obtain pamphlets and the *Journal prophétique* on microfilm.

Following the year in Bologna, a fellowship from the National Endowment for the Humanities made possible a summer of research in London. A sabbatical year in Chicago (1970-71) was supported by grants from the Newberry Library and the Ford Foundation Humanities Fund of Dickinson College.

In a project as diffuse as this one, I have depended on friends and colleagues in a variety of fields for assistance. Among those at institutions other than the ones already mentioned, my thanks go to Louis Lekai, E. P. Thompson, Robert Kreiser, Stephen Marini, Natalie Z. Davis, and especially Elizabeth Eisenstein. While this study is only distantly related to my doctoral dissertation, I have received continued encouragement from my mentors at the University of Wisconsin, Henry Hill and George Mosse. Among my colleagues at Dickinson, the advice and criticism of George Allan, Daniel Bechtel, Michael Kline, Charles Sellers, Ralph and Martha Slotten, Stephen Weinberger, and Henry J. Young have been particularly valuable. Gladys Cashman typed the entire manuscript, with unfailing skill and good humor.

I am grateful to the staffs of several libraries, especially the Newberry Library and the Dickinson College Library. The Archives Nationales, the Bibliothèque de la ville de Lyon, and the Riksarkivet in Stockholm all kindly provided microfilm copies of manuscript materials in their possession. The University of Texas at Austin and Dr. Williams's Library in London gave me permission to quote from manuscripts in the Southcott Collection and the Walton Manuscripts, respectively. I wish to thank the editors of the *Journal of the History of Ideas* and the *Catholic Historical Review* for permission to reprint in revised form the substance of articles that first appeared in their journals.

All translations from the French, unless otherwise indicated, are my own. All quotations retain the capitalization of the original.

Yates and Ida Forbis have lived with Suzette Labrousse and her compeers almost since the book's inception. They have read and commented on most of it, to its great benefit. My deepest thanks go to my family—to my daughters, Amy, Susan, and Margaret, and above all to my wife, Peg—for making the whole process of research and writing a continually companionable and enjoyable one.

Respectable
Folly

Historians
and the
Millennium

THE historical phenomenon of millenarianism has been part of the human experience for several thousand years, but it is only within the last twenty that historians have come to regard millenarianism as worthy of detailed research and analysis. Along with anthropologists and sociologists, they have also become interested in the way in which millenarian movements, *"religious movements that expect imminent, total, ultimate, this-worldly collective salvation,"*[1] seem to recur in times of social and political crisis. They have agreed with the insights of Ernst Troeltsch, Karl Mannheim, and Max Weber that there is a connection between millenarian or messianic ideas and the existence of individuals and groups who find themselves or believe themselves to be "deprived." In the late 1950s, this line of argument was taken somewhat further by several Marxist anthropologists and historians, among them Peter Worsley, Vittorio Lanternari, and Eric Hobsbawm.[2] For them, millenarianism was a pre-political stage in the evolution of popular protest toward a modern, secular, revolutionary consciousness.

It is Eric Hobsbawm who has developed this thesis most fully. In *Primitive Rebels*, he examines three nineteenth-century proletarian movements: the Lazzaretti of Tuscany, the anarchists of Andalusia, and the Sicilian Fasci. While only the third, he admits, successfully made the transition from millenarian escapism to effective revolutionary action, he holds that "millenarians can . . . readily exchange

---

1. Yonina Talmon, "Millenarian Movements," *European Journal of Sociology* 7 (1966): 200. Talmon's italics.
2. Peter Worsely, *The Trumpet Shall Sound* (London: Maggibon & Kee, 1957); Vittorio Lanternari, *The Religions of the Oppressed: A Study of Modern Messianic Cults*, trans. Lisa Sergio (New York: Alfred A. Knopf, 1963); and Eric Hobsbawm, *Primitive Rebels: Studies in Archaic Forms of Social Movement in the 19th and 20th Centuries*, (reprint ed., New York: W. W. Norton & Co., 1965); and Keith Thomas, *Religion and the Decline of Magic* (New York: Charles Scribner's Sons, 1972), pp. 128–50, 389–432.

the primitive costume in which they dress their aspirations for the, modern costume of Socialist and Communist politics."[3] The vision of a new moral order, a world purified and freed from conflict and hatred, is essential to both millenarians and secular revolutionaries. The "essence" of millenarianism, in Hobsbawm's view, is "the hope of a complete and radical change in the world."[4] To the oppressed, the millennium represents the world of their dreams, in which all men live in harmony and in which there are neither masters nor slaves.

Like Engels and Kautsky before him, Hobsbawm sees the more extreme religious movements of the Reformation era essentially as movements of social protest. He is far more careful than his predecessors not to generalize beyond the evidence, but he does make the unexamined assumption that millenarianism was nothing but an attempt on the part of the working classes to articulate their discontent. In Hobsbawm's definition of "the typical old-fashioned millenarian movement," its principal characteristics were "total rejection of the present, evil world," coupled with "a fundamental vagueness about the actual way in which the new society will be brought about" and "a fairly standardized 'ideology' of the chiliastic type."[5] Thus millenarianism might have had importance as an agent for social consciousness and revolutionary action, but as a religious and intellectual phenomenon it was without historical significance or development.

Hobsbawm draws many of his historical analogies from the period of the English Revolution, when millenarian ideas were perhaps more widely disseminated than at any other time or in any other place. The character of English Puritan millenarianism has been a subject of considerable interest for historians, notably for Christopher Hill and his students at Oxford. In numerous books and articles, they have followed a line of interpretation similar to Hobsbawm's,[6] viewing millenarianism essentially as a manifestation of the class conflict that was at the core of the English Revolution and as an expression of the new social and political order that the popular classes envisioned.

This same approach has been followed recently in a more complex and subtle fashion by Henri Desroches and by E. P. Thompson. In a series of articles in the *Archives de sociologie religieuse* and in his book *The American Shakers*, Desroches agrees with Hobsbawm that the origins of Marxist revolutionism are to be found in the religious background of millenarianism and Christian communism.

---

3. Hobsbawm. *Primitive Rebels*, p. 64.   4. Ibid., p. 57.   5. Ibid., pp. 57–58.
6. Most recently, Christopher Hill, *Antichrist in Seventeenth-Century England* (London: Oxford University Press, 1971).

Desroches describes "a socio-religious chain" that stretched from the Reformation to Marx. Early socialists like Wilhelm Weitling and Moses Hess were also millenarians, and conversely, millenarians like the Shakers' Ann Lee expressed in their teachings the alienation and sense of exploitation that the Industrial Revolution had produced in the new factory proletariat of the English Midlands. Desroches sees in Luther's antagonist Thomas Münzer "possibly one of the key links between the mystical millenarianism of the Middle Ages and the social millenarianism that would later take root in nineteenth-century socialism."[7] The crucial transformation, in mid-century, came when socialists throughout Europe repudiated the traditions of millenarianism and biblical communism for a purely secular ideology.

In a rather different interpretation of the same historical development, E. P. Thompson, in *The Making of the English Working Class*, regards the millenarian movements of the English Industrial Revolution as a "chiliasm of despair," the product of the frustrations of the hopes for political and social revolution that the French Revolution had briefly awakened in England.[8] Like the Methodists, the millenarians represented an escape from the hard realities of proletarian existence. The "making" of the working class would come with the development of class consciousness and the evolution of the popular traditions of cooperation, unionization, and political action. Thompson agrees with Hobsbawm that millenarianism was a phenomenon of social protest and economic hardship. It *could* lead believers in the direction of revolutionary action, but it could also lead them to a passive acceptance of repression.

Thompson's interpretation has been continued more recently by Eric Hobsbawm and George Rudé in *Captain Swing*, an examination of popular disturbances in England in 1830–31. In police reports and other contemporary accounts, the authors catch "the millennial note of obscure poor men's discontent,"[9] but for them, as for Thompson, millenarianism was at best a symptom of oppression and a stage in historical and intellectual consciousness that the popular classes would transcend.

7. Henri Desroches, *The American Shakers: From Neo-Christianity to Presocialism*, ed. and trans. John K. Savacool (Amherst: University of Massachusetts Press, 1971), p. 61. See also Descroches, "Micromillénarismes et communautarisme utopique en Amérique du Nord du xviie au xixe siècle," *Archives de sociologie religieuse*, no. 4 (1957), pp. 57–92; and Desroches, "Messianismes et utopies: Note sur les origines du socialisme occidentale," *Archives de sociologie religieuse*, no. 8 (1959), pp. 31–46.
8. E. P. Thompson, *The Making of the English Working Class*, rev. ed. (Harmondsworth: Penguin Books, 1968), pp. 411–40.
9. Eric Hobsbawm and George Rudé, *Captain Swing* (New York: Pantheon Books, 1968), p. 84.

All of these historians, many of whom are associated with Oxford University and with the journal *Past and Present*, have contributed immensely to the historical understanding of millenarianism. They have placed the phenomenon within a social and political context, and they have suggested that millenarian movements are rationally comprehensible when examined within that context. They have also demonstrated the fruitfulness of a comparative approach not only within European history but also between European movements and those in Africa, America, and Melanesia.[10] There are certainly indications that members of millenarian movements share a sense of deprivation and frustration heightened by an awareness that they are living amidst profound social changes—changes that they interpret in millenarian terms. Finally, and perhaps most importantly, the "Marxist" mode of explication has emphasized the progressive, this-worldly, optimistic message which the doctrine of the second coming of a messiah or savior has contained for millenarian and messianic groups.

Two years before Eric Hobsbawm published *Primitive Rebels*, another Englishman, Norman Cohn, offered a very different interpretation of millenarianism in *The Pursuit of the Millennium*, surely one of the most influential historical works of the last twenty years. In it, Cohn has some hard words for what he regards as the distortions and simplifications of the Marxist interpretation of millenarianism. Hobsbawm's work mentions Cohn only in passing, but it is clearly intended as a rebuttal.

If we want to be dialectical about it, Norman Cohn offers a "sociopsychological" antithesis to the Marxists' socioeconomic thesis of the origins and development of millenarianism. Where Hobsbawm praises the "burning confidence in a new world" and the "generosity of emotion" that he believes characterized all millenarian movements,[11] Cohn finds them instead to consist of "disoriented and desperate" and "utterly ruthless" followers of fanatical prophets.[12] Leaders and followers alike "acted out with fierce energy a shared phantasy which, though delusional, yet brought them such intense emotional relief that they could live only through it, and were perfectly willing both to kill and to die for it."[13] Cohn emphasizes that he is studying only one kind of millenarianism, the kind that provided

10. Some very informative comparative studies are to be found in Sylvia L. Thrupp, ed., *Millennial Dreams in Action* (The Hague: Mouton & Co., 1962).
11. Hobsbawm, *Primitive Rebels*, p. 107.
12. Norman Cohn, *The Pursuit of the Millennium*, 3d rev. and expanded ed. (New York: Oxford University Press, 1970), pp. 88, 285–86.
13. Norman Cohn, "Réflexions sur le millénarisme," *Archives de sociologie religieuse*, no. 5 (1958), p. 106.

the rootless poor of Europe during the Middle Ages and the Reformation with a revolutionary ideology, but that this is, after all, the kind that the Marxists had been especially concerned to show had led those same poor in the direction of class consciousness and political revolutionism.

If the vision that shaped the Marxists' perception of popular millenarianism was the masses' coming to revolutionary consciousness, the memory that led Cohn to his approach was that of the Nazis' destruction of European Jewry. The Nazis (and the Marxists, Cohn implies in the recent third edition of his book) were the spiritual heirs of the crowds that burst forth in orgies of murder and destruction during the Crusades, the troubled period of the Black Death, and the Reformation.

There is no question that Cohn's thesis is a bold and startling one. *The Pursuit of the Millennium* is, moreover, an extremely well-written book, in which prodigious scholarship is woven into a powerful and flowing narrative. Cohn gives considerable attention to issues that have only recently received the attention they deserve as topics for historical analysis. For example, he examines both the psychological causation of mass movements and the process by which ideas and beliefs filter down into what he calls "the obscure underworld" of popular religion.[14] It is no wonder that Cohn's book has led a substantial number of scholars and their students to the study of millenarianism.

Certainly Cohn is right to insist that millenarianism must be understood as an ideology that has preserved over the centuries a central core of ideas and beliefs. If it has changed, that change has often been the result of the popularization and vulgarization of conceptions and doctrines first developed in the "high culture" of clerics and academics. Cohn is also right to emphasize the continuing adaptability and vitality of millenarianism. Far from being a transitional stage in man's intellectual development, it has persisted. However vulgarized or even bizarre its ideas might have become, it continues to survive, recurring in different forms and different places right up to the present day.

Despite the very real merits of *The Pursuit of the Millenium*, it has some serious flaws as a comprehensive historical explanation of the phenomenon of millenarianism. It provides, for example, little sense of historical development. Because of its failure to pay sufficient attention to the specific social and political contexts in which medieval millenarian movements grew and flourished, these move-

14. Cohn, *Pursuit of the Millennium*, p. 286.

ments all tend "to happen in a void without real recourse to time and place,"[15] as Gordon Leff complained in a review of the book's first edition. Cohn is also inclined to resort to rather simplistic theories of psychological causation. Millenarian movements are seen as a kind of paranoia; their leaders are often dismissed as insane or are called fanatics acting out Freudian "phantasies." Such statements fail to explain either millenarianism's persistence or its prominence in times of political and social crisis.

Within the past several years, there have appeared a number of studies of millenarian movements that adopt neither the Marxists' socioeconomic interpretation nor Cohn's sociopsychological one. Gordon Leff was led by his objections to Norman Cohn's thesis to trace the development of heresy in the later Middle Ages. He argues that millenarianism should be understood primarily as a protest movement, whose roots were doctrinal and devotional.[16] For example, the Spiritual Franciscans found the institutional church to be corrupt and increasingly out of sympathy with the currents of popular piety to which St. Francis had ministered so well. They therefore elevated the Franciscan ideal of poverty into an absolute principle that not even the Pope could contravene. They also adapted the heterodox, but not heretical, doctrines of Joachim of Fiore to their own situation by assigning to themselves an eschatological role in the prophetic Last Days before the Third Age of the Spirit, in which a perfected church would supersede the sinful one.

Both Howard Kaminsky's *History of the Hussite Revolution* and Donald Weinstein's *Savonarola and Florence* emphasize the ways in which millenarian doctrines developed out of specific contexts that included a religious tradition, a political situation, and social and psychological tensions.[17] Kaminsky specifically denies that the doctrines originated with "the poor," whom both Cohn and Czech Marxist historians make the catalysts of Hussite millenarianism.[18] Weinstein calls it "simplistic" to pretend that Savonarola's message

15. Gordon Leff, "In Search of the Millennium," *Past and Present*, no. 13 (1958), pp. 90, 91. Kenelm Burridge makes a similar criticism of Cohn, from an anthropologist's point of view, in *New Heaven, New Earth* (New York: Schocken Books, 1969), p. 12.
16. Gordon Leff, *Heresy in the Later Middle Ages*, 2 vols. (Manchester: Manchester University Press, 1967), 1: 1–7, 69–79.
17. Howard Kaminsky, *A History of the Hussite Revolution* (Berkeley: University of California Press, 1967), chap. 7 and pp. 287–89; Donald Weinstein, *Savonarola and Florence: Prophecy and Patriotism in the Renaissance* (Princeton: Princeton University Press, 1970), pp. 28–50.
18. Cf. Cohn, *Pursuit of the Millennium*, pp. 208–9; and Ernst Werner, "Popular Ideologies in Late Medieval Europe," *Comparative Studies in Society and History* 2 (1960): 344–63.

was listened to in practical and businesslike Florence solely because of the power of the monk's personality. On the contrary, Savonarola's conception of Florence as a city divinely appointed to lead in the spiritual regeneration of the world was deeply embedded within Florentine civic tradition and popular religion.[19]

William Lamont takes a similar approach in his study of millenarianism during the English Revolution. He rejects both the position of Christopher Hill and his students, for whom millenarian ideas derived from the socioeconomic tensions produced by emergent capitalism, and Norman Cohn's concentration on the extremism of millenarian movements. In his book *Godly Rule* and in two articles in *Past and Present*, Lamont holds instead that belief in the imminence of the millennium was both widespread and perfectly respectable theologically in the seventeenth century. He argues that part of millenarianism's attraction for people of all classes lay in its inconsistency. Even scholarly millenarians like Joseph Mede could hold at one and the same time "the pessimistic belief in an imminent doomsday, and the optimistic expectation of an earthly paradise."[20] The preachers who addressed Parliament in millenarian terms in the 1640s could in the same sermon call upon men to regenerate the world through their own efforts and upon Jesus to transform it through his miraculous intervention. What, Lamont asks, if the belief that they were living in the Last Days brought comfort rather than anxiety? "What if millenarianism meant not alienation from the spirit of the age but a total involvement with it?"[21] Then it would provide a kind of divine assurance in a time of revolutionary change.

John F. C. Harrison's recent study of Owenism, *Quest for the New Moral World*, shares Lamont's premise concerning the normalcy of millenarianism in English popular religion. E. P. Thompson has described the persistence of the traditions of Puritanism, including millenarianism, through the eighteenth century into the nineteenth, but he contends that it was transformed into a psychic escape from intolerable conditions in the early Industrial Revolution. Harrison notes instead the pervasiveness of millenarian ideas and rhetoric within the culture of nineteenth-century England. Since they were not restricted to any social class, the explanation for their wide appeal must lie not in their forming part of an emerging working class con-

---

19. Weinstein, *Savonarola and Florence*, pp. 33–36.
20. William Lamont, "Richard Baxter, the Apocalypse, and the Mad Major," *Past and Present*, no. 55 (1972), p. 70.
21. William Lamont, *Godly Rule: Politics and Religion, 1603–60* (New York: St. Martin's Press, 1969), p. 13; and Lamont, "Puritanism as History and Historiography: Some Further Thoughts," *Past and Present*, no. 44 (1969), pp. 133–46.

sciousness but rather in "the total impact of economic change and the consequent unheaval of social relationships" during the Industrial Revolution.[22]

Recently, both Robert Lerner and Natalie Z. Davis have expressed serious doubts concerning a cherished assumption both Marxist historians and Norman Cohn take for granted—that popular religious movements like millenarianism have a particular attraction for the poor and the oppressed. Having demonstrated that the medieval Heretics of the Free Spirit were not nearly so radical as Cohn and others have believed, Lerner holds that no generalizations concerning the social composition of the movement are possible. Furthermore, the beliefs held by the heretics were essentially mystical and ascetic; they were neither moral anarchists nor social revolutionaries.[23]

Although Natalie Davis was not writing about millenarianism but rather about what she calls the "rites of violence" in sixteenth-century France, her approach and her conclusions are strikingly similar to those of such historians of millenarianism as Kaminsky and Lamont. Religious violence was connected "less to the pathological than to the normal." And, at least in the cities, it was not the vengeance of the poor against the rich. The riots make sense when they are seen as arising out of a complex of traditional actions and beliefs, "derived from the Bible, from liturgy, from the action of political authority, or from the traditions of popular folk justice, intended to purify the religious community and humiliate the enemy and thus make him less harmful."[24]

One scholar who has attempted to bring together a variety of historical and anthropological studies of millenarianism in a sort of synthesis is the sociologist Yonina Talmon.[25] In a series of articles, she describes what can be called the "Cohn" and the "Marxist" schools and then develops a sort of middle ground. She notes the important role played in millenarian movements by "members of a frustrated secondary elite" of priests, intellectuals, and petty officials. Her conclusions complement in an interesting fashion those of Natalie Davis: in all cases, Talmon contends, the emphasis should be

22. John F. C. Harrison, *Quest for the New Moral World: Robert Owen and the Owenites in Britain and America* (New York: Charles Scribner's Sons, 1969), p. 138.
23. Robert E. Lerner, *The Heresy of the Free Spirit in the Later Middle Ages* (Berkeley: University of California Press, 1972), pp. 236–41.
24. Natalie Zemon Davis, "The Rites of Violence: Religious Riot in Sixteenth-Century France," *Past and Present*, no. 59 (1973), pp. 81–82, 90.
25. *International Encyclopedia of the Social Sciences*, s.v. "Millenarism," by Yonina Talmon; and Talmon, "Pursuit of the Millennium: The Relation between Religion and Social Change," *European Journal of Sociology* 3 (1962): 125–48.

placed less on the poor and the oppressed than on the groups and the individuals who, for whatever reasons, see themselves as isolated from society and frustrated in their desire for power and influence within society. She warns against the sort of "reductionism" that makes millenarianism a simple response to economic and social conditions, for her comparative research indicates "the potency and partial independence of the religious factor."[26]

A crucial case demonstrating the "inadequacy" of the reductionist interpretations, according to Talmon, is the Jewish millenarian movement of the seventeenth and eighteenth centuries called Sabbateanism. Historians (including Norman Cohn) have long assumed that the widespread acceptance of the Levantine Jew Sabbatai Zevi as the Messiah among European Jews was the direct result of the terrible pogroms in Poland in 1648-49. Yet Gershon Scholem and Jacob Katz have shown that Sabbatean millenarianism was just as extensive among Jews in countries like Turkey, Italy, and Holland, which were unaffected by the pogroms, as it was in Poland. Sabbatai Zevi's appearance, Katz has written, produced "a spontaneous awakening of forces latent in traditional society at all times—that is, the longing for redemption."[27] Scholem argues that the same kind of mystical undercurrent that flowed through the eighteenth-century Enlightenment was present in Judaism. Sabbateanism's origins should be sought not in the pogroms but rather in the cabalistic tradition and in Lurianic mysticism. The appearance of Sabbatai Zevi transformed the tradition, but his messianic pretensions were still interpreted within the context of the cabalistic and mystical tradition.

Despite harassment by the Christian and Moslem governments and the hostility of the rest of the Jewish community and despite their messiah's apostasy and conversion to Islam, the Sabbateans persisted. Sometimes openly as a Jewish sect, sometimes clandestinely as a kind of mystical brotherhood, they survived until the nineteenth century. The explanation for the survival of Sabbateanism, Scholem argues, is to be found in its capacity to adapt itself to changing conditions while retaining its roots in Jewish mysticism, in the perennial human striving for answers to ultimate questions, and in the recurring dream of social regeneration.

26. Talmon, "Millenarian Movements," p. 190.
27. Jacob Katz, *Tradition and Crisis: Jewish Society at the End of the Middle Ages* (Glencoe, Ill.: Free Press, 1961), p. 215. See also Gershon Scholem, *Major Trends in Jewish Mysticism* (New York: Schocken Books, 1946), p. 301; and Scholem, "Le mouvement sabbataïste en Pologne," *Revue de l'histoire des religions* 143 (1953): 30-90, 209-39.

In Christianity, the equivalent to the messianic tradition within Judaism is the collection of ideas and beliefs associated with the name of the twelfth-century Calabrian abbot Joachim of Fiore. Gordon Leff has given considerable attention to the Joachimist tradition in *Heresy in the Later Middle Ages*, and more recently, Marjorie Reeves has traced Joachimism's persistence through the medieval period and into the sixteenth and seventeenth centuries. During that time, many of Joachim's own ideas were distorted beyond recognition, but what Reeves calls "the essence of the Joachimist view" survived: the belief that the church's greatest persecution must come before the Third Age, the biblical millennium, can take place. And that Third Age is to be above all a time of spiritual blessedness: "*renovatio* on a spiritual level after the most testing battle with evil, yet within history."[28] What persisted was a mood rather than specific doctrines—a mood of optimism, a persistent belief that present sufferings and anxieties would be transcended and the total regeneration of the world accomplished. It is the same apparently contradictory faith both in divine intervention and in human agency that William Lamont finds in seventeenth-century Puritanism, the same sense of inevitable human progress that Ernest Tuveson identifies as new in that same era.[29] However, spiritual Franciscans, Beguines, Jesuits, and a variety of monastic orders, prophets, and heretical sects had all seen themselves as the agents called by God to inaugurate the Third Age of the Spirit long before the Puritans did so. They all preached the reform of the church, the conversion of the Jews and the infidels, and the union of all men into a single body of the faithful: "one flock and one shepherd." For Reeves, this tradition was far more significant historically than the sporadic outbreaks of "left wing" millenarian enthusiasm. In a period of dramatic change such as the Italian Renaissance, for example, "foreboding and great hope lived side by side in the same people. . . . The Joachimist marriage of woe and exaltation exactly fitted the mood of late fifteenth-century Italy, where the concept of a humanist Age of Gold had to be brought into relation with the ingrained expectation of Antichrist."[30]

28. Marjorie Reeves, "Joachimist Influences on the Idea of a Last World Emperor," *Tradition* 17 (1961): 324–25.
29. Marjorie Reeves, *The Influence of Prophecy in the Later Middle Ages: A Study in Joachimism* (Oxford: Clarendon Press, 1969), p. 502. Cf. Ernest Tuveson, *Millennium and Utopia: A Study in the Background of the Idea of Progress* (Berkeley: University of California Press, 1949), p. 28.
30. Reeves, *Influence of Prophecy*, p. 431. See also Weinstein, *Savonarola and Florence*, p. 175.

Three centuries later, in the era of the French Revolution, the memory of Joachim and his teachings was even more indistinct than it had been in the fifteenth century. Yet it is a fact that the Revolution excited millenarian expectations in France and elsewhere, and it is also clear that these expectations were often expressed in forms and phraseologies that resembled those in the prophetic literature of Joachimism. In a few instances, the mingled hope and fear produced by the Revolutionary experience led to the emergence of prophets who declared that the promised era of spiritual regeneration was at hand. It does not matter whether French Revolutionary prophets were aware of Joachim of Fiore; quite probably they were not. What is important is to understand that they represented attitudes and convictions that were centuries old and that they were led to millenarian doctrines because they saw the French Revolution in the context of their own piety.

Millenarianism and the French Revolution is a largely unexplored area for historians, and this study is only a beginning of what needs to be done. Since the Revolution produced no sizable millenarian movement but instead a varied assortment of individuals who interpreted contemporary political events in eschatological terms, I have concentrated my attention on the three figures whose careers seem most to resemble those of the prophets of medieval tradition: two Frenchwomen, Suzette Labrousse and Catherine Théot, and one Englishman, Richard Brothers. Each produced a substantial body of primary material that permits the examination of his or her millenarian ideas as well as the ways in which the French Revolution influenced those ideas. For Richard Brothers, there are his own copious writings plus a number of testimonies written by his followers. For Suzette Labrousse, there is in addition to her own writings a newspaper, the *Journal prophétique*, edited by her chief disciple and dedicated to publicizing her revelations. As for Catherine Théot, the Archives Nationales contains her police dossier, and the dossiers of many of her followers, her sermons in manuscript, and a statement of her beliefs. I have thus been spared a problem that besets many students of obscure religious movements: overdependence on second-hand and often hostile information.

Since one of the central controversies between scholars concerns the social composition of millenarian movements, I should explain why I have not attempted to resolve the issue in this study. In the first place, the same sources that make possible remarkably full descriptions of the ideas of the millenarians and their responses to the events of the Revolution offer relatively few indications of the segments of society from which the millenarians drew their followers. There is one exception: the police records concerning the sect of Catherine Théot contain what appears to be a fairly complete list of her followers; but the group was too small, too diverse, and too emphemeral to justify any meaningful generalizations. In the cases of Labrousse and Brothers, their influence may have been more extensive, but those who believed their prophecies never constituted sects or even coherent bodies of followers. The importance of each rests primarily in the roles he or she played in shaping public opinion during periods in which revolutionary excitement was especially intense. The millenarians I have selected—the three prophets and the millenarian Masons of the Avignon Society, the Convulsionaries of the Lyonnais, and the English Dissenters who interpreted the Revolution apocalyptically—should not be seen as representatives of mass movements or sects-in-the-making but rather as exponents of a theme that is but a single strand in a complex fabric of ideas and attitudes within the popular culture of the revolutionary period.

The decision to narrate what were in most cases careers on the periphery of history had a further justification. Like William Lamont's study of millenarianism among seventeenth-century Puritans or John Harrison's of the Owenites, this study traces the ways in which the millenarian theme was modified and in some cases transformed by events. One secret of the survival of millenarianism for so many centuries has been its ability to adapt its message to changing circumstances and to provide what for believers is a concrete and rational explanation of events in periods of deep social and political crisis. By adopting an essentially biographical approach, I have attempted to demonstrate this adaptability by showing how millenarians were affected by the events that they in turn sought to interpret eschatologically.

I have limited this study to France and England. A full examination of millenarianism in the period would range far more widely, to include central and eastern Europe, Scandinavia, Latin America, and the United States. Since this is an essay in comparative history, a dual study of two cultures that shared certain features promised to uncover more fruitful contrasts and trends than would a more comprehensive survey.

The reasons for focusing upon France should be obvious, but why England? In the first place, cultural interpenetration between France and England in the eighteenth century was both extensive and continuous. In England, the presence of a large reading public and the absence of censorship meant that the French Revolution could have an immediate and profound impact. Since, thanks largely to the Puritan heritage, millenarian ideas enjoyed an exceptional degree of publicity and acceptance, the periodicals, newspapers, sermons, and pamphlets of the revolutionary era offered an unusually promising field for tracing the effects of the Revolution on millenarian thinking. That England's millenarian tradition was Protestant and narrowly scriptural in origin meant that it could fruitfully be compared with the more diffuse Catholic one of France.

I have interpreted millenarianism in the French Revolution as comprising a diverse body of ideas and attitudes. In addition to the prophetic pronouncements of Daniel and of St. John the Divine and the shadowy heritage of Joachim of Fiore, this millenarianism drew equally upon ancient beliefs found in mysticism and popular piety, the doctrines of spiritual regeneration contained in mesmerism, thaumaturgy, and occultism, and the new political consciousness that was a product of the Revolution itself.

Millenarian beliefs, thus broadly defined, were part of many people's "intellectual furniture" in both France and England. Faced with an event of the magnitude of the French Revolution, men and women found in the prophetic books of the Bible and in the literature of popular religion a kind of explanation of what was happening to them. If the Revolution was God's will, if its development had been foretold, then surely, they told themselves, the final outcome would be good, at least for the faithful. Political events became eschatological events, and dangers and misfortunes became simply the chastisements a fallen world must undergo before it could be regenerated at the Second Coming of Jesus Christ. The phrases and the concepts were entirely traditional, even when the actors assigned themselves roles of cosmic significance within the Revolution itself. To dismiss them as insane or to call them fanatics acting out Freudian fantasies is to fail to explain them fully. On the other hand, to see these millenarians as "prepolitical" harbingers of class warfare is to wrench them out of their own time and to distort their teachings. It should not be forgotten, furthermore, that one secret of the survival of millenarian doctrines has been their ability to serve as a comforting explanation of events and conditions that would otherwise be threatening and incomprehensible.

There was considerable variety in the "respectable folly" of French Revolutionary millenarians. Suzette Labrousse, the so-called Prophetess of Périgord, was the millenarian most directly involved in the events of the Revolution. The great act of her life was her 1792 pilgrimage to Rome to convert the Pope to acceptance of her revelation that the Revolution was the agency for God's introduction of an age of spiritual regeneration. Her mental world, as revealed in her extant writings, was one in which mystical piety, eighteenth-century popular culture, and the political realities of the era were all muddled together in a fascinating, if bewildering, fashion.

Catherine Théot was never so directly involved in political developments as Labrousse, and her ideas were both more vague and more bizarre. Yet, once again, a knowledge of the traditions of popular piety within Catholic culture leads one to the conclusion that she too should be understood within that context. Many of Théot's followers came to hear her in hopes of receiving divine assurance in the tense and anxious days of 1794, a time of dictatorship, hardship, and fear of invasion. Her message was one of comfort. France would triumph, the age of the spirit would begin, and the faithful would never die.

The third and last group of millenarians in Revolutionary France that is examined in detail belonged to the Avignon Society, an international body of mystical Freemasons dedicated to propagating the message that the reign of Jesus Christ would soon begin. Like Labrousse and Théot, they were millenarians before the Revolution began, but it was that cataclysm which gave their mission a special urgency. Although they never seem to have numbered more than a hundred, they were remarkably zealous in speading millenarian ideas. Members of the society can be found among the disciples of Labrousse, Théot, and also the English prophet, Richard Brothers. While many of their activities are obscure, they seem to have been influential among mystically inclined circles of the upper classes in most of the capitals of Europe. Their millenarianism represents an amalgamation of ideas derived from a variety of traditions, including cabalism, alchemy, Freemasonry, and Joachimism.

In England, the events of the French Revolution were given eschatological significance through interpretative terms and concepts very similar to the biblicism and prophetism of seventeenth-century Puritanism. The war with France deeply divided English opinion between 1792 and 1795, and one manifestation of the rift was the extensive public controversy over the French Revolution's significance within God's providential plan. The most surprising product of the crisis was the brief but very extensive interest in the prophetic pretensions of Richard Brothers. In 1795 he announced that London would be destroyed by an earthquake, after which the restoration of the Jews to the Holy Land would occur. England was specially called to make that event possible; and he, the Revealed Prince of the Hebrews, would soon lead all the Jews, including those "hidden" within the population of England, to Palestine in order to await the coming of Jesus Christ. Brothers probably *was* mad, but this should not obscure the fact that his followers were not. Those who wrote in defense of Brothers's claims reflected the same mingling of the traditions of popular piety and political awareness produced by the French Revolution as the equally respectable followers of Suzette Labrousse. It is certainly clear that the terrible economic hardship of 1794 and 1795 contributed to Brothers's success, but whether he attracted a significant proportion of attention among the English poor cannot be determined.

The activities of the Avignon Society reveal how the currents of mysticism and occultism within the world of Freemasonry contributed to the dissemination of millenarian ideas. In England, millenarianism enjoyed a continued acceptability within educated circles through its association with a long line of distinguished scholars, including Joseph Mede, Henry More, Isaac Newton, and Joseph Priestley. It is with Priestley that the tradition confronted the French Revolution; in his published writings and his letters, we see especially clearly the ways in which revolutionary political consciousness could be expressed in the traditional imagery of millenarian religion.

I have resisted the temptation to look for secret or unconscious millenarians among the principal actors in the French Revolution. I have preferred instead to concentrate on those who fit the most precise definition of millenarianism and who were led by religious conviction and enthusiasm for the French Revolution to believe that the Second Coming of Jesus Christ would arrive suddenly, miraculously, and soon. Like many of the Puritan millenarians of the seventeenth century, the religious convictions of the French Revolutionary millenarians enabled them to comprehend and to involve themselves in events that they found both exhilarating and ominous.

CHAPTER 1

Millenarian Currents in Eighteenth-Century France

IN 1789 AND 1790, it was widely believed in France that religion and revolution would triumph together. Since the two diverged so sharply afterwards, this is a dimension of the great Revolution that is often forgotten. The convocation of the Estates General, the fall of the Bastille, the abolition of "feudalism" on 4 August were all viewed as God's blessings on his beloved France. Religious rituals accompanied all the great events of the early Revolution—a Te Deum was sung in thanks for the end of feudalism, priests blessed the tricolor flags of the National Guards, and the climax of the Festival of the Federation on 14 July 1790 was the simultaneous celebration of the Mass in churches from one end of France to the other.

When the fall of the Bastille forced Louis XVI to reinstate Jacques Necker as his chief minister, one pamphlet announced that "the Savior of the Republic, the Messiah of France, has returned." The French would now become "the first People of the world." The deputies in the Estates General, now renamed the National Assembly, would "consummate the revolution; and the constitution sealed by the blood of the Citizens [would] assure happiness and liberty."[1] That the return of Necker, the Swiss banker whose most memorable achievement was the siring of Mme. de Staël, should have inspired such effusions may seem strange, but in the context of 1789, it was not exceptional. Albert Mathiez noted sixty years ago that it was "the messianic expectation of regeneration" that inspired the bright hopes of 1789, together with "profound belief in undefined progress, the imminent vision of an age of gold placed in the future and no longer in the past."[2]

1. *A l'heureuse arrivée de M. Necker* (Paris, [1789]), pp. 3–4.
2. Albert Mathiez, *Contributions à l'histoire religieuse de la Révolution française* (Paris: Alcan, 1907), p. 32.

Songs composed by anonymous poets in 1789 announced that "the centuries of gold are going to reappear" and that "at last we are delivered from evils . . . and the good times are already returning—Alleluia."[3] God in his wisdom had brought about the Revolution of 1789, and Louis XVI and Necker were agents of the divine plan. The Revolution was not merely political; it would be the foundation of man's moral and religious regeneration. "Morality, so corrupted in our day, will complete the revolution,"[4] the pamphlet in honor of Necker's return predicted.

Prayers, catechisms, even the Bible were adapted to the mood and the events of the day. In 1788, a collection of prayers included appropriate versions of both the *Ave Maria*—"Mother of our Dauphin, pray for us poor oppressed, now and in the Estates General"—and the Pater Noster—"Our father who is at Versailles, may your name be glorified, your reign be eternal, your will be done in the Provinces as in Paris."[5] A "Magnificat of the Third Estate" praised God by declaring that "Our soul magnifies the Savior of Nations."[6] A pamphlet described "the Passion, the Death, and the Resurrection of the People." As the "plebeian" died on the cross, he cried out, "O my King, O my King, why have you forsaken me?"[7]

The plebeian's cry was the other side of "the spirit of revolution in 1789." In those unsettled times, optimism alternated with anxiety, and confidence in the leadership was often undermined by distrust of those same leaders. There was a tendency to see all issues in blacks and whites. As the National Assembly declared in February 1790, the Revolution was "perhaps the first conflict that has ever been fought by every right principle against every form of error."[8] If right principles should triumph, then, as the future bishop Claude Fauchet wrote in 1789, France would become "the model of nations, and the establisher of true liberty in the universe."[9] Fauchet shared with many of his countrymen the assumption that France was specially blessed—an attitude that was perhaps as old as France. Not long before the Revolution, one English traveler noted: "They have a tradition among

3. Quoted in Cornwell B. Rogers, *The Spirit of Revolution in 1789: A Study of Public Opinion as Revealed in Political Songs and Other Popular Literature at the Beginning of the French Revolution* (Princeton: Princeton University Press, 1949), pp. 78-79; and *A l'usage du temps* (n.p., n.d.), p. 4.
4. *A l'heureuse arrivée de M. Necker*, p. 6.
5. *Prières journalières du Tiers-Etat* (n.p., 1788), p. 2.
6. *Magnificat du Tiers Etat* (n.p., [1788]), p. 4.
7. *La passion, la mort, et la résurrection du peuple* (Jerusalem [Paris], 1789), p. 20; *Gazette de Leyde*, 31 March 1789, supp.
8. Quoted in Rogers, *Spirit of Revolution in 1789*, p. 247.
9. Quoted in ibid., p. 256.

the meaner people that when Christ was crucified, he turned his head towards France, over which he pronounced his last blessing."[10]

It would not be an exaggeration to say that there was a millenarian tone to much that was said and done in 1789, but such a statement must not be given undue significance. There is always the possibility that revolutionary rhetoric was nothing more than that. It is also important to recognize that many Catholics who had initially seen the Revolution as a means to the spiritual regeneration of France had moved into opposition to it by 1790, in disillusionment at the more narrowly secular course it was taking. Pro-Revolutionary sentiment did persist among the devout, but it tended either to abandon the heady visions of 1789 or else to express them within the confines of small circles of believers, such as the millenarians of the Lyonnais or the Parisian sect of Catherine Théot, in which the popular traditions of prophecy and mystical piety survived.

There were a variety of doctrines and ideas flourishing in eighteenth-century France that were clearly millenarian in tendency. None of the manifestations discussed in this chapter fed directly into French Revolutionary millenarianism, nor do they seem to have been transformed by the events of the Revolution. They deserve our attention nonetheless, because their existence does demonstrate the presence of a millenarian sensibility in the decades before the Revolution.

There was, in the first place, a widespread fascination with the miraculous. Robert Mandrou and Geneviève Bollème have found that of the popular literature circulated throughout the countryside by illicit peddlers, a quarter dealt with religious topics. Along with lives of saints, catechisms, devotional tracts, and Bible stories, there was a marked and increasing "taste for the marvelous."[11] This interest extended beyond conventional religion to include astrology, dreams, and the extensive literature of popular prophecies. Nor was interest in the marvelous and the occult limited to the uneducated. Auguste Viatte and Robert Darnton have shown the presence of a similar trend among intellectuals, a trend which increased in intensity

---

10. Hester Thrale Piozzi, *Observations and Reflections Made in the Course of a Journey through France, Italy, and Germany* (1789; reprint ed., Ann Arbor: University of Michigan Press, 1967), p. 16.
11. Robert Mandrou, *De la culture populaire aux 17e et 18e siècles: La Bibliothèque bleue de Troyes* (Paris: Stock, Delamaire & Boutelleaux, 1964), pp. 77, 86-87; Geneviève Bollème, "Littérature populaire et littérature de colportage au 18e siècle," in *Livre et société*, 2 vols. (Paris: Mouton & Co., 1965), 1: 61-92. See also Jeffrey Kaplow, *The Names of Kings: The Parisian Laboring Poor in the Eighteenth Century* (New York: Basic Books, 1972), chap. 5.

during the 1780s.[12] In 1784, the Paris correspondent for the *Journal de Bruxelles* commented on the presence of many "hermetic, cabalistic, and theosophic philosophers, propagating fanatically all the old absurdities of theurgy, of divination, of astrology, etc."[13] Dr. Mesmer's new science also attracted much attention. For some, it seemed to hold the key to solving the secrets of nature. And since mesmerism treated not only the body but also the moral constitution, its application, one of its leading theorists declared, "promised the ultimate moral regeneration of the nation."[14] Because mesmerism seemed to offer tangible evidence of the presence of supernatural forces, it was seen by some as offering the same kind of confirmation of the working of divine providence in the world that many eighteenth-century theologians sought in miracles and in the fulfillment of Scriptural prophecy. To some of its adepts, it was "the demonstrated presence of God."[15]

A similar tendency in Freemasonry characterized the last decades of the century. There was great interest among some masons in varieties of mysticism that were sometimes esoteric and sometimes Catholic. Aided by cabalism, astrology, prophetic lore, and the trances of mesmerized mediums, lodges throughout France prepared for what they believed was an approaching age of spiritual revelation and worldwide unity, perhaps in the near future.[16]

The mood was not always so hopeful. In 1777 the appearance of sunspots led to rumors that they were signs foretelling the end of the world, and unusual and severe weather in the 1780s awakened fears that terrible changes were in store for mankind. The years before the Revolution saw the appearance of a number of novels on the theme of the end of the world, notably those of Grainville and Mercier.[17] Their publication is at least one more indication of a sensibility of mingled anxiety and hope, of a growing belief that either doom or salvation was just around the corner.

None of these trends fits the precise definition of millenarianism. A sense of doom or a belief that great cosmic changes are impending does not necessarily lead to a belief in the Second Coming of Jesus

12. Auguste Viatte, *Les sources occultes du romantisme: Illuminisme-théosophie, 1770-1820,* 2 vols. (1928; reprint ed., Paris: Champion, 1969), 1; Robert Darnton, *Mesmerism and the End of the Enlightenment in France* (Cambridge: Harvard University Press, 1968).
13. Quoted in Darnton, *Mesmerism and the End of the Enlightenment in France,* p. 33.
14. Nicholas Bergasse, quoted in ibid., p. 120.
15. Quoted in ibid., p. 115.
16. See Chap. 5 below.
17. Kaplow, *Names of Kings,* p. 119; Henry Majewski, "Grainville's *Le Dernier Homme,*" *Symposium* [Bruges] 17 (1963): 114-22.

Christ, nor is a mesmerist millennium the same as the Thousand Year Kingdom promised in the book of Revelation. Because Roman Catholic theology continued to follow St. Augustine's doctrine that biblical prophecies should be understood spiritually and not literally, millenarianism in France never enjoyed the kind of informal acceptance it gained in protestant England, where pamphlets, sermons, treatises, and tracts on millenarian themes circulated freely during the eighteenth century. Nevertheless, there were Catholics in France who were millenarians.

Jansenism in the eighteenth century was no longer the force it had been in the days of Port Royal. Harassed by crown and church, its theology condemned by the Pope in the bull *Unigenitus*, it had dissolved into a number of divergent movements.[18] The most notorious were the Convulsionaries, whose pentecostal ecstasies appalled orthodox Jansenists. The Convulsionaries sounded like the spiritual Franciscans of the thirteenth century in assigning to themselves the role of divine agent for the redemption of a sinful world. In their description of the Last Days, however, the Convulsionaries were often more apocalyptical than millenarian. All the emphasis was placed upon God's wrath and the doom that awaited those who rejected their theology.

There had been a millenarian strain in Jansenism before the appearance of the Convulsionaries. In the eighteenth century, there were cells of Jansenists scattered throughout France, generally sympathetic to the "work" of the Convulsionaries but not necessarily associated with them, who met to study biblical prophecy and to pray for the Second Coming. In the decades before the Revolution, they were especially numerous in Paris, Grenoble, Toulouse, Bordeaux, and above all in Lyons. In some cases they disbanded during the Revolution, but they reappeared afterwards.

Some of the same ideas as those expressed during the Revolution by Suzette Labrousse and Catherine Théot and their followers had been advanced earlier by these millenarians. In many cases, the ideas derived from traditions in popular piety that were many centuries old, some of which echo the heritage of Joachimism. Many persons believed, for example, that France was called to perform a divinely appointed mission that would culminate in the reunion of

18. Robert R. Palmer, *Catholics and Unbelievers in Eighteenth-Century France* (1939; reprint ed., New York: Cooper Square, 1961), pp. 24-29; G. R. Cragg, *The Church in an Age of Reason, 1648-1789* (Harmondsworth: Penguin Books, 1960), pp. 193-99; and Bernard Plongeron, "Une image de l'Eglise d'après les 'Nouvelles Ecclésiastiques' (1728-1790)," *Revue d'histoire de l'Eglise de France* 53 (1967): 241-68.

the world in a single purified church. They believed that the Roman
Catholic church must first endure a time of great tribulation and
that this time would coincide with the conversion of the Jews to the
Christian faith and the Jews' restoration to their homeland. They
also expected the coming of Christ to be preceded by the coming of
a heavenly messenger. The Jansenist millenarians awaited the
prophet Elias, or Elijah, who had not died but had been translated to
heaven at the end of his first earthly ministry.[19]

The millenarian strain in eighteenth-century Jansenism was
given more explicit expression in the writings of Jacques-Joseph
Duguet, who died in 1733. He was a millenarian, but he did not expect the Second Coming until the year 2000. He taught that nothing
but the Second Coming could accomplish the spiritual regeneration
of the world. Many developments, all of them prefigured in the Old
Testament, must take place first. The most important of these would
be the conversion of the Jews and their restoration to their homeland, events that many Jansenists after Duguet believed to be imminent. Duguet rejected the contention of orthodox Catholic theology that biblical prophecies concerning the future blessedness of
the Jews referred in fact to the Christians, the new chosen people.
Since they believed that the Roman Catholic church had degener-
ated to a point where it could not possibly be the divine instrument,
Duguet and those who accepted his doctrines looked elsewhere—to
themselves and to the Jews.[20]

During the period when Duguet was developing a doctrine of the
restoration of the Jews, the Huguenot preacher Pierre Jurieu was
advancing similar ideas, with the significant difference that whereas
Duguet placed the millennium in the distant future, Jurieu taught
that it was at hand.[21] Jurieu also believed that after the Jews returned
to the Holy Land, all mankind would be incorporated into a new
Israel. The influence of Jurieu's ideas outside France was considerable. Missionaries spread them in Germany, the Netherlands, and
central Europe. In England, the arrival of the French Huguenot

19. Paul Vulliaud, *La fin du monde* (Paris: Payot, 1952), pp. 147–49; Joseph Lémann,
L'entrée des israélites dans la société française (Paris: Lecoffre, 1886), pp. 276–77;
Felix Vaucher, *Lacunziana: Essais sur les prophéties bibliques*, 2 vols. (Collonges-
sous-Salève: Fides, 1949–55), 2: 67–68.
20. Vulliaud, *Fin du monde*, pp. 159–61; Arthur Hertzberg, *The French Enlighten-
ment and the Jews* (New York: Columbia University Press, 1968), pp. 258–60.
21. Vulliaud, *Fin du monde*, pp. 151–56; Serge Hutin, *Les disciples anglais de Jacob
Boehme aux XVIIe et XVIIIe siècles* (Paris: Denoël, 1960), pp. 92–94; and D. P.
Walker, *The Decline of Hell: Seventeenth-Century Discussions of Eternal Torment*
(Chicago: University of Chicago Press, 1964), pp. 253–56. See also Chap. 7 below.

Prophets had a lasting effect on the development of English millenarianism. However, in France, Jurieu's influence, if it did persist, did so entirely beneath the surface after 1720.[22] On the other hand, while Duguet's views met with continued opposition, the "neo-Jansenism" associated with his name continued to find acceptance well into the nineteenth century.

Even those who disagreed with Duguet's conclusions accepted many of his premises. Rondet, writing in 1776, objected to the recurrent attempts made by Duguet's successors to calculate the date when the millennium would commence. He held that time to be unknowable, but he added that it would probably occur in the middle of the next century. The conversion of the Jews would come then and not before. Rondet also shared Duguet's view that the present was a time when God's hand was very evident: "Our century is memorable for the plagues of all kinds with which humanity has been afflicted; even now, since the middle of this century, our public papers are filled with revolutions in nature, with disasters, with calamities, and with misfortunes, etc. . . ."[23]

Jansenism survived in part because it offered a protest against the values of eighteenth-century society and against the worldliness and complacency that characterized the church in France. Jansenists continued to be harassed and sporadically persecuted by the crown and by the Catholic hierarchy, but they were nevertheless able to disseminate their views quite freely. Some of them continued the work of Duguet, focusing particular attention on the conversion of the Jews and their return to the Holy Land and on the new Jerusalem, which would be the "metropolis of all peoples,"[24] its temple the center of a worldwide church.

The most comprehensive study of Jansenist millenarianism was written after the Revolution by Henri-Baptiste Grégoire, the Lorraine priest whose career as deputy to the National Assembly and Convention and as bishop of the department of Loire-et-Cher made him by far the most eminent cleric who dedicated himself to the Revolution. Grégoire is generally considered to have been a Jansenist himself, but in recent years historians have seen him instead

22. For the reasons for the decline of millenarianism in one Huguenot village, see Patrice L.-R. Higonnet, *Pont-de-Montvert: Social Structure and Politics in a French Village, 1700–1914* (Cambridge: Harvard University Press, 1971), pp. 75–78.
23. Quoted in Vulliaud, *Fin du monde*, p. 168. See also Hertzberg, *The French Enlightenment and the Jews*, pp. 260–62; and Felix Vaucher, *Une célébrité oubliée: Le P. Manuel de Lacunza y Díaz*, new ed. (Collonges-sous-Salève: Fides, 1968), p. 75.
24. Henri-Baptiste Grégoire, *Histoire des sectes religieuses*, new ed., 6 vols. (Paris: Baudouin, 1828–45), 2: 355.

as a theological independent who was warmly sympathetic to some Jansenist ideas.[25] He never declared himself a millenarian, but the tone of the discussion in his *Histoire des sectes religieuses* reveals considerable admiration for them. Both his letters and his memoirs indicate that he was studying doctrines of the millennium on the eve of the Revolution, and the emancipation and conversion of the Jews was the first project that brought him to political prominence.

It was at Lyons that Jansenist millenarianism enjoyed the most zealous support.[26] The explanation for this lies partly in the fact that Lyons had long been a center of religious currents and undercurrents of all kinds and partly in the sympathy and protection that Montazet, the archbishop of Lyons, gave to the Jansenists. The most zealous propagandist for millenarian ideas at Lyons was Claude-François Desfours de la Genetière, one of the three sons of the president of the Cour des Monnaies.[27] Born in 1757, Desfours had studied with Bernard Lambert, a Dominican and a defender of the Convulsionaries.[28] After his conversion, Desfours dedicated his life and his fortune to warning France that the end of the world was at hand.

According to Lambert, one object of the "work" of the Convulsionaries was to bring about "the coming of Elias." Messianic traditions had been growing around the name of Elias since biblical times.[29] Although the Roman Catholic church discouraged such speculations, even some orthodox theologians suggested that the return of Elias would announce the beginning of the end of the world. In the eighteenth century, Convulsionaries found comfort in this idea. Had not the Lord declared to the prophet Malachi: "I will send you Elias the prophet before the great and terrible day of the Lord comes"?

25. P. Gruenebaum-Ballin, "Grégoire convertisseur? ou, La croyance de retour d'Israel," *Revue des études juives* 21 (1962): 389, 394–96; Henri-Baptiste Grégoire, *Mémoires* (Paris: Dupont, 1837), p. 331; Ruth Necheles, *The Abbé Grégoire, 1787–1831* (Westport, Conn.: Greenwood Press, 1971), pp. 10–13; and Necheles, "The Abbé Grégoire's Work in Behalf of the Jews, 1788–91," *French Historical Studies* 6 (Fall 1969): 172–84.

26. Maurice Garden, *Lyon et les lyonnais au XVIIIe siècle* (Paris: "Belles Lettres," 1970), p. 485; Camille Latreille, "Les origines jansénistes de la Petite Eglise de Lyon," *Revue d'histoire de Lyon* 10 (1911): 43–50; and P. Gagnol, *Le jansénisme convulsionnaire et l'affaire de la Planchette* (Paris: Libraire générale catholique, 1911), p. 16.

27. Louis Trénard, *Lyon, de l'Encyclopédie au préromantisme: Histoire sociale des idées*, 2 vols. (Paris: Presses universitaires de France, 1958), 2: 429; Latreille, "Petite Eglise de Lyon," p. 46.

28. Vaucher, *Une célébrité oubliée*, pp. 94–104; Grégoire, *Histoire des sectes religieuses*, 2: 154, 353–55.

29. *The Interpreter's Dictionary of the Bible*, 1962 ed., s.v. "Elijah the Prophet," by S. Szikszai; *The New Catholic Encyclopedia*, 1967 ed., s.v. "Elia (Second Coming of)," by G. J. Dyer.

The Convulsionaries combined the prophecy with Duguet's doctrine of the Jewish restoration, and they declared that Elias would come to regain the Jews' heritage for them. The faithful should pray for Israel in order to escape God's curse against the gentiles for their apostasy.

Ever since the first great outbreak of Convulsionary activity, messianic individuals appeared from time to time who declared themselves to be the expected Elias. The first of these to gain prominence was a priest from Troyes named Pierre Vaillant, whose vehement opposition to the bull *Unigenitus* led to his incarceration in the Bastille. Released in 1731 and ordered to leave France, Vaillant remained in Paris, where he preached the coming of Elias to various Convulsionary assemblies. A popular belief arose that he was Elias or Elias's precursor, a role that Vaillant himself came gradually to accept. In 1734, he and thirty other priests went to Metz to preach in the synagogue and convert the Jews to Christianity. Spurned, the band returned to Paris, where Vaillant was again put in the Bastille. He spent the rest of his life in prison.[30]

In that same year, a group of Convulsionaries were arrested who were followers of a renegade priest who called himself Brother Augustin. He taught that he was Elias's precursor, who, like Jesus Christ, would die for men's sins and be born again. Another member of the group, Sister Restant, claimed to be the woman whom the book of Revelation had announced would "crush the head of the dragon"—the role that Ann Lee, Catherine Théot, and Joanna Southcott would all later assume for themselves. This woman would give birth to a son who "would lead the new Israel, the new Church."[31]

Throughout the rest of the century, rumors spread among the Convulsionaries that Elias was on earth, that he was coming to Paris, that he was in Paris and working miracles. In 1774, a man appeared in the Marais district on the Right Bank who acquired a reputation as a healer.[32] He preached concerning the Last Days and began to attract followers who believed him to be Elias. The prophet disappeared after three years, but the sect survived, keeping alive the memory of his predictions, teachings, and miracles and awaiting his return. An "interpreter" emerged who brought messages periodically

30. Gagnol, *Jansénisme convulsionnaire*, pp. 46–47; Grégoire, *Histoire des sectes religieuse*, 2: 133.
31. Gagnol, *Jansénisme convulsionnaire*, p. 50.
32. Grégoire, *Histoire des sectes religieuses*, 2: 175; Viatte, *Sources occultes du romantisme*, 1: 218–19.

from the absent Elias. In 1792, he brought the artisans and laborers who composed the sect a warning that "the times are at hand. . . . God will send not only a deluge of water and of fire, but also a deluge of evils for many."[33] It is not known what happened to the group in later years, but according to Grégoire, a book written in 1822 asserted that Elias still had disciples who claimed to have spoken with him many times.[34]

In 1773 a group of pious Catholics at Lyons formed a society called the *Amis de la vérité*. Sympathetic to the "work" of the Convulsionaries, they met each month to recite an office for "the conversion of the Jews and the renovation of the Church." They venerated Elias, who was to come and make the world ready to receive Jesus Christ. Grégoire tells us that there were nearly a thousand persons associated with the *Amis de la vérité* in the Lyons area in the years before the Revolution and perhaps two hundred more at Toulouse. Many were men and women of "respectable character," including a number of priests, Desfours de la Genetière and his brothers, and the brothers Bergasse, who were Christian mesmerists.[35]

A similar society, possibly associated with the *Amis de la vérité*, existed at Grenoble. In 1789, a lawyer there described the society in a letter to J.-B. Willermoz, the leading figure in mystical Freemasonry at Lyons. He wrote that this group of "convulsionaries" had made "a rather great éclat in our city." They believed that the return of the Jews was imminent, that "Elias has come, that he is getting ready to carry out his mission very soon," and that the "reign of a thousand years of Jesus Christ is at the point of beginning."[36]

The most famous of the millenarian sects, the Fareinists, was linked with both Convulsionism and the *Amis de la vérité*. It had first formed in the 1780s around two brothers named Bonjour, vicar and curate in the village of Fareins, near Lyons. Desfours de la Genetière had contacted the Bonjours during one of his tours of the countryside in the cause of millenarian evangelization, and it was he who brought them into the *Amis de la vérité*. In 1783, the elder Bonjour resigned his vicarate in favor of his brother, François, in order to devote himself to teaching and manual labor. Under

33. *Journal prophétique*, fourth week of May 1792, pp. 273-74; see also ibid., February 1792, pp. 43-44; and 27 August 1792, pp. 109-10.
34. Grégoire, *Histoire des sectes religieuses*, 2: 185-93.   35. Ibid.
36. Quoted by Antoine Faivre in René Le Forestier, *La Franc-maçonnerie templière et occultiste aux XVIIIe et XIXe siècles*, published by Antoine Faivre (Paris: Aubier-Montaigne, 1970), p. 998.

François's ministry, the parish began to hear and accept the doctrines of Jansenist millenarianism: the apostasy of the gentiles, the conversion of the Jews, the coming of Elias to "restore all things," the extermination of the ungodly, and the earthly reign of Jesus Christ. The ideas spread through the region, as other priests and parishes took them up. Prophetesses appeared; the most zealous of them submitted themselves to crucifixon for extended periods.[37]

Although Fareins, northeast of Lyons, was to be the most notorious center of the new developments, they were also widespread in the mountainous area of the Forez, to the west. The elder Bonjour, Claude, had been transferred to Fareins from there—for having encouraged Convulsionary practices, it was said. The spread of millenarian ideas may have been partly due to the influence of the Bonjour brothers, but the Forez seems to have had strong tendencies in that direction already. The most zealous millenarians of the *Amis de la vérité* were from Boën, in the Forez. Like the entire Lyons region, the Forez had long been a haven for mystical and heterodox popular movements, and when Parisian Convulsionism went underground and spread to the provinces, it, too, found a home in the Forez. By the 1780s, the sect of Brother Augustin had evangelists in the region, who sought above all to convert the clergy to their doctrines of the coming of Elias and the regeneration of the world through the "work" of Convulsionism. The dissemination of these ideas was facilitated by the fact that the Forez was poor and overpopulated, and a great many of its inhabitants migrated to Lyons or Saint-Etienne in search of work. At Saint-Etienne, something of an industrial boom was beginning, based on coal mining, metallurgy, and textile manufacture.[38]

By 1787, a variety of factors—the mystical tradition, the propaganda of the *Amis de la vérité*, and the conversion of a number of bright and talented priests to Convulsionism—had produced a religious situation of considerable embarrassment to the archbishop of Lyons, Montazet. According to a contemporary, the priests involved in the scandal were men of "exemplary piety" and theological attainments who had been "the glory of M. de Montazet."[39] The arch-

37. Claude Hau, *Le messie de l'an XIII et les fareinistes* (Paris: Denoël, 1955), pp. 33-35; Jean-Baptiste Galley, *L'élection de Saint-Etienne à la fin de l'ancien régime* (Saint-Etienne: Imprimerie administrative et commerciale Ménard, 1903), pp. 96-101.
38. Galley, *Election de Saint-Etienne*, pp. 18-19, 38.
39. Taveau's manuscript life of Jacquemont, quoted in Jean-Baptiste Galley, *Saint-Etienne et son district pendant la Révolution*, 3 vols. (Saint-Etienne: "La Loire républicaine," 1903-9), 1: 303.

bishop, in concert with the royal authorities, now moved strongly against them. The priests were removed from their cures; some of them fled to Switzerland; a few, including the Bonjour brothers, were confined in monasteries on *lettres de cachet*. Despite the authorities' continued efforts, however, the movement simply went underground. The younger Bonjour, François, managed to escape to Paris, where he was employed by a Convulsionary publisher and was able to make contacts with the sect of Brother Augustin.[40]

After two years in Paris, the coming of the Revolution encouraged Bonjour to return to Fareins, where he and his followers tried to seize the presbytery by force. The attempt failed, and Bonjour and an associate, a priest named Jean Fialin, were interned by the National Guard for over a year at Trevoux.[41] It was there that Bonjour was visited by one of his female followers, a young widow named Claudine Dauphan, who informed him that she was to give birth to the prophet Elias. After his release from prison, he joined her in Paris.

Claudine had been the servant of one of the more prominent members of the *Amis de la vérité*. Like her mistress, she was a native of Boën in the Forez. Not long after his arrival in Paris, Bonjour explained in a letter to the faithful in Fareins that Claudine, already united in her heart with Jesus Christ, had prayed "to be united by nature": "henceforth, she would be his bride." This request having been granted, she had asked Jesus for "the fruit of his love," and again her prayer had been answered.[42]

On 10 August 1792, the monarchy fell. A week later, Bonjour announced that Claudine, now his wife, had given birth to a son, the new Elias. Bonjour connected the two events by saying that the violence on 10 August marked the onset of the time of troubles that would precede the Second Coming. The child was not just the prophet Elias. At his majority, he would become the incarnation of the Holy Spirit. The birth seems to have divided the Fareins group. One part accepted it as the new Incarnation, while the rest continued to await Elias. Of those who now believed that Elias had come, some went to Paris to join Bonjour. Both his brother Claude and the abbé Fialin arrived, fleeing their enemies in the Lyonnais.

40. Gagnol, *Jansénisme convulsionnaire*, p. 53; Galley, *Saint-Etienne et son district*, 1: 297.

41. Letter of M. Saussier, subprefect of the arrondissement of Trévoux, to M. Ozun, prefect of the department of the Ain, 27 messidor an XI, printed in A. Dubreuil, *Etude historique et critique sur les fareinistes* (Lyons: Rey, 1908), p. 321.

42. Letter of François Bonjour, 20 January 1792, printed in Galley, *Saint-Etienne et son district*, 1: 299.

Claude, who was called Moses by the Fareinists, settled in the suburb of Corbeil, another Convulsionary center, where he worked as a cobbler.[43]

The Fareinists continued to live unmolested in Paris and the Lyonnais for the duration of the Revolution. The Bonjours were suspected of involvement in the millenarian movement in the Forez called the Republic of Jesus Christ;[44] as a result, one of their associates, Fialin, was interned briefly, but the authorities decided that the Fareinists had not instigated the suspected uprising. All three priests could prove their continuous support for the Revolution; in fact, Fialin was a police functionary in his Paris section at the time of his arrest.[45]

In 1805, Napoleon's police rounded up the group. Some of them were allowed to return to Fareins, but the Bonjour brothers were released only on the condition that they leave the country. They went to Lausanne, where some of their followers joined them; "Elias," now a strapping lad of twelve, was placed in an orphans' asylum.[46] Despite the Bonjours' exile, belief in their doctrines and in the coming of Elias persisted in the region around Fareins well into the nineteenth century.

In the world of Catholic dissent, the Bonjour brothers and their followers were unusual in their complete acceptance of the French Revolution. Even they do not seem to have been especially influenced by it. In its essentials, Fareinism was simply a logical culmination of millenarianism as promulgated by Duguet and by the Convulsionaries decades before the Revolution.

Given this continuing millenarian tradition, it is surprising that orthodox Jansenists did not see in the Revolution God's deliverance of them and the world from spiritual bondage, but none seem to have done so. They either viewed the Revolution as God's scourge on wicked France, or else they ignored it. It was a very different group that used Duguet to interpret current developments in a millenarian light—the circle of pious revolutionaries who assembled between 1790 and 1794 under the patronage of the duchesse de Bourbon.

Their spokesman was Pierre Pontard, bishop of the Dordogne, deputy to the Legislative Assembly, and editor of the *Journal prophétique*, a newspaper dedicated to showing that the French

43. Hau, *Messie de l'an XIII*, p. 126.   44. See Chap. 4 below.
45. Hau, *Messie de l'an XIII*, pp. 142–45.
46. Ernest d'Hauterive, *La police secrète du Premier Empire: Bulletins quotidiens adressés par Fouché à l'Empéreur, 1804–1805*, 6 vols. (Paris: Perrin, 1908), 1: 266–67, 308, 369, 440.

Revolution was the herald of the millennium. The newspaper presented a mélange of opinions—Pontard's and others'—on the eschatological significance of the French Revolution. Pontard drew heavily upon Duguet. In July 1792, he devoted several pages of the *Journal prophétique* to an essay on "The Recall of the Jews."[47] It was based on Duguet's doctrines, but it adopted an attitude toward the Revolution that few Jansenists would have shared, certainly not in 1792.

Pontard declared that since the recent French constitution had granted citizenship to the Jews, "we ought to believe that the epoch of the great regeneration is ready to be accomplished." He said that God would "abandon all this corrupted mass which, although in the body of Christianity, is worse than the pagan nations" and turn once again to the Jews as the chosen people. Converted to a purified Christianity, the Jews would assemble in Palestine from all corners of the earth. Then, as St. Peter had promised in his second epistle, God would create new heavens and a new earth, "in the natural realm as in the spiritual."[48] The land would regain its fertility, cities would be built, and the weather itself would change. All this, Pontard never tired of insisting, would come very soon, as the climax of the political revolution France was undergoing.

It was not, however, Duguet or the Convulsionaries who led Pontard to this conviction. It was a village prophetess from his own province of Périgord, Suzette Labrousse, who made him a millenarian by convincing him that her "mission" would bring the world to Christ.

47. *Journal prophétique*, fourth week of July 1792, pp. 49-55.
48. Ibid., pp. 49, 50, 53.

CHAPTER 2

A
Prophetess in
Périgord

WHEN the French Revolution broke out, Suzette Labrousse had been living a solitary life of prayer and good works in the tiny village of Vauxains, in Périgord, for nearly twenty years. Her full name was Clotilde-Suzanne Courcelles Labrousse, but she was universally known by the diminutive Suzette. Her piety was well known in Périgord and neighboring Guyenne, but only a few priests who had served as her spiritual advisors knew that she had had a number of visionary experiences or that she felt herself to be called by God to accomplish a "mission" that would help to bring about the spiritual regeneration of the world.

Holy women like Suzette Labrousse have existed in every century of the Christian era. In the later Middle Ages, such women, who lived like nuns without submitting to the discipline of a religious order, were particularly abundant. Living either alone or in groups, these *Beguines* were the object of much concern to and considerable harassment by both secular and clerical authorities.[1] Accused of a variety of heretical beliefs, frequently imprisoned and sometimes put to death, the Beguines as a religious force were destroyed, by the authorities, but the psychological need that had brought them into existence—the desire for individual mystical experience through asceticism and prayer, outside the sacraments and institutions of the Roman Catholic church—was not eradicated.

This is the religious context in which the career of Suzette Labrousse should be understood. Had it not been for the French Revolution, she would have lived her life quietly in Périgord. Because of it, her message of universal spiritual regeneration, which was to come first to a redeemed and purified France, sounded like prophecy to a diverse body of Christians sympathetic to the Revolution. Labrousse was encouraged to make her spiritual insights public, and she was led to carry out her own "mission" by going to Rome, like a barefoot

---

1. Robert E. Lerner, *The Heresy of the Free Spirit in the Later Middle Ages* (Berkeley: University of California Press, 1972), chap. 2; Gordon Leff, *Heresy in the Later Middle Ages*, 2 vols. (Manchester: Manchester University Press, 1967), 1: 1-7, 69-79.

Beguine, in order to convince the Pope to give his support to France's revolution.

At no time did Labrousse's emergence produce a millenarian movement that can be measured or described. There are indications of extensive interest in her in 1790, but the schism produced in that year by the National Assembly's creation of the Constitutional Church and the papacy's unalterable opposition to it meant that the vision of spiritual regeneration through political revolution that had seemed possible in 1789 was destroyed forever. Interest in Labrousse evaporated almost overnight. When she set out for Rome in 1792, she went with the blessing of a motley group of clerics, mystics, and Freemasons, but her moment in the national spotlight was over. Her career is nonetheless worth examining, for it provides a dimension of the intellectual history of the French Revolution that is too often ignored. Moreover, Labrousse's ideas are a fascinating combination of traditional piety, political militancy, and eighteenth-century popular culture.

The problems involved in tracing the life of Suzette Labrousse are many and complicated. There is no lack of materials; in addition to her own numerous writings, several pamphlets were written about her during the Revolution, and her chief disciple founded a newspaper with the express intention of publicizing her prophecies. This disciple, Pierre Pontard, wrote a short biography of Labrousse in 1792, under Labrousse's own guidance, and ninety years later the abbé Christian Moreau wrote a full-length biography that was based in part on manuscripts of hers that have since disappeared.[2]

The problems remain. The biographies are maddeningly vague about the crucial years of 1790–92. Although the *Journal prophétique* was to be devoted to Labrousse, most of its pages were in fact given over to other issues that interested the editor at the time. On the infrequent occasions when historians of the Revolution have mentioned her at all, they have relied almost entirely on Moreau's biography, despite Albert Mathiez's warning that Moreau's book should be used with "extreme caution."[3] Renzo de Felice, the only historian since Mathiez to give any scholarly attention to Labrousse, called the book "imprecise, superficial, tendentious."[4] Himself a native of Périgord, Moreau reflected the attitude taken in the province toward

2. Christian Moreau, *Une mystique révolutionnaire: Suzette Labrousse d'après ses manuscrits et des documents officiels de son époque, . . .* (Paris: Firmin-Didot, 1886).
3. Albert Mathiez, "Catherine Théot et le mysticisme chrétien révolutionnaire," *Revolution française* 40 (1901): 485 n 1.
4. Renzo de Felice, *Note e ricerche sugli "Illuminati" e il misticismo rivoluzionario (1789–1800)* (Rome: Edizioni di storia e letteratura, 1960), p. 71.

the prophetess since her own lifetime: she was a madwoman, a hysteric, an embarrassment to the respectable people of Périgord. Yet as Felice has pointed out, it explains nothing to dismiss her as mad, since to do so is simply to evade the questions that historians need to ask. She attracted considerable attention in the early years of the Revolution, and she won the support of people who considered themselves to be both Catholic and respectable—as she indeed considered herself. If she had lost most of this public by 1792, the explanation should be sought in the changes that France herself had undergone. In particular, we need to note the disappearance of two widespread convictions of 1789: that state and church would be regenerated together, and that revolutionary zeal and Christian piety were simply two aspects of the same reforming impulse.

Suzette Labrousse's historical significance lies in the fact that she combined traditional Christian piety with a perception of the French Revolution which endowed that event with profound eschatological significance. She believed that the Revolution was the prelude to God's regeneration of the entire world. She felt herself called to perform a divinely appointed "mission" that would be followed by the direct intervention of the Lord in affairs on earth, after which peace and Catholicism would prevail. If this was not precisely the millennium of Revelation, it bore a close family resemblance to it.

Suzette Labrousse was born in Vauxains on 8 May 1747. Her father was an *avocat*; his family, Moreau says, was "one of the most influential in the locality." Her mother was the daughter of a cultivated merchant draper of Libourne in neighboring Guyenne.[5]

In the manuscript notebooks quoted by Moreau in his biography of Labrousse, Suzette recalled hearing her parents say, when she was five or six years old, that God was present everywhere. "These words so seized my heart with love for God, that from that time I had but one desire, to see this God."[6] Suzette's family was large, and her three brothers and above all her mother were hostile to her pious excesses. Predictably, the result was to intensify the young girl's piety.

The great experience that shaped Labrousse's life came when she was about thirteen, not long after her first communion. At prayer in the village church, she felt herself "transported by an access of extraordinary love," and a voice said to her: "Quit the house of your

---

5. Moreau, *Une mystique révolutionnaire*, p. 2; Jean-Baptiste Alexandre Souffrain, *Essais, variétés historiques, et notices sur la ville de Libourne* (Bordeaux: Brossier, 1806), pp. iv, 310; and E. Lairtullier, *Les femmes célèbres*, 2 vols. (Paris, 1840), 2: 213.
6. Moreau, *Une mystique révolutionnaire*, pp. 2-3.

father and of your mother; go into the world unknown and as a beggar, because I wish, by means of a simple girl, to reduce many of the great men of the world and to remedy many evils of my Church." She drew apart from her family and began to dedicate herself entirely to a life of prayer and ascetic practices.[7]

When Suzette was about seventeen, her mother took her to live with two "worldly" aunts in Libourne. They introduced her to a young man who proposed marriage. Despite pressure from her family, Suzette refused him, saying she would never marry. She was sent back to Vauxains and left alone, which was what she wanted. By now she was almost totally alienated from her family. She had grown into a tall, lively, rather pretty girl, but her good looks were marred by a squint that satirical pamphleteers would mock during the Revolution.

Suzette told her confessor of the mission she felt called upon by God to undertake. He warned her against speaking or even thinking about such a thing, and she obeyed. She wrote later that even if an angel had ordered her to set out on her mission, she would not have believed in him, because "the priests are our visible angels."[8]

The confessor had formerly been the chaplain of the Ursulines in Périgueux. In 1769, when Suzette was twenty-two years old, he suggested that she go there and seek to join the convent. She did so and was accepted by the nuns as a postulant. Not long afterwards, she went to the convent's chaplain, the abbé Saint-Geyrac, and told him of the divine mission she was to perform. He heard her coldly, giving her no advice except to trust in God. After two years in the convent, the nuns, probably acting on Saint-Geyrac's advice, told Labrousse that they would not accept her as a novice, since they believed that she had no genuine religious vocation.[9]

Upon her return to Vauxains, Suzette began to live in a hut outside the village, somewhat in the manner of a fourteenth-century Beguine. Despite the Ursulines' rejection of her, she had acquired a reputation in the region for piety, and several other religious communities, even as far away as Bordeaux, invited her to join them. She declined, saying that God wanted her to live alone.[10] Her new life definitely

7. Clotilde-Suzanne Courcelle Labrousse, *Recueil des ouvrages de la célèbre Mlle. Labrousse . . . actuellement prisonnière au chateau Saint-Ange, à Rome* (Bordeaux: Brossier, 1797), p. 24. She repeated her account of the experience in a speech she wrote in August 1792, printed in ibid., p. 202, and in Felice, *Note e ricerche*, p. 170.
8. Labrousse, *Recueil des ouvrages*, p. 31.
9. E. Roux, "Les Ursulines de Périgueux," *Bulletin de la société historique et archéologique de Périgord* 41 (1914): 231–33.
10. Moreau, *Une mystique révolutionnaire*, pp. 16–17.

did not have her family's approval. Many years later, she recalled "how many reproaches" she had received from them for thus making herself into a "public spectacle."[11]

We can get some idea of Labrousse's spiritual development during the years after her decision to live a solitary life of piety from the *Enigmes*, which she wrote down between 1766 and 1779.[12] Pierre Pontard, when he printed them in a collection of her writings in 1797, added explanatory notes to show that Labrousse had foreseen the developments of the Revolution with clairvoyant precision; but to a reader less convinced than Pontard himself, his interpretations are not supported by the *Enigmes* themselves. Some of them do reflect the expectancy of national regeneration that was widespread in France in the decades before the Revolution. Labrousse wrote, for example: "France is going to be the center of great events, and like the cradle of blessed triumphs; my province like the Sanctuary, and my parish like the holy of holies." She also predicted that "the king of France, as oldest son of the Church, will give the crown of the holy Empire to all kings of the earth."

The *Enigmes* show that Labrousse had a very clear idea of the nature of the mission to which God had called her at the age of thirteen. That her project would culminate in the miraculous commencement of a new age for mankind is suggested by the eleventh enigma: "The conclusion of the said plan will be an event of joy that will make mortals cry oh! and ah! without end; it will be manifested to all the earth in the space of 24 hours."

Most of the *Enigmes* are securely within the traditions of popular piety. Men have become corrupted; God must intervene so that they will "return to the primitive order established by the author." The priests must become shepherds of their flocks again, and the Pope must renounce his temporal authority, "a monster" that has "devoured an infinity of peoples."

Felice finds echoes of the Camisard tradition in Labrousse's writings.[13] Her family had been Protestant in the seventeenth century, and the Huguenots were still a sizeable minority in Périgord a century later. Labrousse, however, lacks entirely the apocalyptical imagery of the Camisard prophets, nor can she by any stretch of the

---

11. Clotilde-Suzanne Courcelle Labrousse, *Discorsi recitati dalla cittadina Courcelle Labrousse nel circolo costituzionali di Roma nel mese fiorile dell' anno VI* (Rome: Puccinelli, 1798), p. 200.
12. The *Enigmes* are printed in Felice, *Note e ricerche*, pp. 159-67. Quotations in the next few paragraphs are from the *Enigmes*.
13. Felice, *Note e ricerche*, pp. 84-85.

imagination be interpreted as seeing the Pope as Antichrist. The writings simply do not support Felice's contention.

There really are no intellectual influences that *can* be identified. The tone is reminiscent of the mystical and vaguely messianic tradition of Mme. Guyon, Pierre Poiret, and Antoinette Bourignon, but there is no evidence that Labrousse had read or even heard of any of them. Although she belonged to one of the most distinguished families in her part of Périgord, she had received very little education. She herself wrote during the Revolution that, until the age of twenty, the Gospels, the prayer book, and "an old sacred history" had been her sole reading matter. If she read other books after that time, the evidence is not to be found in her writings. At the conclusion of the confused and rambling book that she published in Rome in 1798, she begged her readers' indulgence, explaining that she was "very little versed in the principles of French grammar [which she spelled *grand maire*], and in all types of literature."[14] Yet, paradoxically, several persons who visited her either at Vauxains or later in Rome commented on the clarity and forcefulness of her speech.

We can say that her writings reflect, in a general way, both traditions of mystical piety already many centuries old and the sense of expectancy concerning France's spiritual and political regeneration that was characteristic of the troubled decades before the Revolution. It would be futile to try to be more precise.

After her return to Vauxains, Labrousse pressed the local clergy to direct the mission that God had given her. The Ursulines' chaplain, Saint-Geyrac, sent her to the abbé Delfau, an ex-Jesuit who in 1789 would represent the clergy of Périgord in the Estates General. He in turn sent her to Grossoles de Flamarens, the bishop of Périgueux, a former artillery officer who spent much more time at Versailles and in Paris than he did in his diocese.[15] Flamarens stalled; he promised to consult Archbishop Beaumont of Paris. Suzette persisted, but none of the clergy was willing to take on the risky task of telling her how she should respond to her "voices."

Then, in 1779, Labrousse met Dom Christophe-Antoine Gerle, prior of the Carthusian monastery of Vauclaire in Périgord. She had written and asked to see him, so one day when he was in

---

14. Labrousse, *Discorsi*, p. 238.

15. Moreau, *Une mystique révolutionnaire*, pp. 16–18; Henri Lacape, *Pierre Pontard, évêque constitutionnel de la Dordogne* (Bordeaux: Bière, 1952), p. 9; and Charles Lafon, "A propos des incidents qui marquèrent l'élection des députés du clergé du Périgord aux états généraux (1789)," *Bulletin de la société historique et archéologique du Périgord* 83 (1956): 80–85.

Vauxains on monastic business, he visited her. Afterwards, he wrote a friend that he had had the pleasure of "seeing and conversing with a young bourgeoise of this locality, born of good parents, and in a state of the most extraordinary piety."[16] Gerle read the manuscripts that she had been writing for thirteen years. He was particularly interested in her prophecies concerning the reformation of the church and the monastic orders. He asked for a copy, which he promised to submit to the general of his order.

Suzette found another clerical supporter in a cousin, Rambaud, a vicar at Libourne. In two pamphlets that appeared in May 1790,[17] when interest in Labrousse and her prophecies was at its height, he described his encounters with Labrousse before the Revolution. She had written him many letters, to which he had responded with "jokes and sarcasms." Then she brought him her writings. He was about to throw them in the fire, when one of them attracted his attention: "It showed me a plan so sublime, so extended, so profound, so well combined that it led me to a delightful perspective; but I had to believe that at some time we would see a new order of things, . . . all men brought together, the Orders suppressed, the Church reformed."[18] Henceforth Rambaud was not only a believer in her prophecies but also the intermediary in her continued stormy relations with her family.

In 1787, Rambaud wrote, Labrousse had come to see him again. She told him that within three years, the king would call an Estates General and that then "the happiest of revolutions would end all misfortunes."[19] He added that she had told him that when these great events took place, Dom Gerle would have a special role to play in Paris.

From the collection of her pre-Revolutionary writings that Pierre Pontard edited and published in 1797, it is clear that in the years immediately preceding 1789, Labrousse's conception of herself and her mission became more exalted than before. She wrote that she was free from "temptations of the body" and desired only "to become wholly in God and with Him." She expected to be "transformed into a new being," miraculously, and then she would be "visible to the whole universe, in order to draw everyone to God."[20]

---

16. Quoted in D. de Lage, "Le mysticisme révolutionnaire en Périgord," *Revue du Périgord* (1910), p. 46.
17. *La prophétesse du Périgord* (Paris, n.d.) and *Suite de la grande prophétesse* (n.p., n.d.).
18. *Prophétesse du Périgord*, p. 5.   19. Ibid., p. 6.
20. Quoted in Pontard, "Précis de la vie de Mlle. Labrousse," in Labrousse, *Recueil des ouvrages*, pp. 60, 65, 69.

Apparently Dom Gerle did not see Labrousse very often during the decade after their first visit. She never told him directly that he would be called to sit in the Estates General, although he understood that she had said this to Rambaud. One gets the impression from a pamphlet Gerle wrote in 1790 that he was less interested in Labrousse's predictions concerning himself than he was in her vision of "a new society" that would supplant the existing monastic orders.[21] His Carthusian order was exceptional in pre-Revolutionary France for its strictness and piety, and Gerle, a man of education and ability, had enjoyed a career of solid accomplishment and increasing responsibility within it.[22] There is no question that he felt a genuine sense of vocation for the monastic life; only after his acceptance of the National Assembly's reorganization of the French church had led to his exclusion from the Carthusians did he drift into the world of mysticism and heterodoxy that brought him ultimately to the bar of revolutionary justice as the chief disciple of "Mother Catherine": Catherine Théot.

In 1789, Dom Gerle represented his monastery at the electoral assembly of the clergy of Riom. At its conclusion, he was chosen second alternate to the Estates General that was to convene at Versailles a little over a month later.

Jacques-Louis David's great painting of the Tennis Court Oath depicts Gerle in the foreground, dramatic in his white robe and hood. Moreau assures us that on that day Gerle "distinguished himself by his vehemence and his patriotic fervor."[23] In fact, he was not even present. He became a deputy only on 11 December, when a second resignation in the deputation created a vacancy.

Gerle made his first speech to the National Assembly on the day after he was sworn in as a deputy. He offered a "patriotic gift" from the Carthusians to the nation and declared that the fact that the assembly allowed a monk to sit in its midst proved that it wanted "all to be witnesses to the regeneration of this empire." Referring to recent decrees that had placed ecclesiastical property at the disposal of the nation, provisionally suspended monastic vows, and offered "freedom" to those monks who wished to leave their houses, Gerle expressed the disquiet of his brother monks of the cloistered

21. Christophe-Antoine Gerle, *Renseignemens donnés au public par Dom Gerle . . . sur des faits relatifs à Mlle. La Brousse* (Paris, [1790]).
22. On Gerle's life, Francisque Mège, *Révolution française: Notes biographiques sur les députés de la Basse-Auvergne . . . Dom Gerle* (Paris: Aubry, 1866), is reliable. Further useful information is in Lairtullier, *Les femmes célèbres*, 2: 222–23.
23. Moreau, *Une mystique révolutionnaire*, p. 63.

orders who saw in the decrees "the loss of their houses or of their estate."[24]

He proposed a sensible three-part program: sufficient monastic houses for those who wanted to continue living in them; pensions for monks who preferred "to live in society;" and an orderly procedure to enable monks who wanted to leave their houses to do so. Gerle's address met with considerable approval, and his proposal was referred to the Ecclesiastical Committee, to which Gerle himself was soon appointed. Thus the fifty-three-year-old monk did seem to fulfill Labrousse's prediction. Not only was he a deputy, but he even attained, almost immediately, a position of some prominence. He took his seat on the Left of the assembly and joined the Jacobin Club. In meetings of the Ecclesiastical Committee, and occasionally in the National Assembly, he continued to speak for the interests of his fellow monks.

It is impossible to say what effect the events of 1789 had on Labrousse herself. None of her extant writings date from that year, and neither Moreau nor Pontard has anything to say about her thoughts or activities at that time. It is perhaps significant, however, that when reports of her prophecies began to circulate in 1790, the predictions they contained were far more specific and more political than the pre-Revolutionary notebooks and *Enigmes* had been.

The tiny province of Périgord had long prided itself on its stability and social conservatism, and in general it avoided serious disturbances in 1789. The elections of deputies of the nobility and the Third Estate to the Estates General went off without incident, but the assemblies of the First Estate revealed serious tensions between higher and lower clergy. Bishop Flamarens of Périgueux made one of his rare visits to his diocese in order to preside over the clergy's deliberations. When the lower clergy opposed one of his rulings, he adjourned the session and withdrew from the hall, followed by a third of the delegates. On the advice of the royal seneschal, Césare Pierre Thibault de Labrousse, marquis de Vertaillac, the clergy continued its meetings. They elected a new president, an aged Augustinian monk named Penchenat, abbot of Chancelade. Along with Dom Gerle's Carthusian house of Vauclaire, Chancelade was an exception to the general decay of monasticism in Périgord. It should be added that Penchenat was also one of the clerics of the region who had for some time been in contact with Suzette Labrousse and knew of her predictions and

24. *Le Point du jour*, 15 December 1789, pp. 105–7; *Réimpression de l'ancien Moniteur*, 32 vols. (Paris: Bureau Central, 1840–54), 2: 383.

her mission. The assembly of the clergy concluded its business without incident. As its deputies to the Estates General it chose two village priests, one of whom was Suzette Labrousse's longtime acquaintance, the ex-Jesuit Guillaume Delfau.[25]

In Périgord, as in the rest of France, the aftermath of the fall of the Bastille brought a mood of both expectancy and anxiety. On 30 July Périgord experienced its "Day of the Fear." The marquis de Vertaillac's agent reported rumors that thousands of escaped prisoners were coming to ravage the province. Messengers arrived to announce that the brigands were at this or that town, and ten thousand people came to Périgueux for safety. When the rumored invaders did not appear, affairs in the province soon returned to normal.[26] Although one of the invading armies of brigands was supposed to have been in the province of Saintes, only a few miles from Vauxains, the events of 1789 may have had no effect at all on Suzette Labrousse, who was entirely absorbed in mystical contemplation and the fulfillment of her mission. What is highly probable, however, is that the alternation of hope and despair that characterized the first months of the Revolution produced, in the province of Périgord, a more receptive audience for the prophecies of the Vauxains Beguine than they might otherwise have had.

The evidence is fragmentary, but late in 1789 or at the beginning of 1790 a group of priests from Périgord and Guyenne apparently began to discuss Labrousse in letters and conversations. She promised the regeneration of both France and the Catholic church, and in those anxious times her prophecies must have offered an assurance —of sorts—that all would be well.

The priests who became Labrousse's advocates could select from her vague and diffuse ideas those that conformed to what they wanted to believe. Those who, like Gerle, supported the Revolution wholeheartedly, could find therein the prophecy of an age of political and ecclesiastical democracy, in which all men would live as

25. Lacape, *Pierre Pontard*, pp. 7-8; R. de Boysson, *Le clergé périgourdin pendant la persécution révolutionnaire* (Paris, 1907), pp. 59-60, 74-79; Lafon, "A propos des incidents," pp. 80-84; and Lafon, "Périgourdins à l'Assemblée nationale," *Bulletin de la société historique et archéologique du Périgord* 67 (1940): 233-37.

26. G. Bussières, "La Révolution en Périgord: L'organization spontanée, mai à octobre 1789," *Révolution française* 21 (1891): 385-92, 423; Bussières, "La Révolution en Périgord: Fin d'un vieux municipe," *Révolution française* 31 (1896): 140-62, 193-224; Jean Joseph Escande, *Histoire du Périgord*, 2 vols. (Cahors, 1934), 2: 290-307; and G. Lavergne, "Les préliminaires de 1789 à Périgueux: Lettres de Chilhaud de la Rigaudie et du marquis de Labrousse-Verteillac," *Bulletin de la société historique et archéologique du Périgord* 82 (1955): 57-58.

Catholics and as brothers. Others could find assurance that their epoch was a brief and painful ordeal that would be followed by peace and the moral regeneration of mankind. As one of her most active propagandizers, a Lazarist missionary at Bergerac, abbé Gastaudias, wrote to her: "I have always regarded our present misfortunes as passing and transitory chastisements of divine providence which wants to humiliate us and not to lose us."[27]

In February 1790 Labrousse met with several priests who had become interested in her prophecies. One of them reported in a letter to his friend Gastaudias that she was surely inspired by God and that she was in correspondence with many members of the National Assembly, some of whom urged her to come to Paris.

There are several indications that copies of letters such as the one Gastaudias received circulated in manuscript in the regions of Périgord and Guyenne and in Paris. In addition to statements written on her behalf by priests who knew her, some of Labrousse's own letters were circulated. At Bergerac, midway between Périgueux and Bordeaux, this sort of publicity was sufficiently widespread to lead some citizens to complain about it to the municipal authorities.[28] A few of these letters were printed as pamphlets in 1790, but there was never the flood of pamphlets and testimonies that later characterized the careers of both Richard Brothers and Joanna Southcott. In England this kind of religious literature, cheap and easily procured, had been a staple of popular culture since the seventeenth century; in France in 1790, it seems to have been rather exceptional.

In Paris, meanwhile, a few individuals who knew Labrousse talked about her and circulated copies of the letters about her. In March 1790 Baron Grimm reported the campaign to publicize Labrousse's prophecies in his *Correspondance littéraire*. He quoted at length from a letter written by a professor at the seminary in Périgueux who said he knew Labrousse well. The letter said that she had predicted the troubles that France had experienced during the past year. Soon, "a phenomenon as extraordinary as the deluge and the Last Judgement [would] reestablish peace and tranquility in 24 hours," after which religion would flourish as never before. Therefore, the

27. Gustave Charrier, ed., *Séances municipales faisant suite aux jurades de la ville de Bergerac: Extrait des registres de l'Hôtel de ville*, 14 vols. (Bergerac: Castanet, 1892–1904; reprint ed., 1941): 14: 21–22.
28. Ibid.; Périsse-Duluc letters, 19 and 23 March 1790, ms 5430, Bibliothèque de la ville de Lyon.

professor concluded, despite France's troubles, Labrousse was "joyous in seeing the epoch of the Revolution arrive."[29]

Several pamphlets state that the two clerical deputies from Périgord, Laporte and Delfau, were active in publicizing Labrousse and her prophecies. So too was Dom Gerle. Another deputy, Périsse-Duluc, one of the leading mystical Masons of Lyons, wrote his friend and spiritual mentor in Lyons, Jean-Baptiste Willermoz, that writings about Labrousse were being circulated by both Gerle and a seminary professor whom he did not name. Périsse-Duluc had first learned of Labrousse from Louis-Michel Gombault, a retired royal official whose name recurs again and again in the correspondence and memoirs of the mystics and occultists of the revolutionary period. Gombault had sent Périsse a "bulletin" that was being distributed "in the circles of Paris." Périsse was interested in what it had to say, for he had much admiration for the "excellent Carthusian deputy" who was mentioned in it and who, like himself, sat with the "Patriots."[30]

A pamphlet appeared in Paris in the spring of 1790 that indicated the high level of interest in Labrousse. The author had misgivings about her, but her views were "so widespread" and the events she predicted were of "such great importance" that he thought it important to publish two letters that were circulating concerning her.

In one letter, a priest named Ducheron wrote that Labrousse lived in retreat in the country and wrote copiously: "The rapidity of her pen is as surprising as the variety of objects of which she speaks." She expected to be called to Paris soon; then, in May, the great event would occur which would "put the seal to the revolution which will restore peace and happiness to France." The message contained in the other letter was similar, but it threatened great sufferings to France if Labrousse's ideas were not adopted: "it will cost our Nation THE MOST TERRIBLE BLOODBATH." If all went well, she would go to Paris, return to Vauxains, and then "disappear," after which there would be no more news of her.[31]

Another letter, which Bernard Plongeron discovered a few years ago in the archives of the seminary of Saint-Sulpice, was addressed to the duchesse de Bourbon by a priest in Bordeaux. The duchesse was interested in all mystical and spiritual novelties, and the letter was probably written in response to inquiries from her concerning

29. Melchior Grimm, *Correspondance littéraire, philosophique et critique*, ed. Maurice Tourneux, 16 vols. (Paris: Garnier, 1882), 15: 597.
30. Périsse-Duluc letters, 19 and 23 March 1790.
31. *Prophéties de Mademoiselle Suzette de la Brousse concernant la Révolution française* (n.p., n.d.), pp. 11–12.

Labrousse. It contains the fullest physical description of the prophetess that we have. She always wore a coarse grayish gown and
a white cord around her waist, to which were attached a wooden
rosary and a crucifix. Her headdress was of coarse cloth, covered
with black gauze. The priest wrote that "she seems to me to be of
a modestly gay character." She spoke "with clarity, justice, and great
precision," and could talk to "the most renowned philosopher with
as much tranquillity as to the smallest child of her village."[32]

Two letters from Labrousse herself indicate more fully the state of
her thinking during February and March 1790.[33] One letter was addressed to Gastaudias, who had written her to ask about the future
of the king. The other letter, published several times during the Revolution, was written to her "cousin," a deputy to the National Assembly. The cousin is not named, but there was a Labrousse in the
assembly, Bernard de Labrousse de Beauregard,[34] who had gone to the
Estates General as a deputy for the clergy of Saintes, just north of
Périgord. He was a native of Périgord, and he may have had a role
in the distribution of news about the prophetess. He was a canon of
the abbey of Chancelade, which several printed letters indicate was
a center for activities designed to popularize Labrousse's prophecies,
and his address in Paris was the same as that of the Périgord deputy
Laporte.

Both letters are entirely consistent with Suzette Labrousse's pre-
Revolutionary views, but they reflect a heightened expectancy of a
great supernatural event: "What is called a revolution today is only
the necessary preliminary of what after it is to lead to the expected
event, and is in effect only a symptom of it."[35] She told Gastaudias
that her prophecies were all conditional, and in the letter she frequently prefaced them with the phrase "si je ne me trompe pas."
These prophecies had been "revolving constantly in my stomach for
thirty years," she said. In answer to Gastaudias's query about the
king, she repeated the prophecy contained in the *Enigmes*: he was
the eldest son of the church and would give "the crown of holy-
empire" to all other kings.[36] She wrote her cousin that her "plan con-

32. Letter of the abbé Monturon, vicar of Saint-Rémi in Bordeaux, to the duchesse
de Bourbon, 14 April 1790, quoted in Bernard Plongeron, *Conscience religieuse en
révolution: Regards sur l'historiographie religieuse de la Révolution française* (Paris:
Picard, 1969), pp. 140–41.
33. Charrier, ed., *Séances municipales*, 14: 23–26; reprinted in Felice, *Note e
ricerche*, pp. 167–70.
34. Lafon, "Périgourdins à l'Assemblée nationale," p. 236.
35. Felice, *Note e ricerche*, p. 168.
36. Charrier, ed., *Séances municipales*, 14: 25, 27.

cerned the whole universe, would bring about good laws and consti-
tutions," and would culminate in the spread of the Gospel throughout
the whole world. She referred in a mysterious fashion to the "event"
that would persuade unbelieving men that her mission was divinely
inspired and would at the same time initiate the totally new era in
which the clergy would be reformed, France would flourish, peace
would reign throughout the earth, and "bodies [would] take on a
new vigor" and enjoy "a new state of health."[37] She predicted that
the National Assembly would soon call her to Paris, where a council
of bishops would examine her writings in detail and discuss them
with her. She would not undertake her mission without their approval. She was still, apparently, the docile girl to whom priests
were "angels."

Meanwhile, as Suzette awaited the call from Paris, her other kins-
man, Rambaud, wrote in a letter that appeared in another pamphlet:
"Tranquil in her retreat, she maintains a fatiguing correspondence
with some distinguished persons, all the deputies of her province
and almost all parts of the Kingdom; she expects them to call her,
and believes that she will receive the order to set forth."[38]

The advent of the Prophetess of Périgord also inspired a number
of satires. She was called a "sibyl," a new Joan of Arc, and "the
Pythoness, Labrousse, new Delilah," who would destroy the strength
of the aristocratic opposition in the National Assembly. One
pamphlet sarcastically thanked the deputies of Périgord for offering
in Labrousse a gift to the nation even more precious than the truffles
and patés for which the province was famous. The most extended
attack on Labrousse, a play in which Dom Gerle and Robespierre
competed for her hand, dragged through several issues of a satirical
review called *La Chronique du manège*. In the end, she agreed to
marry Gerle in order to save the life of her "True Love" from Périgord, who was to be guillotined. In the concluding lines of the not
very amusing comedy, Labrousse said to Gerle:

> Et nous, allons former une douce union
> Qui peut seule assure la constitution.[39]

Labrousse's were not the only prophecies to evoke public interest
in 1790. Although the vogue for finding and reprinting old prophecies

---

37. Felice, *Note e ricerche*, pp. 167–68.
38. *La prophétesse du Périgord*, pp. 2, 6; *Suite de la grande prophétesse*, p. 7.
39. *La chronique du manège*, no. 24, p. 13. The other satires are *Le pucelage; ou,
La France sauvée* (n.p., n.d.); *Les actes des capucins* (n.p., n.d.); *La dinde au truffes*
(n.p., n.d.); and *L'Observateur*, no. 106 (10 April 1790), pp. 856–57, and no. 109
(17 April 1790), p. 88.

that seemed to predict current political developments never reached the pitch in France during the Revolution that it did in England, where the discussion of prophecies and their significance was a surprisingly common feature of the newspapers and pamphlets of 1794 and 1795, it is clear that the same sort of interest was present. A variety of old mystical and prophetic texts were printed which somebody must have bought. Both Robert Darnton and Robert Mandrou have emphasized the traditional nature of popular culture in eighteenth-century France, which the new philosophical currents of the Enlightenment only barely penetrated.[40] The interest in Suzette Labrousse perhaps reflects this older culture, for her prophecies explained and justified the Revolution in the rhetoric of the tradition of mystical and biblical piety.

The vague astrological predictions of Nostradamus were particularly attractive to those who sought prophecies concerning the French Revolution. He seemed to say, for example, that persecutions in the Christian church would last until 1792, when there would be a great "renovation." In his epistle to Henry II, Nostradamus had predicted a spring (1790?) in which there would be "omens, and thereafter extreme changes, reversals of realms and mighty earthquakes." The new Babylon would appear, to last for seventy-three years and seven months. This passage is still singled out by his commentators as referring to the French Revolution.[41] One pamphlet contended that Nostradamus had predicted that in 1790 or 1791 an event without parallel in the history of the world would take place, when "one of the most powerful peoples of the world" would see its government weakened "by the very people who were charged with preserving it."[42]

Noting in the spring of 1790 that one of Nostradamus's predictions was being circulated in Paris, the *Journal général de la cour* wrote that "a part of this oracle is accomplished; let heaven preserve us from the rest." In July the journal urged its readers to procure copies of a new pamphlet called *Prophéties anciennes et nouvelles* in which they would find "perfect correspondences . . . between the ancient prophecies and present events."[43] The pamphlet described

40. Robert Darnton, "Reading, Writing, and Publishing in Eighteenth-Century France: A Case Study in the Sociology of Literature," in Felix Gilbert and Stephen R. Graubard, eds., *Historical Studies Today* (New York: W. W. Norton & Co., 1972), p. 249; Robert Mandrou, *De la culture populaire aux 17e et 18e siècles: La bibliothèque bleue de Troyes* (Paris: Stock, 1964), p. 145.
41. Edgar Leoni, *Nostradamus: Life and Literature*, 2d ed. (New York: Nosbooks, 1965), pp. 332, 340; Colin Wilson, *The Occult: A History* (London: Hodder & Stoughton, 1971), pp. 253–61.
42. *Le petit Nostradamus; ou, Predictions pour l'an de grace 1789 et suivans* (n.p., n.d.), p. 1.
43. *Journal général de la cour*, 28 April 1790, p. 222, and 1 July 1790, p. 8.

Nostradamus's prediction that the climactic period in world history would begin in 1780 and last until 1792. Foreign armies would invade France and wreak terrible carnage. The papacy would move from Rome, probably to Avignon. Then three popes would be elected at once, and all the earth would tremble. The pamphlet also cited a fourteenth-century Franciscan, Jean de Roquetaillade (John of Rupescissa), who, the author said, had predicted that in 1792 an angel "would come to reform the priesthood, recall the priests to the life of the apostles, and convert the Saracens, the Turks, and the Tartars." The angel would rule over a pacified earth for a thousand years, but first there must be "evils" throughout the world.[44] It is not surprising that someone should have rediscovered Roquetaillade. A Gascon, born at Aurillac not far from Périgueux, he managed to write copiously during the twenty years he spent in ecclesiastical prisons. All his writings were millenarian; they all predicted the coming of Antichrist, who would be destroyed by the true pope and the king of France in alliance.[45]

A similar vision of a millennium of universal peace through the agency of France and a reformed church had appeared in the *Mirabilis Liber*, a prophetic anthology first printed at Venice in 1514. According to Auguste Viatte, when the book was republished during the French Revolution it enjoyed "a totally unexpected reputation."[46]

Some of these old prophetic writings had the same essentially hopeful tone as the prophecies of Labrousse and Catherine Théot. They emphasized the future bliss that would conclude the trials France was then experiencing. The rest of the prophetic literature of the 1790s reflected instead the apocalyptic message of Nostradamus. One pamphlet specifically attacked Labrousse for expressing hope for the future at a time when God was punishing France for her sins.[47] Quite possibly, those who reflected on ancient prophecies and current events during the spring of 1790 found these predictions more believable than Suzette Labrousse's vision of national and universal regeneration. A priest in Angers may have depicted the mood

44. *Prophéties anciennes et nouvelles, avec réflexions sur les rapports parfaits qu'elles ont entre elles* (Paris, 1790), pp. 39, 41, 68.
45. Marjorie Reeves, *The Influence of Prophecy in the Later Middle Ages: A Study in Joachimism* (Oxford: Clarendon Press, 1969), pp. 225–28, 416–21.
46. Auguste Viatte, *Les Sources occultes du romantisme: Illuminisme-théosophie, 1770–1820*, 2 vols. (1928; reprint ed., Paris: Champion, 1969), 1: 238: See also Charles Nodier, *Mélanges tirées d'une petite bibliothèque; ou, Variétés littéraires et philosophiques* (Paris, 1829), p. 234; and Reeves, *Influence of Prophecy*, p. 443.
47. *La sybille gallicane* (n.p., n.d.), pp. 4, 16–17; Claude-François Desfours de la Genetière, ed., *Recueil de prédictions intéressantes faites depuis 1733*, 2 vols. ([Lyons], 1792), esp. 2: 270–71, 323.

of many Frenchmen when he reflected, in the register of his parish, that the old prophecies were coming true: "great earthquake in 1755, an outpouring of God's wrath in 1790, with revolution, famine and war close at hand—a prelude to the stars going out in 1799 and the end of the world."[48]

The first six months of 1790, when interest in the prophecies of Suzette Labrousse was at its height, was the period in which the National Assembly was at work on the reorganization of the French church that culminated in the Civil Constitution of the Clergy and the schism that nearly tore France apart.

On 13 February, after bitter debate, the National Assembly abolished monastic vows. The action caused relatively little outcry in France, even among the monks. The assembly seemed simply to be continuing the process of reorganizing of the regular clergy that Louis XV had begun in 1768. The next step came in May, when the monks were given the choice of either leaving the communal life and receiving pensions from the state or moving into "houses of union" with monks from other cloisters and even other orders. In a few of the poorer and stricter orders, notably the Carthusians, the majority chose to remain in communities; but in general, faced with uncertain futures and an indifferent, if not hostile, society around them, the monks of France chose the securer option of pensions.[49]

It was Dom Gerle who precipitated the first major controversy on the religious issue of which the reorganization of the monasteries was only a part. On 17 April, he proposed that the National Assembly decree that "the Catholic, apostolic, and Roman religion is and will remain forever the religion of the nation and that its rites will be the sole authorized ones."[50]

His intention was to show that the Ecclesiastical Committee was not prejudiced against Roman Catholicism, but Camille Desmoulins,

48. Quoted in John McManners, *French Ecclesiastical Society under the Ancien Régime* (Manchester: Manchester University Press, 1961), pp. 277-78.
49. Two recent studies that revise somewhat the traditional view of monastic decay are Bernard Plongeron, *Les réguliers de Paris devant le serment constitutionnel* (Paris: Vrin, 1964); and Louis J. Lekai, "French Cistercians and the Revolution, 1789-91," *Analecta Cisterciensia* 24 (Jan.-June 1968): 86-119.
50. *Réimpression de l'ancien Moniteur*, 4: 103; Camille Desmoulins, *Révolutions de France et de Brabant*, 8 vols. (Paris, 1789-91), 2: 348. A particularly clear and concise report is found in *Les "Bulletins" de Poncet-Delpech, député du Quercy aux états généraux de 1789 par Daniel Ligou* (Paris: Presses universitaires de France, 1961), pp. 275-77. Also useful are Mège, *Révolution française*, pp. 10-15; Pierre-Jean-Baptiste Nougaret, *Anecdotes du règne de Louis XVI*, 6 vols. (Paris, 1791), 6: 161-67; and John McManners, *The French Revolution and the Church* (New York: Harper & Bros., 1969), chap. 4.

in his journal, *Révolutions de France et de Brabant*, described the motion as "a lighted match in a barrel of powder." The problem, as Gerle's fellow Jacobins angrily pointed out to him that evening, was that the anti-Revolutionary faction would use his proposal to foment disorder. There had already been armed clashes between Catholics and Protestants in the Midi and Languedoc. If the motion were to pass, so its critics argued, it would strengthen the clergy's efforts to keep their lands out of the hands of the state. If it were defeated, the Right could claim that the assembly was indeed anti-Catholic. The next day, in tears, Gerle withdrew his motion. Despite protests from the Right, the assembly then passed a substitute motion, which stated that while the assembly had great "attachment" for the Roman Catholic religion, it could not compel the consciences and religious opinions of the nation.

As the Jacobins predicted, the extreme Right used the Gerle motion to attack the Revolution. The abbé Maury, whose demagogic oratory had already embittered many debates, was as effective as ever; the hostility of the crowd was such that only the intervention of troops enabled him to leave the hall in safety after the session. The abbé Salamon, secret agent of Cardinal Zelada, the papal secretary of state, reported to Rome that the debate on the Gerle motion had been "among the stormiest that there have yet been."[51]

In the course of the debate, the comte de Virieu attempted to repropose Gerle's motion, but without success. Virieu was not a member of the extreme Right but rather a respected moderate and a Christian mystic closely associated with various illuminist groups in Paris, Lyons, and his native Dauphiny. Now, however, he joined the leaders of the Right in drawing up a declaration affirming that Roman Catholicism was the religion of the state.[52] Three hundred and twenty-three deputies signed the declaration, including Delfau and Laporte of Périgord.

In the provinces, the rejection of the Gerle motion provoked demonstrations hostile to the Revolution in a number of places.[53]

---

51. Quoted in Charles Ledré, *L'abbé Salamon, correspondant et agent du Saint-Siège pendant la Révolution* (Paris: Vrin, 1965), pp. 55–57.

52. F. Bussière, "Le constituant Foucault de Lardimalie," *Révolution française* 22 (1892): 232–35; *Déclaration d'une partie de l'Assemblée nationale sur le decret rendu le 13 avril 1790, concernant la religion* (Paris, n.d.).

53. Ledré, *L'abbé Salamon*, p. 57; Périsse-Duluc letters, 27 April 1790; James Hood, "Protestant-Catholic Relations and the Roots of the First Popular Counterrevolutionary Movement in France," *Journal of Modern History* 43 (June 1971): 245–75; and Gwynn Lewis, "The White Terror of 1815 in the Department of Gard: Counterrevolution, Continuity, and the Individual," *Past and Present*, no. 58 (1973), pp. 108–115.

Clergy and laity who had paid little attention to the nationalization of church property and the reorganization of the monasteries began for the first time to wonder if the Revolution were compatible with religion. Patriots and Catholics began to drift into separate camps.

The religious issue was dividing Périgord as it was the rest of France. An address in the name of the electors of the province, now renamed the department of the Dordogne, congratulated the National Assembly for refusing to make Roman Catholicism dominant. "Religion," the address declared, "has not been instituted in order to dominate; it has been created to console and to instruct." With the rhetoric that the revolutionaries loved so well, the electors of Périgord described the assembly's task as the creation of the "Code of the universe."[54]

A bill proposing the complete reorganization of the French church was introduced on 29 May. Dom Gerle, as secretary of the Ecclesiastical Committee, must have been in the midst of the National Assembly's deliberations on the document that became the Civil Constitution of the Clergy when he gave his third and last major speech on 13 June. Having requested and received the National Assembly's permission to address it concerning "a person to whom are attributed predictions and in which I am named," he told the deputies about Suzette Labrousse and her prophecies. These included, he said, "the convocation of the National Assembly, the cessation of monastic vows, the reform of abuses, the recall of the clergy to its primitive purity, the federation of all the peoples of the earth."[55] Some of the deputies began to mutter their disapproval, and the Assembly decided to pass to the order of the day. On this pathetic note, Dom Gerle's political career came effectively to an end.

Why did Gerle attempt something as rash as a speech about prophecy, after the disastrous outcome of his April motion to make Roman Catholicism the national religion? Francisque Mège argued a century ago that Gerle, finding himself isolated in the assembly, scorned by the bulk of his fellow clergy as a radical and a renegade, yet at the same time distrusted by the Left, came to see himself as a prophet called to lead the National Assembly to truth.[56] A close reading of the pamphlet Gerle wrote a week after his speech, however, suggests instead a man of simple and uncomplicated piety, neither

54. *Adresse des électeurs du département de la Dordogne présentée à l'Assemblée nationale dans la séance du 12 août* (n.p., n.d.), pp. 3-4.
55. *Réimpression de l'ancien Moniteur,* 4: 621.
56. Mège, *Révolution française,* pp. 14-15.

prophet nor visionary. He did not have "full confidence" in all Labrousse's predictions, he wrote, because some of them seemed "too extraordinary." Yet, he concluded, "I have not rejected them because I believe firmly, that nothing is impossible for God."[57]

Gerle was sincerely committed to Christianity, to his Carthusian order, and to a moral and spiritual renovation of the Church. He believed that the French Revolution was the first step toward that renovation and that Suzette Labrousse was its herald. The evidence suggests that he continued to believe all these things, even after he had drifted into the more unconventional circles first of the duchesse de Bourbon and then of Catherine Théot. Gerle became more explicitly millenarian, but essentially his convictions did not change.

On 27 December, Gerle was one of the sixty deputies of the clergy who took the oath of loyalty to the Civil Constitution of the Clergy. The general of the Carthusians declared him apostate. Expelled from the Carthusians' Paris house, he went to live with Louis-Etienne Quevremont La Motte, a physician and mesmerist who, like his patient and friend, the duchesse de Bourbon, had become interested in the prophecies of Suzette Labrousse.[58]

The issue of the oath made the growing sense of estrangement between the church and the Revolution irreversible. For the majority of the clergy, the great task faced by the National Assembly in 1789 was less the reform of the state than the reform of the church by means of the state. In 1789 and early 1790, the difference was obscured by the battle against privilege, the enemy of "patriot" lawyers and parish priests alike.[59] The idea that one had to choose—either France and the Revolution or Rome and the church—was not yet taken for granted. Only gradually and painfully would the belief that religion and revolution were compatible and interrelated at last disappear.

For some priests in 1790 the conviction that religion and revolution would triumph together was as strong as ever. When the greatest of these, the abbé Henri-Baptiste Grégoire, took the oath in the National Assembly, he declared simply that "we are Christians and patriots."[60] A priest in Libourne declared: ". . . The Eternal has pre-

57. Gerle, *Renseignemens donné au public*, p. 7.
58. Plongeron, *Réguliers de Paris*, p. 292. Plongeron's information on Gerle is undocumented and in some places erroneous; that they were friends at this time is also indicated in the manuscript journal of the Swedish Count Reuterholm (G. A. Reuterholm, "Resejournaler," 17 May 1790, Riksarkivet, Stockholm).
59. M. G. Hutt, "The Role of the Curés in the Estates General of 1789," *Journal of Ecclesiastical History* 6 (1956): 220; Plongeron, *Conscience religieuse en révolution*, pp. 285–90; McManners, *French Ecclesiastical Society*, p. 272.
60. *Spectateur universel*, no. 28, 28 December 1790, p. 114.

sided over the decrees of our legislators. . . . I shall die content, with my dear country free of the yoke of servitude."[61]

On the other hand, for many of the clergy who regarded themselves as "Patriots," the Civil Constitution of the Clergy was not the moral reformation and spiritual regeneration of the French church for which they had hoped. By making it in effect a department of the state, the Civil Constitution destroyed the special relationship that the Church had enjoyed with both crown and papacy. Dom Gerle's motion in April had played a large part in forcing French Catholics to recognize what was going to happen. For many of them, the new situation was entirely unacceptable.

Dom Gerle accepted the Civil Constitution, but both his April motion and his subsequent retreat deeper and deeper into mysticism suggest that it was an inwardly distressing decision. Of Suzette Labrousse's other clerical supporters who can be traced, all of them rejected the Civil Constitution. Périgord's deputies, Laport and Delfau, refused to take the oath in December, explaining later that they had not wished to see their church "deprived for the first time of its prerogatives and confounded with all the sects."[62] In Libourne, although a majority of the clergy there took the oath, Labrousse's cousin Rambaud not only refused but also sent a letter to the municipal authorities declaring his resignation from all public office.[63] The abbé Gastaudias at Bergerac also refused to take the oath; he was subsequently interned at Bordeaux, then deported to Guyana with sixty-one other priests from Périgord.[64]

For Suzette Labrousse herself, however, the Civil Constitution of the Clergy seems to have presented no problem at all. That it was part of God's plan for the regeneration of man and the Church would be a principal theme of her writings and speeches in 1791 and 1792.

Labrousse and her prophecies attracted none of the public attention after 1790 that they had formerly enjoyed. Nor did this have any effect on her. The month of May 1790 came and went without the miraculous sign in the heavens she had more or less predicted, but

61. Quoted in Marc Besson, *Histoire de la Révolution à Libourne, 1789-1795* (Libourne: Imprimerie Libournaise, 1968), p. 90.
62. Guillaume Delfau and François Laporte, "Compte rendu à leurs commetans," in *Collection de pièces intéressantes sur les grands événemens de l'histoire de France pendant les années 1789, 1790, et 1791*, 12 vols. (Paris, 1801), 8: 97.
63. Besson, *Histoire de la Révolution à Libourne*, p. 88; Souffrain, *Essais . . . sur la ville de Libourne*, pt. 4, p. 310.
64. H. Brugière, *Le livre d'or des diocèses de Périgueux et de Sarlat; ou, Le clergé du Périgord pendant la période révolutionnaire* (Montreuil-sur-Mer: Notre-Dame-des-Prés, 1893), pp. 105-6; Lafon, "Périgourdins à l'Assemblée nationale," pp. 233-34; and Charrier, ed., *Séances municipales*, 14: 18-19, 35.

she simply postponed the time of its occurrence. According to a letter from a follower in Périgueux, she had predicted that the "present calamities" would climax in 1791. In 1792 a sign would appear in the heavens, the papacy would move to another place, and there would transpire "a thousand other events" she was "not permitted to reveal."[65] In July 1790 a newspaper reported Labrousse's prediction that "in 1792 there will be in heaven a meteor that all the inhabitants of the earth will see, that it will remain visible for a year, that then justice will reign on earth; the Pope will renounce his temporal power. . . . If this does not happen, there will be great bloodshed in Europe."[66]

Despite these announcements, Labrousse apparently remained at her retreat in Vauxains; nothing more was reported concerning her for over a year. Then, in the fall of 1791, she met her most zealous and faithful supporter—Pierre Pontard, Périgord's bishop of the Constitutional church, recently chosen to represent his department in the Legislative Assembly that was about to convene. Ignoring the advice of those who dismissed her as ridiculous, he called on Labrousse shortly before his departure for Paris; he came away convinced.

Pontard's advocacy of the prophetic claims of Suzette Labrousse is impossible to explain on the basis of what we know about his career up to that point. He had apparently taken no part in the campaign to publicize her prophecies in Périgord and Guyenne in 1789 and 1790. Unlike the priests who had been her first propagandizers, Pontard had committed himself completely to the Revolution. Forty years old when the Revolution began, he had served in a parish in Bergerac after having received a doctorate in theology from the seminary at Périgueux in 1774. Six years later he was named to a particularly lucrative post at Sarlat, where he rapidly became the most trusted advisor of the Bishop of Sarlat. Clearly, Pontard was a man on the move in the church—at least as far as it was possible for a commoner to rise, which was not much farther. Never one to wallow in humility, Pontard said later that he had been "beloved" at Bergerac and "esteemed beyond all expression." The same, he continued, had been true during his ten years at Sarlat.[67]

Although he was not elected, Pontard had been a leading candidate to represent the clergy of Périgord at Versailles in 1789. Then came

65. *Prophéties anciennes et nouvelles*, pp. 73-74 n.
66. Quoted from the *Archives de Dresde*, 13 July 1790, in A. Geffroy, *Gustave III et la cour de France*, 2 vols. (Paris, 1863), 2: 475.
67. *Journal prophétique*, fourth week of May 1792, p. 278.

the troubled summer of the fall of the Bastille and the Great Fear. Sarlat, like practically every town in France, underwent a "municipal revolution" in which the local patriots supplanted the old municipal corporation. In the new commune, Pontard served as secretary and his bishop as mayor. When the National Assembly's decree required priests in government employment to take an oath to the Civil Constitution of the Clergy, Pontard did so without reservation, recalling later that he had acted "with courage" in the midst of forty-four priests who did not take the oath.[68]

It is hardly surprising, therefore, that after the bishops of Périgueux and Sarlat had refused to take the oath, the departmental electors should have chosen Pontard to be bishop of the department of the Dordogne on 27 March, 1791. Pontard arrived in Périgueux the next day, and in a rather aggressive address, having affirmed his attachment to "Religion, *La Patrie*, and the Constitution," denounced the nobility and the "ecclesiastical aristocracy."[69] His prestige with the patriots of the Dordogne remained high; when the departmental electors met that fall to choose deputies to the Legislative Assembly, Pontard said Mass for the electors, presided over the assembly, and was the first to be selected as a deputy.

Pontard wrote voluminously during the Revolution. In addition to sermons and addresses to the faithful in the Dordogne, he produced a life of Suzette Labrousse and an edition of her writings, and he was the editor and principal contributor to two journals: the *Journal prophétique*, which he published in Paris between January and September 1792, and the *Journal de Pierre Pontard*, which appeared between January and July 1793, after his return to Périgueux. These writings reveal a man of intense if rather naive piety, pedantic, uncritical, given to windy digressions on whatever topic captured his interest. As a result, Pontard provides a useful if sometimes peculiar potpourri of the ideas of one who considered himself a partisan of both philosophy and religion, of the Revolution and the church. Furthermore, it is primarily because of Pontard that we know as much as we do of Labrousse's career after 1791.

It was probably with Pontard's approval that in the fall of 1791 some of Suzette Labrousse's writings appeared in print.[70] Her first published work was a defense of the National Assembly's actions

---

68. Quoted in Brugière, *Livre d'or des diocèses de Périgueux et de Sarlat*, p. 190.
69. Pierre Pontard, *Instruction pastorale de M. l'évèque du département de la Dordogne avec la lettre de communion au Pape* (Périgueux, 1791).
70. Moreau, *Une mystique révolutionnaire*, p. 28.

concerning the church, including the Civil Constitution of the Clergy,[71] written in response to one of the pamphlets of the abbé Maury, by then an emigré but still a skilful rhetorician against the Revolution. Labrousse's *Réponse* was neither millenarian nor mystical. It was a rambling, detailed refutation of Maury's pamphlet; the soporific style and the run-on sentences mark it as her own work. Its only effect upon public opinion, as far as we know, was to provoke a rather nasty reply from Maury three months later.

Late in 1791, soon after the publication of her *Réponse*, Labrousse came to Paris. Her purpose, as Pontard explained, was to meet with a committee of bishops in order to receive their permission for her to undertake her "mission." It is clear that the mission was still to be a pilgrimage to Rome, culminating in the conversion of the Pope, through a miraculous sign, to an acceptance of the French Revolution. As Pontard hinted in the *Précis* of her life that he wrote to publicize both her arrival in Paris and the launching of his *Journal prophétique*: "In effect, a solitary girl, unknown, going to . . . , in order to . . . , and then to ascend. . . ."[72]

Shortly after her arrival in Paris, Labrousse became the guest of the duchesse de Bourbon, the sister of the duc d'Orléans. A mystic of immense wealth, it was she who paid for the publication of the *Journal prophétique* and also provided some funds for Labrousse's pilgrimage. The duchesse had long lived apart from her husband, a bitter opponent of the Revolution and an emigré. Probably with more sincerity than her brother, she supported the Revolution while continuing to immerse herself in a passive, quietist religion much influenced by the works of Madame Guyon. Before the Revolution, she had offered her hospitality to all the luminaries of the occult Enlightenment, including Mesmer, Puységur, and Lavater. Now, in 1791, the doors of her country house at Petit-Bourg were again open to all who shared her interest in what might be termed revolutionary Christian mysticism.[73]

The mystical and occult circles of Paris had first become interested in Labrousse in 1790, and the duchesse herself, it will be recalled, had written to a priest in Bordeaux to inquire about her. One of the

---

71. Clotilde-Suzanne Courcelle Labrousse, *Réponse de Mlle. Labrousse à l'opinion de M. Maury* (n.p., 1791).
72. Pontard, "Précis de la vie de Mlle. Labrousse," in Labrousse, *Recueil des ouvrages*, pp. 72–74. Labrousse's 1798 description of her arrival is in *Correspondance des directeurs de l'Académie de France à Rome . . .*, ed. Anatole de Montaiglon and Jules Guiffrey, 18 vols. (Paris: Charavay, 1887–1912), 16: 475.
73. P. E. T. Ducos, *La mère du duc d'Enghien, 1750–1822* (Paris, 1900), pp. 258–61 et passim, with caution; Viatte, *Sources occultes du romantisme*, 1: 238–45. On the

regular visitors to Petit-Bourg was the retired royal official Louis-Michel Gombault; he had helped Dom Gerle to publicize the prophecies of Labrousse in 1790, and it may have been he who brought Gerle into the group. It was probably at Petit-Bourg that Gerle met the mesmerizing physician Quevremont La Motte, with whom he lived after his expulsion from the Carthusians. And it was probably also through the duchesse and her friends that he was introduced to Louis-Joseph Louvain de Pescheloche, formerly an *avocat* to the Parlement of Paris and now an officer of the National Guard. Later, Pescheloche would introduce Gerle to Catherine Théot.[74] Clearly, the religious crisis of 1790 did not shatter the Petit-Bourg group's belief that religion and revolution would triumph together, nor did it decrease their interest in Suzette Labrousse and her message.

In his biography of Labrousse, the abbé Moreau quoted a passage from what he said was an autobiography written by the prophetess in 1792 in which she recounted how the duchesse de Bourbon had told her about "Calliostro," alchemy, and the healing science of animal magnetism.[75] The "autobiography" was probably a fraud, since Labrousse was already practicing magnetic healing when she came to Paris. Although Périgueux, Bergerac, and Bordeaux were all centers of mesmerist activity, it is more than a little surprising that she had learned of Mesmer's fashionable science; yet there are statements in the 1790 pamphlets concerning Labrousse that mention her activities as a healer. Gerle admitted that her mesmerist activities had led many to criticize her, but he added that she considered magnetic healing "a gift common to all men." It might also be noted that whereas the duchesse's circle was particularly interested in mesmerism as a path to spiritual knowledge, Labrousse never showed interest in any aspect of mesmerism save healing. She continued to practice it on her pilgrimage to Rome in 1792, and she devoted a long section of the book she wrote there in 1798 to the evils of medicine and the virtues of animal magnetism, a "natural remedy" that led to a "natural restoration."[76]

duchesse's wealth, see Beatrice F. Hyslop, *L'apanage du duc d'Orléans* (Paris: CNRS, 1965), p. 161.

74. Michel Eude, "Points de vue sur l'affaire Catherine Théot," *Annales historiques de la Révolution française* 41 (1969): 610, 614 n 33, 616–17; Archives Nationales, F⁷4722, doss. Gerle, and F⁷4775²⁷, doss. Théot. Louis Joseph Louvain de Pescheloche (1751–1805) was a colonel in the dragoons when he was killed in the Battle of Austerlitz; see Eude, "Points de vue sur l'affaire Catherine Théot," p. 615 n 34.

75. Moreau, *Une mystique révolutionnaire*, pp. 76–77.

76. Labrousse, *Discorsi*, pp. 30–40, 210; Gerle, *Renseignemens donné au public*, p. 5; *Prophéties de Mlle. de la Brousse*, p. 9; and Pierre Barrière, *La vie intellectuelle en Périgord, 1550–1800* (Bordeaux: Delmas, 1936), pp. 422–23.

Another member of the circle at Petit-Bourg who played a part in the events that followed Labrousse's arrival there was Jean-Baptiste Miroudot, formerly bishop of Babylon and one of seven bishops to accept the Civil Constitution of the Clergy. Born in 1716, Miroudot had had a long, varied, and undistinguished career in the church.[77] The author of several books on agriculture and at one time chaplain to the deposed king of Poland (Louis XV's father-in-law), he was abbot *in partibus* of the Cistercian monastery of Jerpoint when, in 1770, the king named him bishop of Babylon and French consul in the same region, the deltas of the Tigris and Euphrates. Miroudot visited his see only once, eleven years after his appointment to it. He spent much of his time as a political agent at the court of Versailles for his Cistercian order and an equal amount of time writing letters to Rome demanding higher revenues from his bishopric.

Miroudot was a zealous mesmerist. It was probably this interest that brought him into the circle of mystical Christians at Petit-Bourg, for in 1790 Nicholas Bergasse was still a leading figure there, and his mesmerist theories were one of the duchesse's principal enthusiasms. The *Journal de la cour* reported that Miroudot had a somnambulist prophetess of his own at his residences in the Cloîtres de Notre Dame, adding that "Madame la duchesse de BOUR——goes there three or four times each week."[78]

A fairly dispassionate historian, the abbé Pisani, has described Miroudot as "devoid of any personal merit and even of all moral worth."[79] Neither the sordidly self-serving character of his ecclesiastical career nor the querulous letters he wrote after his arrest in 1794 do anything to contradict this impression. Some of his contemporaries agreed. When Miroudot assisted Talleyrand at the consecration of the first bishops of the new Constitutional Church in February of 1791, the *Journal de la cour* remarked that "Holy Scripture calls Babylon the harlot of nations. The bishop thus will not change his diocese."[80]

Miroudot's part in the consecrations that enabled the Constitutional Church to maintain the apostolic succession did give the aged bishop

77. Frédéric Masson, *Le Cardinal de Bernis, depuis son ministère, 1758–1794* (Paris: Plon, Nourrit, 1884), pp. 428–30; *Abrégé chronologique pour servir à l'histoire de l'église gallicane, pendant la tenue de l'Assemblée nationale* (Paris, 1791), pp. 60–61; and Louis J. Lekai, "The Cistercian Order and the 'Commission des Réguliers' (1766–1783)," *Analecta Cisterciensia* 23 (July–Dec. 1967): 199–201.
78. *Journal de la cour*, 10 March 1791, p. 90.
79. Paul Pisani, *L'Eglise de Paris et la Révolution*, 4 vols. (Paris: Picard, 1908–11), 1: 208–9.
80. *Journal de la cour*, 7 May 1791, p. 62; Paul Pisani, *Répertoire biographique de l'épiscopat constitutionnel (1791–1802)* (Paris: Picard, 1907), p. 445.

a sudden prominence and inspired great hopes for him among his friends. Gombault wrote a friend that the Civil Constitution marked the beginning of "the Reign of the New Jerusalem," when the clergy would be chosen by the people, as in the primitive church. When a new bishop of Paris was chosen, Gombault said, "I shall not be surprised if it is our good bishop."[81]

Miroudot was not even in the running for the Paris post. He was a candidate for election as bishop in one department, Lot-et-Garonne, just south of the Dordogne, but he lost. He did fulfull his obligations as a citizen during the Revolution more assiduously than he had fulfilled his obligations as a bishop before it. After his arrest, the revolutionary committee of his section testified that he had always contributed money to patriotic collections and, despite his age, had served in the section's armed guard.

Pierre Pontard never said how he came to join the circle at Petit-Bourg, but it must have happened soon after his arrival in Paris from Périgueux. He rapidly gained ascendancy over the duchesse, who seems always to have needed a spiritual advisor. After his return to Périgueux in 1793, Pontard recalled how he had "guided a Bourbon, with a firm step, into righteousness." It was he who brought Suzette Labrousse to Paris, where she lived as the guest of the duchesse. It was at Petit-Bourg that Pontard devised the idea for the *Journal prophétique* (which the duchesse partially financed) and thus began the literary career in which he said he had "inundated the republic" with his writings. On Sundays, instead of attending the sessions of the Legislative Assembly, he went to Petit-Bourg, where, after saying Mass for the duchesse's household and guests, he would edit his *Journal.*[82]

The launching of the *Journal prophétique* was intimately connected with the mission of Suzette Labrousse. In a prospectus for the new journal, Pontard announced that he had "some very authentic information on the new order that God is going to establish in his church," to which "our revolution is only an unimportant prelude." The writings of Labrousse had prophesied that "the new order, presently established in France" would be the beginning, and "the rest of it is like an inevitable continuation." Then, with the mixture of zeal and practicality that gives the *Journal prophétique* a certain charm, he added that Jacobin Clubs might be interested in subscribing, since they were "already the image of the first Christian

81. Archives Nationales, F⁷4728, doss. Gombault, and F⁷477447, doss. Miroudot.
82. *Journal de Pierre Pontard*, May 1793, pp. 129, 133–35, 136.

societies, where there reigned that spirit of equality that the Constitution has just reestablished among us."[83]

Through frequent reports from their spy in Paris, the abbé Salamon, the papal authorities were fully informed of Labrousse's presence in Paris and her intention to come to Rome. They were especially interested in her because she was mentioned in letters seized by the Roman police after the arrest of a prophet named Ottavio Cappelli. One letter described her predictions in detail, including the fall of the temporal power of the papacy. The letter added that Labrousse planned to make a pilgrimage to Rome "to give the news to the Pope."[84]

By the time Labrousse arrived in Paris, the abbé Maury, whose pamphlets against the Civil Constitution of the Clergy had been the subject of her first published work, was in Rome, serving as ambassador of the Coblentz emigrés to the Holy See. He now wrote an attack on her. After heaping scorn on the three clerics he said were her advisors—Gerle, Pontard, and Miroudot—he warned Labrousse that should she come to Rome, "the gentlemen of the Holy Office" would ask her to "take an apartment with the *illuminé* Cagliostro in the Castello Sant' Angelo."[85]

Ironically, there seems to have been more interest in Labrousse's proposed pilgrimage in Rome than in Paris. Aside from Maury's riposte, only one pamphlet, a feeble effort at Voltairean humor called *Le suédois à Paris*, took note of her presence. Excepting of course the *Journal prophétique*, none of the newspapers so much as mentioned her. This is not to say, however, that interest in the prophetic interpretation of the Revolution had entirely disappeared. For example, the author of one pamphlet extracted from the angels' proclamation to the shepherds in the book of Luke the letters that were also Roman numerals: "gLorIa In eXCeLsIs et In terrae paX huMInIbVs bonae VoLVntatIs." He added them up, and their total was 1792! The author concluded, "Glory will be to God in the Heavens and Peace on earth to men of good will in the year 1792. . . . Tremble, impostors who criticize our Representatives; the word of God will not pass away; Religion triumphs, the Constitution does not fear your attacks."[86]

83. *Projet d'un journal intitulé "Journal prophétique"* (n.p., n.d.), pp. 1–2.
84. Felice, *Note e ricerche*, pp. 228–29. Cappelli's letters are printed in ibid., pp. 215–30. See also Ledré, *L'abbé Salamon*, p. 10.
85. Jean Siffrein Maury, *Lettre de l'abbé Maury à l'incomparable demoiselle Suzette Labrousse* (n.p., Jan. 1792), p. 15; Maurice Andrieux, *Les français à Rome* (Paris: Fayard, 1969), pp. 189–90.
86. *Prophétie contenue dans le Gloria in Excelsis, qui fixe le triomphe et la stabilité irrevocable de la Révolution française à l'année 1792* (n.p., n.d.), pp. 2–4. The

There was also a pamphlet called *Prophétie de Nostradamus accomplie* and another in which "le prophète national" appointed himself Nostradamus's successor and predicted the doom of Paris, "this superb Babylon."[87] The greatest number of prophetic texts appeared in Lyons, the pre-Revolutionary center of Convulsionist millenarianism. It was there that Desfours de la Genetière published a two-volume collection of "interesting predictions," most of them by Convulsionaries. He concluded that all the prophecies were now coming true, and terrible times awaited France. The clergy of the Constitutional Church were false prophets, as were the "hysterics, the Martinists, and the other *illuminés* of all kinds with which Paris abounds." They all "preach, like Mlle. La Brousse, in favor of the new order of things, and predict that the whole universe is going to gather the happy fruits of them,"[88] when in truth all that France could look forward to was God's wrath.

Labrousse still believed that the climax of the Revolution would be glorious for both France and the church. And she still wanted her own mission to have clerical direction. Since before the Revolution, she had desired to present her "plan" to a committee of bishops. This was the final point Gerle had made concerning her in his pamphlet in 1790, and it may possibly have been to urge the formation of such a committee that he had tried to address the National Assembly in her behalf.

On 13 February 1792 Pontard was able to convene an approximation of the committee Labrousse had envisaged. He had already given his approval, as her bishop, but she "desired that the other bishops should know of her *affaire*. . . . I have fulfilled the object of her desires and I have satisfied my desire in consulting all of my colleagues."[89] Pontard wrote about the meeting some weeks later in his *Journal prophétique*. Gerle had once again recounted the story of

---

prophecy was reprinted in *Journal prophétique*, third week of February 1792, p. 63, and in *Amende honorable de l'année 1791 en expiation de ses forfaits* (Paris, 1792), p. 14.

87. *Prophétie de Nostradamus accomplie*, 2d ed. (n.p., 1792); *Prophéties pour les huit derniers mois de l'année 1792* (Paris, 1792), pp. 4, 13.

88. Desfours de la Genetière, ed., *Recueil de prédictions interéssantes*, 2: 330-39; Henri-Baptiste Grégoire, *Histoire des sectes religieuses*, new ed., 6 vols. (Paris: Baudouin, 1828-45), 2: 146-48; and Louis Trénard, *Lyon, de l'Encyclopédie au préromantisme: Histoire sociale des idées*, 2 vols. (Paris: Presses universitaires de France, 1958), 2: 429.

89. *Journal prophétique*, third week of February 1792, p. 64. See also Albert Mathiez, *Contributions à l'histoire religieuse de la Révolution française* (Paris: Alcan, 1907), pp. 104-6; and Louis Siffrein de Salamon, *Correspondance secrète . . . avec le cardinal Zelada*, ed. E. O. M. R. Panan Desbassayns, comte de Richemont (Paris: Plon, Nourrit, 1898), pp. 363-64.

the predictions Labrousse had made to him, and she in turn had described her mission. One bishop had opposed the project. The other six, while not specifically approving it, had not said no to what Labrousse told them was "the commencement of the great works of God, the signal of the return of the Jews, and the conversion of all the peoples of the world." She had added some new prophecies that even Pontard found difficult to accept, including the prediction that both Mirabeau and the Dauphin would return to life. Pontard thought this very doubtful, but then had not Dom Gerle been "dead" in his monastery before he met Labrousse and learned of his future political career?[90]

A few days after her meeting with the bishops, Labrousse boarded the public carriage for Bordeaux, together with her servant Marie, who was to accompany her to Rome. "We said our last farewells to her there with feelings difficult to describe," Gerle wrote to her brother afterwards. "You will understand them, if you are persuaded how dear this being is to us and how she has served to revive our hopes."[91] In a letter written after her return to Vauxains, Labrousse asked a friend to tell her brother that "the sway of the interior movement" to which she was destined was such that she had had to overcome all that nature had inspired in her for him.[92]

She left Vauxains at about three in the morning on the last day of February, barefooted and dressed in rags. One who had seen her reported to Pontard that she had set forth "in a perfect gaiety," having told her servant "that all men would soon be happy." Pontard told his readers that there would be no more news of her "until we see her beside the prodigy that she has announced to us." He added: ". . . if she was not mistaken."[93]

90. *Journal prophétique*, first week of March 1792, pp. 81–84.
91. The letter is printed in P. J. Crédot, *Pierre Pontard, évèque constitutionnel de la Dordogne* (Paris: Delhomme & Briguet, 1893), p. 519.
92. *Journal prophétique*, fourth week of March 1792, pp. 135–37. A badly garbled account, including some peculiar statements attributed to Labrousse, is in Moreau, *Une mystique révolutionnaire*, pp. 59–60.
93. *Journal prophétique*, fourth week of March 1792, p. 136.

CHAPTER 3

A
Respectable
Folly

SUZETTE Labrousse's pilgrimage to Rome had only the most marginal connection with the great events that were transforming France in 1792. As the Legislative Assembly pursued its momentous policy of war against the rest of Europe, the monarchy sank into a morass of ineffectiveness and duplicity from which it never recovered. The new structures of government created by the new constitution and the Civil Constitution of the Clergy proved inadequate to the desperate crisis of the summer of 1792. Meanwhile, the Prophetess of Périgord made her way on foot across the south of France. It was an act hardly appropriate to the spirit of the times. More surprising still, in over twenty towns and villages along her route, she was given the use of a church or a Jacobin Club in order that she might address the citizens on her religious and political views. It was in these speeches that Labrousse worked out most completely her conception of a revolution that would be both political and spiritual.

Meanwhile, the faithful Pierre Pontard filled out his *Journal prophétique* with old prophetic texts and scriptural exegeses that borrowed heavily from the Jansenist theologian Duguet. The *Journal* also evinced an increasingly militant antipapalism. It need hardly be said that neither Labrousse nor Pontard was a thinker of much depth, but their writings do help to indicate what had happened to the message of millenarian regeneration since 1790.

Not much is known of the pilgrimage from Vauxains, which Labrousse called "the smallest village in the universe," to Rome, "the greatest city,"[1] where she was imprisoned seven months later. Pontard printed a few letters from people who had seen and heard her, and Labrousse herself described the trip when she paused at Lyons in June to write down the substance of the discourse she had delivered along the way.

---

1. Quoted in *Biographie des hommes vivants*, 5 vols. (Paris, 1818), 4: 12.

Pontard printed the first reports in late March. A villager at whose home Labrousse had stayed on the first night of her pilgrimage told how she had accepted his offer of hospitality, and soon his "house was full." She had told the gathering that there would probably be no war but that if war did break out, the "antipatriotic party" would be obliged to surrender and "religion would triumph." She had exhorted everyone to go to the Mass of the Constitutional Clergy.[2] Pontard commented that many Parisians said the mission was folly, but at least it was "a very respectable folly." Perhaps, he added, it was more than coincidence that since her departure the Emperor Leopold of Austria had died, the king of Prussia had fallen ill, and the Spanish ministry had been overthrown.

A few weeks earlier, one of the members of the Petit-Bourg circle, Gombault, had written a friend in Avignon that the group was "daily expecting great events." Noting Leopold's sudden death, he commented that just when "the Emperor was ending his career, Mlle. LaBrausse [sic] was beginning hers." Gombault had encountered many people who shared his belief that "the new reign" was near at hand. Then, in the alternation of despair and hope so typical of millenarianism, he added: "The spirit of vertigo and of impiety which rules here . . . is inconceivable. People generally agree that it is impossible that all this will end without the greatest misfortunes. . . ." He believed that those misfortunes would come soon.[3]

The first public meeting that Labrousse addressed took place in Montauban, a month after she had set out. It was to have been held at a priest's home, but the house became too crowded. At the priest's suggestion, everyone moved to the church, but only after he had overcome Labrousse's objection that "it was not customary for women to speak in church."[4] Two weeks later, in April, she arrived at Narbonne.

Her stay in Narbonne was described in a letter to Pontard from Gabriel Chefdebien, captain of the National Guard.[5] The letter is a

2. *Journal prophétique*, fourth week of March 1792, pp. 137, 139, and fifth week of March 1792, p. 145.

3. Gombault-Baron Corberon, 16 March 1792, in Archives Nationales, F⁷4728, doss. Gombault.

4. Preface to Labrousse's 1792 *Discourse* in Renzo de Felice, *Note e ricerche sugli "Illuminati" e il misticismo rivoluzionario (1789–1800)* (Rome: Edizioni di storia e letteratura, 1960), pp. 170-72; C. Daux, *Une voyante révolutionnaire à Montauban en 1792* (Montauban: Forestié, 1901), pp. 8-14, 19-20.

5. *Journal prophétique*, first week of May 1792, pp. 231-32. On the Chefdebiens, see Alain Le Bihan, *Loges et chapitres de la Grande Loge et du Grand Orient de France* (Paris: Bibliothèque nationale, 1967), pp. xxv, 170-72; and René Le

further indication of the interest that Labrousse continued to inspire in mystical and occult circles. The Chefdebien family, long prominent in the Masonic world, had established in Narbonne a lodge based on a "primitive rite" of their own devising. According to the letter, Chefdebien's mother had learned that the prophetess would arrive during Holy Week and on the eve of Holy Thursday had found her praying in the church. Labrousse performed many charitable works during her stay, elucidated the true principles of religion, and gave treatments by magnetism, "which, practised by her with complete confidence in God, could not but produce very good effects." On the day after Easter, the pious mesmerist and revolutionary Beguine resumed her journey.

In May, Pontard noted in the *Journal prophétique* that the hand of God seemed to have been at work against the enemies of the Revolution since Labrousse's departure. Leopold's death had been followed by the assassination of the king of Sweden, and there had been many other "remarkable deaths," especially among the clergy. The deepening religious crisis was causing serious dissensions in Pontard's bishopric of the Dordogne.

Pontard found an outlet for his frustrated zeal in his *Journal*, which gradually took on a tone of militant anticlericalism reminiscent of Jansenist or even Protestant millenarians. As the Revolution became politically more radical and more intolerant of opposition, so did Pontard. He predicted that Pius VI was "at the end of his career of abuses" and would suffer the fate of other European rulers. He saw the hand of God in the war that had broken out between France and the powers of the First Coalition. As Peter had prophesied in his second epistle, the present times of war and blindness would lead to "a pleasant society of brothers," after the wicked had been destroyed. "The epoch of the recall of the Jews is near," Pontard declared. "God is going to bring them together by the noise of war." Soon Jews and Gentiles would be "reunited in a single sheepfold."[6]

The fall of the monarchy on 10 August 1792 had been predicted by Isaiah, according to the first issue of the *Journal prophétique* which appeared after the event. Isaiah had said that Jerusalem (meaning, Pontard said, the Catholic church) would be renovated in the present age. "Here is the moment for seeing executed all that I have announced since the first of January, 1792," he declared. "The trans-

---

Forestier, *La Franc-maçonnerie templière et occultiste aux XVIIIᵉ et XIXᵉ siècles*, published by Antoine Faivre (Paris: Aubier-Montaigne, 1970), p. 625.
6. *Journal prophétique*, third week of May 1792, pp. 270-71.

formation of peoples into a single family; universal peace after indispensable shocks; a spiritual regeneration preceded by the recall of the Jews." All things were possible: "New heavens, a new earth; everything is leading toward the end."[7]

Meanwhile, Labrousse continued to make her way across France. Writing six years later, she recalled that her words had been so well received at Montpellier that her portrait had been done, "to put in the club." She said that almost everywhere she went, crowds of people met her and took her to the place of assembly so that she could "explain the Constitution to them." In none of the places where she had spoken had there been "either guillotine or massacre" during the Reign of Terror; that fact repaid her infinitely for her labors.[8]

At the end of May Labrousse arrived at Lyons, where she spent two weeks writing down the speech she had given so often during her pilgrimage. She left for Grenoble on 2 June, and there she added further arguments in support of the Civil Constitution.

At about that time, Pontard received a letter from a village priest who declared that within forty days, "truth [would] be recognized, iniquity unveiled." The Pope would be vindicated by his response to Labrousse, and as a result, the bishops would "recognize the sovereignty of the Nation. . . . I am not a prophet, but my love for the fatherland says what is and what ought to be."[9]

The discourse that Labrousse wrote down at Lyons is a rather good indication of her own very similar intermingling of prophecy and patriotism. The Civil Constitution was "holy," she told her audiences in 1792. It was "more the work of God than of man."[10] Six years later in Rome, she said that she had always believed that "the Revolution and the Constitution come from on high" and would "go from one end of the universe to the other."[11]

The 1792 discourse began: "I am that demoiselle Labrousse of Périgord, of whom the public papers have spoken so much since the beginning of the Revolution." The written version would take several hours to read, and much of it is tedious; perhaps the oral presentations were briefer and more effective. As an indication of her fusion

7. Ibid., 27 August 1792, p. 98.
8. Clotilde-Suzanne Courcelle Labrousse, *Discorsi recitati dalla cittadina Courcelle Labrousse nel circolo costituzionali di Roma nel mese fiorile dell'anno VI* (Rome: Puccinelli, 1798), pp. 88, 90.
9. *Journal prophétique*, third and fourth weeks of June 1792, pp. 361–63.
10. Printed in Christian Moreau, *Une mystique révolutionnaire: Suzette Labrousse d'après ses manuscrits et des documents officiels de son époque . . .* (Paris: Firmin-Didot, 1886), p. 176. The text of the *Discourse* is printed on pp. 170–224.
11. Labrousse, *Discorsi*, p. 108.

of religious and political convictions, however, the discourse is a revealing document. Labrousse declared, for example, that Jesus Christ had anticipated the Civil Constitution of the Clergy's provision for a clergy elected by the local citizenry when he said that "the sheep recognize the voice of their shepherd."[12] All France's troubles were the work of an "aristocratic spirit" contrary to the law of God and of man. It was "the nation" that created the nobility, and it was the nation that could "destroy them, because it is sovereign." Let everyone support those whom Labrousse called the patriots: "The spirit of patriotism is nothing but the spirit of fraternity; the spirit of fraternity comes from charity; and the spirit of charity comes from God."[13]

Labrousse denied that she was hostile to the Pope, who was "the father of Christians," adding: "Let us always recognize that the Roman Church is holy and pure in its faith . . . despite the corruption of its court and of its clergy." She referred to her "mission," but not to the miraculous climax which she expected it to have: "If I succeed in my projects, I shall lead [the Pope] in triumph to the National Assembly, to rejoice with the Nation in the favors that God wants to confer on the earth; if I do not succeed, I shall try at least to induce him to come by himself to show to France, in person, his good wishes for the welfare of the Nation."[14]

After her departure from Grenoble in mid-June of 1792, Labrousse must have crossed the mountains into Italy. Two months later, when she entered Bologna, she crossed into papal territory.

The papacy had been increasingly concerned over the possibility of subversion by revolutionaries in its territories, particularly in the turbulent province of Romagna and in the Legations of Ferrara and Bologna. Ferrara had already experienced a small revolt in 1790, and Bologna had been the scene of the first of two pathetic appeals to local and national patriotism led by a young student named Luigi Zamboni. Political clubs on the French model had formed in many cities, including Bologna. Especially after Mirabeau's prediction in July of that year that the Revolution would spread to all countries, the papacy had been fearful that French agents would infiltrate its territories.[15]

In fact, support for the French Revolution was confined to members of the merchant and professional classes and to the petty nobility.

12. Labrousse, *Discourse*, in Moreau, *Une mystique révolutionnaire*, p. 215.
13. Ibid., pp. 177–79.   14. Ibid., pp. 193, 203.
15. Ludwig von Pastor, *The History of the Popes, from the Close of the Middle Ages*, ed. Frederick Ignatius Antrobus, 40 vols. (London: Routledge & Kegan Paul, 1898–1953), 40: 215–22; Robert R. Palmer, *The Age of the Democratic Revolution*,

The influence of "subversive" groups was extremely limited, since local particularism and class privilege usually outweighed revolutionary ardor in the scale of values of opponents of the papal regime. Nevertheless, the disturbances within the Papal States continued. The authorities blamed French agents for them, and in one case, there were indications that trouble was fomented by emissaries of the National Assembly.[16]

It is hardly surprising, therefore, that Suzette Labrousse's mission to Italy was regarded by the papal regime as one of subversion. Not long after receiving word from the abbé Salamon of Labrousse's meeting with the bishops, the papal secretary of state wrote the governors of Ancona, Città Vecchia, and Viterbo that the sect of *illuminés* in Paris had sent her to Rome. He ordered them "to forbid the pontifical territory to the *illuminée* Suzette Labrousse."[17]

Bologna, at whose gates the prophetess arrived in mid-August, was the leading commercial and industrial city in the Papal States and the principal point of entry from the north. On 8 August, a few days before Labrousse's arrival there, the papal legate in Bologna issued an edict requiring citizens to report all "foreigners" who came to the city, giving names, places of birth, and occupations.[18] Rome had that summer discovered another alleged plot in the Romagna, this one to be followed by an incursion of French troops at Ancona on the Adriatic. The man whom the papal authorities believed to be the principal French agent in the plot was known to be at Bologna. He was arrested, then released for lack of evidence. According to Canon Leflon, such French agents "swarmed" in the papal states, posing as merchants, artists, tourists, "even as pilgrims en route to the holy sanctuaries."[19]

Some information on Labrousse's activities is found in the historical dictionary written by the abbé Feller, a Belgian Jesuit scholar-

2 vols. (Princeton: Princeton University Press, 1959-65), 2: 275-84; Umberto Marcelli, "Movimenti politici a Bologna durante la Rivoluzione francese e l'impero napoleonico," in Marcelli, *Riforme e rivoluzione in Italia nel secolo XVIII* (Bologna: Patron, 1964), pp. 121-24; and Franco Cristoforo and Andrea Emiliani, eds., *I Giacobini a Bologna* (Bologna: Edizioni Alfa, 1966), pp. viii-xiv.

16. Pastor, *History of the Popes*, 40: 218, 222; Jean Leflon, *Pie VII, des abbayes bénédictines à la papauté* (Paris: Plon, 1958), pp. 246-50.

17. Georges Bourgin, ed., *La France et Rome de 1788 à 1797: Registres des dépêches du Cardinal Secrétaire d'Etat* (Paris: Fontemoing, 1909), p. 19.

18. Pastor, *History of the Popes*, 40: 233; decree of the Legate in Bologna: Archivio di Stato, Archivio del Legato, Bandi speciali dei Legati, vol. 68; and Archivio dell'ambasciata bolognese in Roma, Registri di lettere dell' ambasciatore al Senato, vol. 480 (July-2 Dec. 1792).

19. Leflon, *Pie VII*, pp. 246-49.

journalist who spent much of the Revolutionary period in Rome. According to him, Labrousse preached in the streets of Bologne, but she could not have selected a town where the people were less devout. The legate ended the "comedy" by expelling her from the city, and she made her way south across the mountains to Viterbo. At nearby Montefiascone, she was arrested.

According to Feller, Labrousse was brought to Rome but was not imprisoned. She was therefore able to make speeches "against the Pope and against the nonjuring clergy," climaxing with a speech delivered in what is still one of Rome's most popular gathering places, the Piazza Navona.[20] Late that night, she was placed in Castello Sant' Angelo, where she remained until the French army freed her five and a half years later.

Within a few weeks the news of her arrest reached Paris, where it was even reported in one newspaper, the *Gazette national.* The Petit-Bourg circle received further information in letters from a friend in Lyons. The papal authorities in Rome had released several French citizens from prison, and one of them, the sculptor Gabriel Chinard, returned to his native town of Lyons and told of Labrousse's imprisonment in Sant' Angelo. He had occupied a cell near hers and had been able to contact her with the help of an Italian domestic servant employed in the prison. Labrousse had asked him to report her plight to her friends in France. Chinard said that he had heard her cry out, "Oh! my dear Frenchmen, do not abandon me." The correspondent went on to say that everyone who had seen her at Lyons, including Chinard, was urging the diplomatic committee of the National Convention to work to secure her release. It would be wise to say nothing of her religious ideas, he continued, and to emphasize instead her role as "an exalted patriot, who had gone to Italy to preach liberty and equality." And it was true, "that she had no other occupation on all of her route from Périgueux to Bologna."[21]

The French government did try to free Labrousse from Sant' Angelo, but all attempts met with frustration in the devious and mysterious channels of papal bureaucracy. It was not until eight months after her arrest that the French chargé d'affaires, Cacault, was able to inform the Convention of her precise whereabouts and of the charges against her. From a series of letters from the French representatives in Rome during the next several years, one can piece

20. François Feller, *Dizionario storico ossia Storia compendiate* (Venice, 1830–36). See also Bourgin, ed., *La France et Rome de 1788 à 1797*, pp. 33–34.

21. Unknown-Gombault, 25 December 1792, and ibid., undated, Archives Nationales, F⁷4728, doss. Gombault.

together the story of her imprisonment and learn something of Roman justice. After numerous interviews, the authorities finally confirmed that Labrousse was one of three French citizens incarcerated in the fortress. She had "attracted the suspicions of the papal government by wandering through Italy with a pilgrim's staff in her hand." She was being held without trial, "as a madwoman." This was not Labrousse's view; Cacault reported that another Frenchman who had briefly occupied her original cell had found written on the wall: "I Courcelle La Brousse, of Périgord in France, I am held prisoner here for the cause of God and of his people, in September, 1792."[22]

From about the time of Labrousse's arrest, Pierre Pontard's own fortunes began to go rapidly downhill. The voters failed to elect him as a deputy to the Convention in the fall of 1792. Then, after a brief and unsatisfactory spell as a collaborator on a journal called *La Poste du matin*, he returned to Périgueux, where, in *Le Journal de Pierre Pontard*, he resumed his efforts to interpret the French Revolution as the manifestation of millenial prophecy and the promised regeneration of the church. Still a convinced Jacobin, he continued to be involved in local politics and to maintain his links with Paris officialdom and with the mystical and millenarian circles in the capital.

In September 1793, Pontard became one of the few constitutional clerics to marry. Two months later, he left the priesthood. Like his friend Dom Gerle, he spent the rest of his life seeking government posts and involving himself in unsuccessful journalistic and educational projects in the "Grub Street" of the Parisian literary underworld.

A letter Pontard wrote Gombault in the spring of 1794 describing his precarious situation in Périgueux shows that he retained the same sunny if superficial optimism that characterized the writings of his salad days in Paris at the salon of the duchesse de Bourbon.[23] The letter was apparently intended for all the members of that "society" to which he had occasionally referred in the *Journal prophétique*. He told his "dear fraternity" that he had two prospects for employment: one as an overseer in a spinning mill and the other as a supervisor in a hospital. He had also been offered a place as a librarian in Paris, through the influence of an uncle. Pontard's main concern was that the post he took be "stable and solid and above all peaceful," for

22. *Correspondance des directeurs de l'Académie de France à Rome* . . . , ed. Anatole de Montaiglon and Jules Guiffrey, 18 vols. (Paris: Charavay, 1887-1912), 16: 295-98, 304, 316, 319, 362.
23. Pontard-Gombault, 19 pluviôse (year II), Archives Nationales, F⁷4728, doss. Gombault. Quotations in the next few paragraphs are from this letter.

he had learned that "the most advantageous post for a true patriot is the one in which he can do good without exciting jealousy." He did in fact hold the hospital post for the next several years.

Pontard referred humorously but affectionately to his new wife, whose name was Sophie. He predicted that "Brother Lamothe [sic] in the epoch of the New Jersualem [would] take a Sophie" and so would "Brother Saint-Martin." He continued: "A Sophie is a very interesting piece of furniture [meuble]. My own is completely lovable. . . . We are very cheerful despite our misfortunes and *vive la République* is our cry of joy. Gerle would be scandalized. . . . and Catherine [Théot] would accuse us of a lack of courage; but we are far from deserving this reprimand." Sophie was expecting a child, and this had deepened their attachment for each other still further. Despite everything, he said, "we live *à la sans-culotte* and we live happily."

By the time the Petit-Bourg circle received Pontard's letter, the group was much absorbed in the teachings of a prophetess very different from Labrousse, the aged "Mother Catherine" Théot. When she was arrested a few weeks later, Théot told the police that Pontard had visited her religious services, but he had been neither arrested nor interrogated—perhaps because the Revolutionary dictatorship ended too soon.

In a postscript to his letter, Pontard thanked Dom Gerle for sending him a copy of the "catechism." He probably referred to an essay the police seized at Gerle's apartment after his arrest, a statement of belief in an imminent millennium which would be followed by the reign of the "Mother." Pontard made no further comments on the "catechism," and it is unlikely that Théot's teachings would have much interested him. His own religious beliefs had always been rather practical and earthbound, even if some of his best friends were mystics.

Pontard's letter to the Petit-Bourg circle shows that his hopes for the regeneration of religion were as strong as ever, but it also indicates that he had moved rather far from Christian orthodoxy. "Truth is going to put everything in balance," he wrote. "The priesthood is no more." The news that Islam, too, was "threatened with annihilation" meant that men would soon realize that "every cult is an absurdity and that man needs only himself to be all that he ought to be."

Given the drastic evolution that his beliefs had undergone since 1791, it is a little surprising that Pontard was still convinced that Labrousse's mission, when completed, would inaugurate the transformation of the world. That does seem to have been the case, although it must be said that Labrousse's prophecies served more and more to support Pontard's own views. In the *Journal de Pierre Pontard*, he gave vent to a thoroughly Jacobin detestation of kings and aristocracies that derived less from Rousseau than from the prophet Daniel. Pontard wrote that Suzette Labrousse had announced that total equality would prevail in the world and that all peoples would "form a single family." Now, at last, that prophecy was in the process of being fulfilled. "The universe is in movement," he continued. "The kings are withering with fright. . . . Nothing is therefore more believable than the imminent fall of those heads that cause this universal trouble."[24] In the next issue of the *Journal de Pierre Pontard*, he declared that the chief "head" destined to fall was that of "the holy king, the bishop of Rome, who covers the earth with blood, not only in this war, but ever since the world has existed."[25]

A sermon delivered in August 1793 shows that Pontard's Jacobin millenarianism had by then lost its Christian origins: "Sublime Revolution! You cannot be the work of men; the destruction of egoism . . . is the work of the common principle of the great whole. It is by this great work that he wants us to reunite into one great family."[26]

Despite his own personal troubles and his own religious evolution, Pontard continued to concern himself with Labrousse's fate, maintaining contact both with government officials in Paris and with her family. He continued his efforts to propagate her teachings and in 1797 published a collection of her writings, which included the biography he had first issued in 1792.

In September 1796, chargé d'affaires Cacault in Rome reported to Paris that he had at last been permitted to interview the prophetess Labrousse. Thouin, of the Commission of the Arts, had accompanied him. They had "verified" that she was "mad," for she was obsessed with the project of reforming the Catholic church and persuading the Pope to renounce his temporal power. She was clearly a woman of good breeding; "infinitely honest and gentle; her head, overexcited on one sole point, is wise on all the rest." She told her visitors that she was perfectly content and that she would not leave Rome until the century had ended. Her room in Castello Sant' Angelo was "vast"; her servant Marie was still in attendance.[27]

24. *Journal de Pierre Pontard*, second fortnight of April 1793, p. 112.
25. Ibid., first and second fortnights of May 1793, p. 154.
26. Ibid., second fortnight of August 1793, p. 247. Five pages later, in the middle of a sentence, the *Journal de Pierre Pontard* ends.
27. *Correspondance des directeurs de l'Académie de France à Rome*, 16: 473–76.

Labrousse told Thouin and Cacault that after her arrest she had undergone five long interrogations, during which she had been accused of having come to Italy to murder the Pope. This she had denied, saying that her sole aim was to persuade the Pope to abdicate his temporal authority so that he could fulfill his true role as spiritual head of all Catholic Christians. She told Thouin that she must remain in Rome until 1800, because the divine will had destined her "for great things."[28]

A year later, another French visitor received substantially the same impression of the prophetess. "She maintains her good sense in her conversation as in her correspondence," Joseph Bonaparte wrote Talleyrand, "except on the object of her pretended mission. She is destined, she says, to be witness to a great event that will bring happiness for the human race." The Pope must abdicate his temporal power, since it was incompatible with the maxims of Jesus. If he did not, "an inevitable catastrophe" would take it from him.[29]

In February 1798, the French army occupied Rome. Labrousse was now free to leave her prison, but for the next year she was content to remain there, going out daily to walk in the streets and deliver her speeches to the people of Rome. She became a well-known figure in the city and the center of a small circle of disciples. Perhaps because of jokes directed at her and her followers by the French troops at Sant' Angelo, she moved at the beginning of 1799 to the Corsini Palace, site of the French Embassy, and then to the palace formerly occupied by the Holy Office.[30]

As had been the case in Paris in 1792, Labrousse developed an acquaintance among mystically inclined members of the upper classes, and once again she involved herself in politics. Following the French occupation, the commanding general, Saint-Cyr, had established a club, the Circolo Costituzionale, to "spread enlightenment among the People and to make it virtuous."[31] The group was to discuss law, Roman history, and related topics, but it was forbidden to concern itself with current political issues. In Northern Italy, particularly at Milan and Bologna, political clubs on the Jacobin model had proved to be effective and reliable agencies of Revolutionary and French propaganda. In Rome, however, the Circolo Costitu-

28. Ibid.   29. Ibid., 17: 110–11.
30. Felice, *Note e ricerche*, pp. 144–48; Labrousse, *Discorsi*, pp. 5–6.
31. *Gazetta di Roma*, 19 May 1789, p. 23. On the Circoli, see Umberto Marcelli, "Giacobini ed insorgenti in Romagna (1796–99)," in Marcelli, *Riforme e rivoluzione*, pp. 157–75.

zionale almost immediately made itself unacceptable to the ruling coalition of Roman aristocracy and French army, and within a month, Saint-Cyr had shut it down. According to the editor of Labrousse's *Discorsi*, Labrousse intervened with the general and persuaded him to allow the club to reopen. He agreed, on the condition that its speakers refrain from criticizing the government. He soon closed the club again, however, and Labrousse herself was accused of saying "incendiary things."[32] According to a contemporary chronicler, she had been a frequent speaker at the Circolo Costituzionale, and she had also "tainted Rome with the ridiculous printing of her vagaries."[33] Labrousse had published the substance of her speeches at the Circolo, together with a defence of her conduct in Rome.

Printed on facing pages in appallingly ungrammatical French and in a fairly good Italian translation, the Roman *Discorsi* are frequently vague and sometimes incoherent. They reveal a mind of little depth, full of a haphazard collection of ideas that had been current in pre-Revolutionary France. It is easy, on the basis of the *Discorsi*, to say that Labrousse was eccentric, but not that she was mad. Unlike Richard Brothers, confined after 1795 in an asylum in London, the experience of imprisonment did not produce new fantasies concerning her divinely ordained role. She wrote that all Rome called her a prophetess but that she was "no more a prophetess than anyone else."[34] Her references to the miraculous sign by which she would inaugurate the final age were very guarded, although her belief in the event, which she now expected in 1800, had not changed. She wrote that she had not wished to leave her "apartment" in Sant' Angelo for "personal" reasons, which she hoped that time would make apparent. She had no more to say about it, but there is no reason to doubt that she was still convinced that at the time of the Pope's conversion to support of the French Republic, she would herself announce the regeneration of the world through her miraculous elevation in the sky. She had always been rather circumspect about this part of her mission, but she had been expecting such a climax for over twenty years, ever since she had written in her *Enigmes* that a miraculous sign in the heavens would cause mankind to say oh! and ah! for twenty-four hours. In the preface to her *Discorsi* of 1798, one of her associates wrote: ". . . She hopes that soon the People . . . will understand everything: *May Heaven make it come quickly.*"[35]

32. Felice, *Note e ricerche*, pp. 147–48; Labrousse, *Discorsi*, pp. 5–6.
33. F. Valentinelli, *Memorie storiche sulle principali cagioni e circonstanze della rivoluzione di Roma e di Napoli* (n.p., 1800), p. 280.
34. Labrousse, *Discorsi*, p. 196.   35. Ibid., pp. 8, 284.

Labrousse was still a French patriot, but she was critical of many of her government's actions in Italy. She spoke of her "degenerate nation," which allowed the old Roman aristocracy to remain in power; yet she insisted that France was still capable of the "regeneration of the nations." France's wars were against despots, not against peoples. "France does not seek to be mistress of all the world." She "seeks solely to assure her tranquillity [and] to draw the people out of slavery."[36]

While it is true that the *Discorsi* contain none of the violent antipapal and anticlerical rhetoric that dominates the *Journal de Pierre Pontard*, Labrousse's experiences after her arrest had strengthened her conviction that the Pope must either reform his church and abandon his temporal authority or else face God's continued wrath. She had come to Rome to tell the Pope to get rid of those things that were false in the church, "because they were displeasing to God." He had refused to see her, had imprisoned her, had spread lies about her. He was being punished for his blindness: "You see how heaven treats him as if it wants to swallow him up." Despite her sufferings, there is no evidence that Labrousse ceased to regard herself as an entirely orthodox Roman Catholic. She recalled that she had taken daily Communion for more than thirty years, "and always with a new eagerness and an indescribable joy."[37]

Perhaps the most surprising thing about the *Discorsi* is that so little of it is millenarian, mystical, or even spiritual. It is entirely unlike the works of Labrousse's more conventionally prophetic contemporaries, Catherine Théot, Richard Brothers, and Joanna Southcott. In an unsystematic way, Labrousse dealt with a variety of topics that interested her. One section of the book, for example, concerns the four "principles" that theretofore had "dominated the earth": "despotism, modern theology, medicine, and *ridiculisme*." By despotism, she meant kingship. Like Pontard, she was able to find biblical evidence that God himself had opposed the rule of kings. By her strange term *ridiculisme*, she referred to the aristocrats, who she said had caused the French Revolution by ridiculing any who "opposed their conduct."[38] The passage on "modern theology" is so incoherent and so full of typographical errors that it is impossible to understand. Most curious of all is the long attack on medicine. "It is incontestable that the theory of medicine is false," she began. "It is the sick person himself who ought to be his own doctor."[39] Having

36. Ibid., pp. 164, 244.   37. Ibid., pp. 96, 106.
38. Ibid., p. 74.   39. Ibid., p. 30.

discerned the causes of his own illness, he can be healed by the techniques of animal magnetism.

Another of her medical theories concerned the raising of children. Here her views clearly owed something to the widespread contemporary interest in education and child rearing (of which Rousseau's *Emile* is the finest example) and something to her own stormy relations with her mother and brothers. As children grow up, she wrote, "NEVER PROVOKE THEM." Left to develop as they would, "like flowers," they would "succeed in being men powerful as gods."[40] Men would be healthy and happy if they would but exercise what Labrousse called their "liberty." They should eat only when hungry, consult their own inner nature, and "follow it in everything, because . . . it will indicate everything that will be necessary."[41]

The late eighteenth century produced several prophetesses who taught that the regeneration of the world was the special calling of members of their sex. In this, Labrousse is no exception, although her conception of woman's role was considerably more worldly than that of Ann Lee of the Shakers or of Jemimah Wilkinson, the Universal Friend. For too long, Labrousse wrote, the education of women had been neglected. They had been made to believe that "they were good for nothing but making babies." She had long believed that soon women would govern the world, since they "sympathize more with suffering humanity than do men."[42]

Finally, after two hundred and ten pages, Labrousse's curious mixture of private revelation, popular culture, and political observation ends with a characteristic touch. In order to show that what she said was "not in vain," she signed the work with her "four names . . . CLOTILDE SUZANNE COURCELLE LABROUSSE."[43]

In the fall of 1799, military reverses elsewhere led the French Republic to withdraw its troops from Rome. On 26 November the prophetess of Périgord was arrested again, but after an interrogation she was allowed to return to France. She left Rome on 3 December, only weeks before the advent of the year 1800 for which she had waited for so long.

Preferring not to go back to Périgord, she returned instead to Paris. There she lived quietly, in a pension in Montparnasse operated by Pierre Pontard, until her death in 1821. The only sources of information on her last years, the contemporary biographical dictionaries, rely mainly on hearsay and tend to repeat one another, but they all agree that she retained a small circle of followers. Ac-

40. Ibid., pp. 56–58.   41. Ibid., pp. 60–62.
42. Ibid., p. 190.   43. Ibid., p. 210.

cording to some of them, she abandoned Roman Catholicism in order to explore occultism and alchemy. The credulous Moreau accepted this story, on the basis of what informants told him.[44] There is no evidence, however, in the writings of Labrousse or Pontard that either of them was ever interested in the sorts of spiritualist and alchemical projects that absorbed the intellectuals of the Avignon Society.

The two fullest and most sympathetic biographical sketches, in *Les Femmes célèbres* and *Biographies des hommes vivants*, say that Labrousse continued to study the Bible, especially the Apocalypse, and that she continued to believe herself called to a special mission connected with the reform of the church. She lived a life of quiet piety, retaining her health, her memory, and her "mental health" until her death, at the age of 74, "in Pontard's arms." In her will, she named him her heir. Her family took the will to court on the grounds that she was incompetent, but Pontard won the case and received her small inheritance.

The information on Pontard's last years is equally fragmentary.[45] It is known that he resigned his hospital post in Périgueux and went to Paris at the end of 1795. He may have operated a school there until about 1801, when he became a toll collector. Like many others of his generation, Pontard's sudden rise to prominence on the crest of the Revolution was followed by an equally abrupt fall and decades of hardship, obscurity, and frustration. After his death, one story current in Périgueux held that Pontard had collaborated with the novelist Pigault-Lebrun (who had also worked as a Paris toll collector) on some of his works. Another story insisted that Pontard had been reduced to cleaning the streets of Périgueux, accompanied by a donkey that was known in the town as "Pontard's ass." He did publish a book, an elementary French grammar, in 1812. In the preface, he said that he had been teaching in a school for girls in Paris. Sometime after 1815, he received a pension from his old friend and benefactress, the duchesse de Bourbon. And in 1832 he died, at the age of eighty-three, in a rest home near Paris.

With the death of her most loyal disciple, the story of Suzette Labrousse reaches its conclusion. She left no other followers, no intellectual legacy. Twice in her life, between 1790 and 1792 and again in 1798, she had enjoyed considerable notoriety; but it did not

44. Moreau, *Une mystique révolutionnaire*, pp. 234-36.
45. Henri Lacape, *Pierre Pontard, évêque constitutionnel de la Dordogne* (Bordeaux: Bière, 1952), pp. 59-60; P. J. Credot, *Pierre Pontard, évêque constitutionnel de la Dordogne* (Paris: Delhomme & Briquet, 1893), pp. 604-6; and H. Brugière, *Le livre d'or des diocèses de Périgueux et de Sarlat; ou, Le clergé du Périgord pendant la période révolutionnaire* (Montreuil-sur-Mer: Notre-Dame-des-Prés, 1893).

last. Even before she set out on the "respectable folly" of her pilgrimage to Rome, interest in her prophecies had declined. The address she delivered as she crossed France in the spring of 1792 made no mention of the glorious eschatological event she expected to initiate when she reached her destination, and it may be that the popular interest she does seem to have aroused reflected fascination less with Suzette Labrousse herself than with the prophetess of Périgord as a pious Jacobin, a phenomenon that was not yet unthinkable in 1792. It is impossible to know whether the spectacle of a barefooted pilgrim on her way to convert the Pope was merely a curiosity or whether, instead, she recalled to the people who saw her a memory of the religious practices of earlier and more pious centuries.

It was possibly the modesty of her claims for herself and the moderation of her views that explain why Labrousse left no disciples to carry on her work. A woman exceptional only for her piety, she was responding to specific political circumstances, first in Périgord and later in Paris and Rome, when she attempted, in her writings and speeches, to reconcile her essentially conventional Catholic beliefs with her deep sense of the Revolution's moral and eschatological significance. She made few exalted claims for herself, and she offered to those who heard her none of the promises of glory and sanctification of a Southcott, a Brothers, or a Théot. She practised mesmerist healing, but she claimed no miraculous powers. Her "mission," at least the part that involved her suspension in the sky for twenty-four hours, as a sign to the Pope and the Catholic faithful that the Third Age of the Spirit had arrived with the French Revolution, was certainly "exalted"; but even here, the vagueness and the secretiveness of her allusions to it and her failure to elaborate more fully on the nature of the expected world regeneration suggest that she herself was slightly uncomfortable with the role she believed God had intended her to play in the working out of the divine plan.

Her failure to leave any spiritual heirs should not obscure the fact that the vision of a spiritualized revolution that Labrousse and Pontard articulated did not fade entirely after terror, aggressive war, and military dictatorship had supplanted the ideals of the early Revolution. Something of their dream of "one flock and one shepherd" can be seen in the utopian socialisms of Saint-Simon, Fourier, and Cabet. The call for the moral and political regeneration of France lived on, at least until mid-century, in the writings of Buchez, Boullan, and above all Lamennais. None of them imagined that the advent of the millennium would be as simple and miraculous as Labrousse and her followers had thought, but the dream, the possibility, was still vital.

CHAPTER 4

The
Popular Piety
of Catherine
Théot

THERE is no evidence that Suzette Labrousse and
Catherine Théot ever met. They probably did not, for during the
months Labrousse spent in Paris in early 1792, Théot was living ob-
scurely on the rue des Rosiers in the Marais, attended by a few
disciples. It was after Labrousse had set out for Rome that some of her
own followers, most notably Colonel Pescheloche and Dom Gerle,
began visiting the worship services conducted by the aged former
domestic servant who called herself "Mother Catherine."

Catherine Théot's prominence as a prophet was never as great as
Suzette Labrousse's had been in 1790 nor as great as Richard Brothers's
would be in 1795. It is ironic, therefore, that the political machinations connected with the overthrow of Robespierre should have given
her not only brief prominence in 1794 but also a celebrity in the his-
tories of the French Revolution that Labrousse and Brothers will
never enjoy. Also, thanks to the scrupulous care with which the Paris
police and the surveillance committees of the Paris sections recorded
and filed their interrogations of suspects, it is possible to know in
considerable detail who Théot's followers were and what she and they
believed.

Albert Mathiez pointed out fifty years ago that Catherine Théot
deserved more respectful attention from historians than her contemporaries had given her. Relying on the materials (now in the Archives
Nationales) collected on the Théot "conspiracy" by the Committee of
General Security, the police, and the committees in the sections, he
argued that she represented the end of that "Christian revolutionary
mysticism . . . which had moved one part of the masses at the beginning of the Revolution."[1] The "regeneration" that 1789–90 seemed

1. Albert Mathiez, *Contributions à l'histoire religieuse de la Révolution française*
(Paris: Alcan, 1907), p. 142. For the fullest accounts of the Théot affairs and its political
implications, see ibid., pp. 107–42; and Mathiez, "Robespierre et le procès de
Catherine Théot," *Annales historiques de la Révolution française* 6 (1929): 392–97.

to embody was translated into Christian terms. Men would become moral, the church would return to its ancient simplicity and purity, and finally, Jesus Christ would return to rule for a thousand years.

More recently, Albert Soboul has called attention to the emergence of cults of the Revolutionary martyrs Marat, Dugué, and Chalier.[2] These cults, he contends, differed profoundly from the bourgeois and official expressions of revolutionary religion that Mathiez studied in that they derived from the traditional religion of popular culture, with its veneration of saints and martyrs. Olwen Hufton has recently taken Soboul's argument one step further. The shocks of 1792, she maintains, produced among the women of the poor a religious fervor of an intensity "without parallel in the eighteenth century." The object of this fervor, which lasted into 1794, was the revolutionary nation. But hunger, unemployment, and the failure of the social revolution gradually led the women to turn away from the Revolution and to revive a "visceral" popular Catholicism, which "owed its strength to the rigours of the times, the imminence of death from disease or under-nourishment, shame, failure, the sense of contrition which sought as solace . . . the sort of expiatory religion which defies rooting out."[3]

Unfortunately, in concentrating on revolutionary religion as an expression of working-class consciousness, Soboul and Hufton have ignored an implication of Mathiez's work that does have significance for the study of the religious history of the French Revolution. Théot and her followers represented the persistence into the French Revolutionary period of that tradition of devotion, sometimes heretical, often anticlerical, that can be described as "popular piety." George Mosse defines the phrase as "the hopes and aspirations of the multitude, whose religious awareness tends to be immediate and naive. . . . There is a sameness about such popular piety which preserves the traditional texture of its modes of thought and expression from the Middle Ages into recent times."[4]

In a recent article, Michel Eude questions Mathiez's interpretation of the Théot affair. He contends that there was a genuine "inquiétude" in 1794 among the members of the ruling committees of the National Convention concerning the extent of mystical religion ("Points de vue sur l'affaire Catherine Théot," *Annales historiques de la Révolution française* 41 [1969]: 606-29).

2. Albert Soboul, "Sentiment religieux et cultes populaires pendant la Révolution: Saintes patriotes et martyrs de la liberté," *Annales historiques de la Révolution française* 29 (1957): 193-213.

3. Olwen Hufton, "Women in Revolution, 1789-1796," *Past and Present*, no. 53 (1971), pp. 106-7.

4. George L. Mosse and H. G. Koenigsberger, *Europe in the Sixteenth Century* (New York: Holt, Rinehart, and Winston, 1968), p. 87. See also Gordon Leff, *Heresy in the Later Middle Ages*, 2 vols. (Manchester: Manchester University Press, 1967), 1: 13-22.

In the case of Suzette Labrousse, the traditions of popular piety can be seen in her mission—a pilgrimage to the holy city, made barefoot, begging, in the dress of a Beguine. These traditions may be supposed to underlie the *Enigmes* and her other writings, but vagueness, her miscellaneous notions on politics and science, and the guiding hand of Pierre Pontard make it possible to perceive them only dimly. With Catherine Théot, whose sermons and letters were copied out by faithful secretaries, the persistence of popular piety into the French Revolution is seen much more clearly. And while it is only a guess it is at least arguable that Théot's circle was not unique; that throughout France there were similar groups which accepted the Revolution just as wholeheartedly, which also met to read the Bible, sing, hear sermons, and pray for the salvation of themselves and the French nation.

Catherine Théot was born at Barenton, near Avranches, in Normandy on 6 May 1716.[5] Her parents were illiterate peasants. It is unclear whether Catherine knew how to read and write. She was unable to sign her name to the police interrogation in 1794, but by then she was severely crippled by a palsy. Like Labrousse, her sense of religious vocation had begun in earliest childhood. She wrote during the Revolution that she had been "given to God from infancy"; one of her disciples recalled hearing her say that when she was only four years old, "God had made known to her that he would make an alliance with her."[6]

Having acquired a reputation in her village for piety, Théot was sent by her parish priest to Paris and placed her under the spiritual direction of the abbé Joseph Grisel. After having left his native Normandy, Grisel won some eminence both at the court of Louis XV and as the author of mystical tracts aimed primarily at an audience of women. Grisel placed her in the Convent of the Miramionnes, where she worked for many years as a domestic servant.[7] At one point she returned to Normandy and sought admission to a convent near her home, but God told her to return to "the greater world that there is in Paris," where she "would be all the joy of Israel" and "would deliver his people from the wiles of Satan."[8] She returned to Paris, where she spent the rest of her life.

---

5. Gustave Lenôtre [pseud.], *Robespierre et la "Mère de Dieu"* (Paris: Perrin, 1926), p. 85 nn. 1, 2.
6. Archives Nationales, T604[2], and F[7]4768, doss. Lauriston.
7. F. P., *Notices sur les inspirés, fanatiques, imposteurs, béates, etc., de la département de la Manche* (Saint-Lô, 1829), pp. 10–11.
8. Archives Nationales, T604[2].

Théot became convinced that God had called her "to do penance for all the nation." She submitted herself to an austere penitential regimen, which included wearing a hair shirt and a barbed crown. Until she abandoned the sacraments in about 1769, she had taken daily communion at 5 A.M. Since she had to work during the day, she spent part of each night carrying out the penances she imposed upon herself.[9]

It was in 1769 that Théot met Michel Hastain, a writer and former royal official from Saint Lô, not far from her native village in Normandy; for twenty-five years, he would be her disciple and sometimes her secretary.[10] In April 1779, Théot, Hastain, and three aged followers were arrested.

According to a nephew, Raphael Théot, a vicar at the church of Saint Roch in Paris until he abjured his vows in 1794, Catherine had been inspired by reading the lives of Saints Teresa of Avila and Catherine of Siena and had come to believe that she alone could understand the Scriptures. He complained that she had filled his life "with bitterness and vexation, by the public scenes she had caused at different times, by her stubbornness in making proselytes," and that she had hampered his career by prejudicing the archbishop, Christophe de Beaumont, against him.[11]

Beaumont, despite his distaste for her activities, had a use for the pious domestic servant. Knowing that she "ran to all the sermons," he wrote her a letter inquiring about them and about "the knowledge that God had given her." She cherished the letter and soon began to get up in church and preach against the preachers. She spoke, her nephew wrote, "against the priests and their doctrine, until a curé of Paris of the parish Gervais obtained an order to have her sent to the Bastille."

After six weeks in the Bastille, Théot was moved to the mental hospital of the Salpétrière, where she remained for three years. Very little is known of her activities between 1782 and 1793. She went to live in the Marais with Marie Madelaine Amblard, the widow Godefroy, a middle-aged seamstress with whom she had probably been acquainted before her arrest. The widow Godefroy continued to care for the increasingly infirm Mother Catherine until they were both arrested in

9. Chenon, *Vie privée de Catherine Théot, se disant Mère de Dieu* (Paris, 1794), p. 4. Chenon was *commissaire de police* at the Bastille in 1779, and the *Vie privée de Catherine Théot* is his report prepared at the time of Théot's arrest in that year. He was still *commissaire* in 1789 (Robert Darnton, communication in *Annales historiques de la Révolution française* 42 [1970]: 666).

10. Chenon, *Vie privée de Catherine Théot*, pp. 2-3; Archives Nationales, F⁷4739, doss. Hastain; and Eude, "Points de vue," p. 608.

11. Archives Nationales, F⁷4775²⁷, doss. Théot.

1794. Perhaps Théot again attracted a circle of followers, but only one of the persons interrogated in 1794 (aside from Godefroy and Hastain) had known her before the Revolution. When asked by the police how they had learned about her, they all said that a friend, relative, or neighbor had invited them to one of her meetings initially.

Théot's next brush with the authorities came in January 1793. When neighbors complained about the number of people observed going in and out of her apartment on the rue des Rosiers, the police investigated. In February, the public prosecutor of the Commune of Paris, Anaxagoras Chaumette, had Théot's dossier brought to the Hôtel de Ville. Chaumette, future apostle of the Cult of Reason, was apparently fascinated with the letters and sermons that it contained. He contacted Hastain, who obligingly provided him with a "Précis des sentiments et de la religion de la Citoyenne Catherine Théot," transcribed from the words of Mother Catherine herself and concerned primarily with the age of the Reign of God, which she said was "very near."[12]

All these documents show that Théot, like Labrousse, interpreted the French Revolution as part of a divine plan by which true morality and the true church would triumph and the way be prepared for Christ's return. Théot, however, claimed that she never commented on "affairs of the time," because, as she told her followers in October 1791: ". . . We are not of this world." Her references to events are vague: men should trust in God. One disciple recalled that she had urged those who attended her sessions "to fulfill their duties as citizens . . . and to observe the law."[13] Her only political activity was dictating letters, which she sent not only to the clergy but also, according to her nephew, to the different presidents of the National Convention.

The same disciple, a retired banker named Delaroche, told his interrogators in 1794 that Théot had said "it was God who had permitted the year 1789." She also claimed that it was because of her that the Swiss troops had left Paris after the crisis at the Champs de Mars in 1791. Delaroche had been attending her sessions for three years. A servant named Marie Bousquet, who had been going to them even longer, said that Théot had predicted that all nations would

12. The letters and sermons are included with Chaumette's papers in the Archives Nationales, T604². The "Précis" is in F⁷4775²⁷, doss. Théot. See also Eude, "Points de vue," p. 608.
13. Archives Nationales, F⁷4775²⁷, doss. Théot, and F⁷4667, doss. Delaroche. Mathiez summarized the Delaroche dossier and quoted substantial portions of it in *Autour de Robespierre* (Paris: Payot, 1925), pp. 128–35.

submit to France and the world would become "a family of brothers. . . . The French are destined to bring happiness to all nations, because they are the people chosen by God."[14]

This sense of France's special destiny was intensified when France declared war on Austria and Prussia in April. In one of her letters, Théot called on the Legislative Assembly, the king, the municipality of Paris, and the bishop of Paris to sign a statement urging the soldiers to pray to "le Seigneur de Nous" to bring peace and "to make us triumph over the enemies of Our Safety."[15]

There were more complaints about the daily assemblies at the widow Godefroy's in June 1793, and she and Théot were again interrogated by the police. They were again released, but when Hastain went to the surveillance committee of the section to protest the behavior of the agents who had raided Godefroy's apartment, he was sent to the Hôtel de Ville for further questioning. The committee suspected Hastain of believing doctrines similar to those of "the counterrevolutionaries of the Vendée"—doctrines that could be "disastrous to the republic."[16] About a week earlier, Théot had moved across the river to the rue Contrescarpe, near the Pantheon, so that she could continue to hold meetings without interference.

It is surely not coincidental that Théot's new lodgings were a few blocks away from those of Dom Gerle on the rue des Postes. The principal leaseholder of the building to which Théot and Godefroy moved was Colonel Pescheloche, the man who not long before had first brought Gerle to meet Mother Catherine. Gerle's involvement with Théot was known to the police, for at the time of Hastain's interrogation, he had been asked if he knew Gerle's address. He had answered (incorrectly, it seems) that Gerle lived "chez Cambeau."[17] Apparently the bustling Gombault, who knew everybody in Paris's mystical underground, had taken the exmonk into his charge.

Théot was allowed to continue her meetings for nearly a year without further interference, despite the rather extensive dossiers concerning her which had been collected by the Revolutionary security network. Furthermore, many of her followers in the Marais continued to come to sessions at the new location across the river. Although the new neighbors also complained about the activities in Théot's apartment, the authorities took no action until May 1794, when two gendarmes, acting either on their own authority or on that of the Com-

---

14. Archives Nationales, F⁷4768, doss. Lauriston.   15. Ibid., T604².
16. Ibid., F⁷4735, doss. Hastain.
17. Lenôtre, *Robespierre et la "Mère de Dieu"*, pp. 102, 104; Archives Nationales, F⁷4775²⁷, doss. Théot, and F⁷4722, doss. Gerle.

mittee of General Security of the National Convention, denounced Catherine Théot once again. This time, the Committee of General Security itself ordered two of its agents, Heron and Senar, to infiltrate the group and to arrest any members who seemed to be politically suspect.

Five days later, on 17 May, the agents attended a session at the rue Contrescarpe. During the service of worship, they called in the police who were waiting outside on the street. Fourteen of those present were charged and jailed, including Théot, Godefroy, and Gerle. These suspects were interrogated, and they in turn led the Committee of General Security and the section committees to other persons allegedly associated with the aged prophetess. Most of those arrested were artisans and working people, but the list also included Michel Hastain and a number of veterans of the duchesse de Bourbon's circle at Petit-Bourg, among them Quevremont, Bishop Miroudot, and Madame Law de Lauriston. In August, warrants were signed for the arrest of Pontard, Madame Pescheloche, and Claude de Saint-Martin, but they were saved by Robespierre's fall and the abrupt dismantling of the machinery of revolutionary justice.[18]

Théot and her followers were now made into a political issue by Robespierre's rivals and enemies in the two ruling committees. On 15 June, the fierce old atheist Marc Guillaume Alexis Vadier, in a speech to the National Convention, denounced "a primary school of fanaticism" which, while centered in Paris, had infected all of France and even the armies. He claimed that Théot, its leader, was known to the faithful variously as "Mother of God," "Mother of the Word," and "the New Eve" and that she promised "immortality of the soul and the body to those whom she has initiated into her mysteries." And in the rhetoric of the Terror that was either paranoid or hyperbolic or both, he further claimed that the sect was in fact part of a conspiracy that included royalists, mystics, emigrés, "fools, egoists, fops," William Pitt, and the King of Prussia.[19]

Although he did not dare say so, Vadier deplored Robespierre's religious policies. For him, Robespierre's projected Cult of the Supreme Being, Roman Catholic orthodoxy, and the millenarian fantasies of Catherine Théot were at bottom alike; all were fanatical, and all were fit only for mockery and contempt. By implicating Robespierre in

18. Eude, "Points de vue," pp. 609, 614–15; Archives Nationales, F⁷4775²⁷, doss. Théot.
19. Marc-Guillaume-Alexis Vadier, *Convention nationale: Rapport et Project de decret présentés à la Convention nationale, au nom des Comités de Sûreté générale et de Salut public* (Paris, 1794), pp. 4–5, 8–9, 17–19, 21. The report is also printed in *Réimpression de l'ancien Moniteur*, 32 vols. (Paris: Bureau Central, 1840–54), 20: 737–42.

some fashion in the activities of the rue Contrescarpe, he could then portray him as a fanatic who sought dictatorship for himself.

Robespierre managed to persuade the Committee of Public Safety to keep the case from coming to trial, although the National Convention had supported Vadier's request that Théot and the four he named as her chief disciples be brought before the Revolutionary Tribunal. Perhaps Robespierre sensed in the whole affair a trap that was being laid for him; certainly he believed the prisoners to be a harmless group of zealots without political importance. Tensions increased within the ruling committees as the anti-Robespierre faction sought to destroy his prestige and power.

In the climactic session of 9 Thermidor, Vadier claimed that a letter addressed to Robespierre had been discovered under Théot's mattress; it announced that his mission had been "predicted in Ezekiel" and that he would establish a "new cult."[20] It is unlikely that this revelation was crucial in persuading the convention to vote for Robespierre's arrest. After Vadier's speech, Robespierre's other adversaries quickly shifted the attack to other, more tangible grievances.

It is doubtful, indeed, that the letter even existed. Robespierre and Dom Gerle had had a few casual contacts in the years since they had both sat on the Left in the National Assembly in 1790–91. Robespierre had written a letter stating that Gerle was a "bon patriote" after Gerle had been refused a *certificat de civisme* by the surveillance committee of his section because of his ill-fated motion, in 1790, to make Roman Catholicism the state religion.[21] Gerle had also tried unsuccessfully to persuade Robespierre to get him an administrative post to supplement his small pension, but there is no evidence either that Robespierre belonged to Catherine Théot's sect or that Théot knew him. There are three contemporary accounts that claim to quote Théot's letter to Robespierre,[22] but their versions of its contents vary so widely that one suspects the whole story to have been a fabrication by the Committee of General Security and its secret agents.

20. *Réimpression de l'ancien Moniteur*, 21: 329, 334.
21. Christophe-Antoine Gerle, "Mémoire," printed in Francisque Mège, *Révolution française: Notes biographiques sur les députés de la Basse Auvergne . . . Dom Gerle* (Paris: Aubry, 1866), pp. 33–34.
22. In addition to Vadier in *Réimpression de l'ancien Moniteur*, 21: 334, they are Gabriel Senar, *Révélations puisées dans les cartons des Comités de Salut public et de Sûreté générale; ou, Mémoires (inédits) de Senart* [sic] *publiés par Alexis Dumesnil*, in Saint-Aldin Berville and F. Barrière, *Collection des mémoires*, 2d ed., 53 vols. (Paris: Pastu, 1824), 27: 182; and Joachim Vilate, *Les mystères de la Mère de Dieu dévoilés*, vol. 3, *Les causes secrètes de la Révolution du 9 au 10 thermidor* (Paris, 1795), p. 57.

One of the accounts is Vadier's. The other two were written by men who had worked for the ruling committees during the Reign of Terror. Both Gabriel Senar and Joachim Vilate had direct knowledge of the Théot affair. Senar had in fact been one of those who arrested and interrogated Théot and her followers in May, but his version of that episode, written and published while he was in prison in 1795, differs markedly from the report he signed at the time of the arrests. Both he and Vilate were primarily concerned with exculpating themselves from "the crimes of Robespierre." Both invented details to make their stories more interesting, and both tended, like Vadier, to use the rhetoric and preconceptions of deism to describe the doctrines of Mother Catherine and her followers. The uneducated Jacobins in the sections who interrogated Théot's believers were no more sympathetic with what they heard, but at least they transcribed as faithfully as they could what they were told by the suspects. Therefore a reliable estimate of the religious ideas of Théot and her group will depend almost entirely on the police records in the French Archives.

These records show that certain significant changes took place in the ideas and practices of Théot's sect after 1793. Mathiez believed that these modifications derived from the influence of Dom Gerle,[23] but it may have been that the sense of revolutionary excitement, the alternations of hope and despair that the Revolution produced in the spring of 1794, penetrated in a vague way to Théot and her followers. She had been a millenarian at least since the 1770s; at her interrogation in 1779, she had described herself as "the virgin who would receive the little Jesus, who would come from heaven to earth . . . to bring peace to all the earth and to receive all nations." But as late as 1791, her message was primarily that the time had not yet come and that all would be well.[24]

There was a heightened and more precise sense of eschatological urgency in the "Précis" that Hastain prepared for Chaumette in 1793, but by 1794 Théot was alluding directly to the book of Revelation. The gendarme Pidoux, in his denunciation of her to the Committee of General Security, reported her claim that "all the nations [would] be obliged to come to her, that there [were] seven seals and the sixth had been broken, and that she had received the power from God only a month [before] to break the seventh." The moment was near and all the events would come to pass at Paris, which God had chosen as the greatest city.[25]

23. Mathiez, *Contributions*, pp. 111–13.
24. Chenon, *Vie privée de Catherine Théot*, p. 4; Archives Nationales, T604[2].
25. Archives Nationales, F[7]4774[27], doss. Théot.

Why are there not more indications in the police records that Théot expected an imminent Second Coming? The reason may be that she had only recently come to that conviction. It may also be due to the failure of the interrogators to ask her disciples the right questions.[26] Their main concern was to find the names of other disciples and to discover if Théot had expressed politically subversive sentiments or taught doctrines that were either aristocratic or pessimistic. That the doctrines were all within a Christian tradition, partly orthodox and partly heretical, was of no interest to them.

France's war against the monarchs of Europe continued to have God's blessing, according to Théot. One disciple told the authorities that Mother Catherine had said that "all the Children of the Fatherland would be his own and that they . . . would shed their blood in order to speed Liberty and that they would return victorious" and that there would be no more kings. God would preserve the National Convention from harm.[27] Senar and Heron reported that one of the hymns sung at the service they attended proclaimed that "the armies of the Serpent" would be conquered and that God was the general in command of the French armies.[28]

In 1792, "the Serpent" meant the devil or, perhaps, Antichrist. Théot's letters of 1791 had promised that the Reign of God would begin soon. "Satan will have no power to hold us because death will be destroyed and the Serpent will lose his life." By 1794 she also identified that serpent with the enemies of France. The French, on the other hand, according to one disciple, were destined "to bring happiness to all the Nations, because they are the people chosen by God."[29]

Théot had believed for some time that the school of law, near the Pantheon, was specially favored by God. In one of her letters, she declared that New Saint Geneviève (as the Pantheon was still known) should be the house of prayer for the school "until God comes into his Reign." As her millenial expectations intensified, the role of the school of law became still more exalted. It would be the site "for rallying around Mother Catherine as the daughter of God," said one disciple. Another declared that Théot lived near the Pantheon so that when the time came, she could "give her instructions publicly there." Senar and Heron reported hearing Godefroy say that after the minis-

26. This point is suggested by Claus-Peter Clasen, "Medieval Heresies in the Reformation," *Church History* 32 (Dec. 1963): 392-414.
27. Archives Nationales, F⁷4720, doss. Gautherot.
28. Ibid., F⁷4775²⁷, doss. Théot. The Heron-Senar report from the Théot dossier was printed by Mathiez in "Catherine Théot et le myticisme chrétien révolutionnaire," *Révolution française* 40 (1901): 515.
29. Archives Nationales, F⁷4768, doss. Lauriston.

ters and armies of the serpent had been destroyed, Théot herself would govern the world. In another report, however, a disciple declared that God would rule.[30]

An innovation in 1794 was a ceremony of ritual kisses, which Senar believed to be a rite of initiation into a secret society. The rite consisted of making the sign of the cross on the believer's forehead and kissing him on the two eyes, the two cheeks, the forehead, and the chin. Those interrogated all agreed that the ceremony, which one follower said Théot called "the sign of the Christian," had been practiced for a short time, two months at most.[31] The significance of the ceremony may have been to assure the faithful that they would be preserved at the time of the Second Coming. This might explain why both Théot and Gerle admitted at the time of their arrest that many soldiers had come to her sessions before leaving for the front. Like the sealed letters that Joanna Southcott would issue to her followers in England a decade later, the ceremony of the kisses might thus offer the promise of personal immortality to men and women in whom intensified hopes for the millennium were accompanied by an increasing fear of death. And according to one disciple, Théot said the rite "would accomplish a great movement which will end the war."[32]

A disciple who was asked in June 1793 what sorts of people came to hear Théot replied, "des riches et des pauvres."[33] The police reports indicate that there were indeed a few wealthy followers. A "farmer-general" and his wife were arrested with Théot, and also three persons "living on their income." The majority, however, were artisans, petty shopkeepers, and servants living either in the environs of the Marais or in the immediate neighborhood of the rue Contrescarpe on the Left Bank. Listed in the police reports were a lacemaker, a worker in linen, two lemonade sellers, a seller of meat at Les Halles, two cafe owners, two architects, a baker, and several shopkeepers. The great majority of the disciples were women.[34]

It is not clear when or how completely the duchesse de Bourbon's circle took up Catherine Théot. Pescheloche seems to have been the first to learn of her; he brought Gerle, who in turn may have brought Pierre Pontard. The time was mid-1792, after Suzette Labrousse had set out on her pilgrimage. One disciple said he had heard Gerle tell Pontard at about that time "that it is better not to die than to die,"

30. Ibid., F⁷4775²⁷, doss. Théot, and F⁷4768, doss. Lauriston.
31. Ibid., F⁷4768, doss. Lauriston.
32. Ibid., F⁷4775²⁷, doss. Théot.   33. Ibid., F⁷4739, doss. Hastain.
34. Ibid., F⁷4775²⁷, doss. Théot, and F⁷4768, doss. Lauriston; Eude, "Points de vue," pp. 600–615.

and that if the Legislative Assembly recognized Théot "for what she seemed to be, we would be at the end of the corruption of morals." She "would crush the head of the serpent," and there would be no more death and no more war.[35] This testimony suggests that Théot did not replace Labrousse in the hearts of the prophetess of Périgord's chief disciples. The nature of Mother Catherine's spiritual pretensions was quite different, offering as they did both spiritual knowledge and the assurance of personal salvation. It was entirely possible to believe in both Labrousse and Théot.

The absence of references to Théot in the *Journal prophétique* and the bantering tone of the reference to her and Gerle in the letter Pontard wrote to Gombault at the time of his marriage suggest that for him, at least, the interest was rather casual. There is another possible line of connection between the old prophetess and the Bishop of the Dordogne. When Pontard returned to Paris on business in 1793, he told the readers of the *Journal de Pierre Pontard* that he could be reached at the presbytery of the Church of Saint Roch.[36] Saint Roch at that time had three curés who had taken up arms and joined the Jacobins on the night of 10 August 1792. One of the three was Raphael Théot.

Pontard was never arrested and interrogated about his relationship with Catherine Théot. Neither was Pescheloche, who was serving with the army. Pescheloche's wife, too, escaped arrest. The duchesse de Bourbon had been under arrest at Marseilles for some months but was not interrogated about Théot. Among the members of the Petit-Bourg circle who were arrested, several denied any but the most casual acquaintance with the aged prophetess. Miroudot, Quevremont, and Gerle all sent statements from prison protesting their innocence, although Gerle's declarations conflicted pathetically with his own candid testimony to the police at the time of his and Théot's arrest. A much more open and cooperative witness was Madame Jeanne Carvalho Law de Lauriston, a frequent guest at Petit-Bourg. She told her interrogators that she had seen Gerle, Quevremont, and Miroudot at Théot's religious services and added that Théot and Godefroy had spent August 1793 at Petit-Bourg, where Pescheloche and Gerle were also staying.

Another visitor to the palace at that time had been Claude de Saint-Martin, the old friend and spiritual advisor of the duchesse. After the

35. Archives Nationales, F⁷4667, doss. Delaroche.
36. *Journal de Pierre Pontard*, second fortnight of April 1793, p. 124.

Revolution, Saint-Martin recorded his recollections of the "Cateri-
nettes." He rejected Théot's doctrines (just as he had rejected those
of Labrousse the year before), but at the same time he was drawn to
Mother Catherine because of "the strong attraction" that she radi-
ated.[37]

Senar claimed in his *Mémoires* that "the number of disciples of this
sect is inconceivable; it has spread everywhere."[38] Senar certainly
exaggerated wildly. About thirty persons were present when Théot
was arrested in 1794, and half of these were released because they
said they had only come out of curiosity. A casual visitor to Mother
Catherine's meetings in 1793 said that there had never been more than
fifteen persons present.[39] In all, some seventy individuals were named
in Heron and Senar's report and in the various interrogations by the
sectional surveillance committees.

There is no evidence that Théot's disciples in any way constituted
a secret society. Nor, despite the involvement of the Petit-Bourg
mystics, does it appear that Théot had any interest in mesmerism,
Masonic ritual, and occultism. Hers were essentially lay prayer meetings, and they changed little in the course of the Revolution. They
consisted of short sermons by Théot, readings from the Bible and the
missal, and singing. Occasionally, the widow Godefroy or Dom Gerle
would speak to the assembly.

In some ways, Théot's activities anticipated the revival of popular
Catholicism that occurred in France in 1795. More striking, however,
are those aspects of her beliefs that connect her with the heresies of
the later Middle Ages.

There is, for example, her anticlericalism, which included a denial
of the efficacy of the sacraments. Sounding very much like a Spiritual
Franciscan, Théot contended that God's elect must break with the
guilty church. After she had quarrelled with her confessor in about
1769, God told her that "she no longer needed to take communion,
and that he would lead her himself."[40] It was her denunciations of
priests that put her in the Bastille in 1779. One disciple told the
police in 1794 that Théot had in effect converted him from the usages
of the Roman Catholic Church. She had "enlightened him," he said,

37. Archives Nationales, F⁷4768, doss. Lauriston; Louis-Claude de Saint-Martin, *Mon
portrait historique et philosophique (1789–1802)*, ed. Robert Amadou (Paris:
Juilliard, 1961), pp. 220–21.
38. Senar, *Mémoires (inédits) de Senart*, p. 186.
39. Archives Nationales, F⁷4739, doss. Hastain, and F⁷4775²⁷, doss. Theot.
40. Chenon, *Vie privée de Catherine Théot*, p. 4.

concerning "the uselessness of confession and priests and of the sufficiency of looking to God himself for the remission of sins."[41] Another disciple said that Théot had told her followers to pray and to seek the temple of God only within their own hearts.[42] Théot wrote in the "Précis" that the true church, which had not yet been established, would be for all the world, something that the Roman Catholic church had never been: "Of all the churches, has it ever been universal? . . . It is to his elect that the Lord speaks when he says . . . go out, my people, from this guilty Babylon, for fear of sharing with it the punishment that I am preparing for it."[43]

It is not clear exactly what Théot conceived her own role to be. She had told the police in 1779 that she was the "virgin who would receive the little Jesus," that God had revealed his "mysteries" to her alone, and that it was she who was "destined to accomplish them." In one of her 1791 letters, she announced: "I am the first of the Christians; I am the first who has received from God his spirit and grace." God had given her knowledge of the past, the future, and "the true Religion that is not established and that is to be established only at the end of the times in which we are now."[44]

There is no evidence that Théot (unlike Joanna Southcott twenty years later) ever believed that she would give birth to a baby. Senar said to her at the time of her arrest, after he had received the ceremonial kisses and before he called in the police: "It is you, then, mother divine, who protects us . . . so that we will not die." Théot responded, "Yes, . . . I am sent from God. The Virgin has spiritually conceived Jesus Christ and I produce the Word of God, which is the same thing."[45] Asked by her interrogators if it were not true that Théot expected to give birth to a child, a disciple replied that it was not "a carnal childbirth" but rather a "spiritual" one that gave "the knowledge that everything that comes from God is spiritual."[46]

Théot did regard herself as the New Eve. She stated in one letter that "God has announced a New Eve who will deliver us from the iniquity into which the first Eve led us by her disobedience." Gerle told Senar that she was "destined by God to give happiness to the world and to repair the misfortune of the first Mother." He wrote a verse in her honor that concluded with the lines:

41. Archives Nationales, F⁷4667, doss. Delaroche.
42. Ibid., F⁷4720, doss. Gautherot. Cf. Leff, *Heresy in the Later Middle Ages*, 1: 7–8.
43. Ibid., F⁷4775²⁷, doss. Théot.
44. Chenon, *Vie privée de Catherine Théot*, pp. 4, 6; Archives Nationales, T604².
45. Archives Nationales, F⁷4775²⁷, doss. Théot.
46. Ibid., F⁷4768, doss. Lauriston.

Ni culte, ni prêtre, ni roi
Car la nouvelle Eve, c'est toi.[47]

Concerning the New Eve, Théot was probably influenced by the ideas of Guillaume Postel, a native of her own village of Barenton and one of the leading scholars of sixteenth-century France.[48] Postel had met an old lady in Venice who claimed to be inspired by God, and in 1553 he published a book in which he contended that this woman, "Mère Jeanne," would redeem the human race, an act only a woman could accomplish, by freeing men from the damnation imposed by Adam's fall. This is precisely what Théot promised to do as the New Eve. Like Postel,[49] she declared that there would be a new gospel for the new dispensation, and like him she said that the prophets, the apostles, and Christ himself were only "figures" who presaged the spiritual era that would come soon. It may have been Michel Hastain who introduced this notion into her doctrines. In any event, the similarity of Postel's doctrines to those of Théot's "Précis" is striking.

Théot's growing millennial expectations had little to do with the nature of the world after the Second Coming. In the "Précis," she declared it false to say that all human beings would die at the last judgement. God "in his omnipotence will sweep iniquity from the earth, as the autumn wind sweeps the dust and the leaves, so that the face of the earth will be purified to be the eternal abode of man." And elsewhere in the "Précis" she stated: "the reign of God that I announce to you is therefore the reestablishment of the earth in its first degree of beauty and felicity," as it was when "Adam lived in it before the fall."[50]

The idea of a new gospel did not originate with Théot or Postel; the notion of an "Eternal Gospel" which would supersede the two Testaments and serve as the final revelation of God to man in the Third Age that was to be the culmination of human history dates back to the thirteenth-century followers of Joachim of Fiore. Like Postel

47. Archives Nationales, T604², and F⁷4775²⁷, doss. Théot; Gerle, "Mémoire," in Mège, *Révolution française*, p. 32. Gerle claimed that the subject of this verse was "truth."
48. F. P., *Notices sur les inspirés*, pp. 5–6, 11; William Bouwsma, *Concordia Mundi: The Career and Thought of Guillaume Postel* (Cambridge: Harvard University Press, 1957), pp. 15–18, 154–58.
49. Guillaume Postel, *Le thrésor des prophéties de l'univers*, ed. François Secret (The Hague: Martinus Nijhoff, 1969), pp. 40–41; Archives Nationales, F⁷4775²⁷, doss. Théot. Joachim of Fiore also spoke of "figures" which hid true reality: Leff, *Heresy in the Later Middle Ages*, 1: 76. It will be recalled that Duguet and other Jansenist millenarians also believed that the prophetic events promised in the New Testament had been prefigured in the Old.
50. Archives Nationales, F⁷4775²⁷, doss. Théot.

and others in the Joachimite tradition, Théot conceived her mission to be that of a prophet not only of the millennium but also of a new and final revelation from God. In a letter, she referred to "the gospel of the Reign of God," which "contains the word of God entirely pure; it was announced since the beginning; it is going to appear only with the Religion of Jesus Christ."[51] In the next letter, she explained that God had reserved knowledge of his gospel and his religion "to the last times." Madam Law de Lauriston and Marie Bousquet both believed that Théot intended to present the new gospel to the National Convention at the proper time. Then, if the Convention accepted it, "all the earth would be happy" and "wars would cease throughout the earth." If they did not, "things would be otherwise."[52]

What was the message of the eternal gospel? None of the interrogators thought to ask. Quite possibly Théot expected it to contain teachings similar to a passage in the "Précis" she had submitted to Chaumette: "Why will the Elect be saved? It is that they will have the true faith in the name of the Lord which I announce to them; it is by their good works, their charities, and their patience."[53] Here the vision is not very different from that of Pierre Pontard and Suzette Labrousse. At last there would be one religion for all men and one gospel. Their reception by mankind would constitute "the beginning of the Reign of God which will be established in our hearts and our spirit which will form the church of Jesus Christ and which will be universal."

According to the comtesse de Bohm, an inmate of the prison to which Théot and her female disciples were taken in 1794, the group's arrest did not shake their conviction that the millennium was at hand. One of them told the comtesse that soon everything in France would be transformed. Mother Catherine died in prison, a month after Robespierre had died on the scaffold. She never lost her serenity or her faith, the comtesse wrote, and when she died, her followers lighted candles and patiently awaited her miraculous resurrection.[54]

There were a few alarms in 1794 that sects similar to Théot's had appeared elsewhere in France. The district of Tanargue, in Provence, reported that "a new Catherine Théot" was winning converts in the countryside there, but the local authorities vowed that she would not escape arrest. Senar claimed that shortly after he had taken Théot

51. Ibid., T604².
52. Archives Nationales, F⁷4768, doss. Lauriston; Marjorie Reeves, *The Influence of Prophecy in the Later Middle Ages: A Study of Joachimism* (Oxford: Clarendon Press, 1969), pp. 108–9, 187–90, 494; Leff, *Heresy in the Later Middle Ages*, 1: 79–80.
53. Archives Nationales, F⁷4775²⁷, doss. Théot.
54. Lenôtre, *Robespierre et la "Mère de Dieu"*, pp. 321–24.

prisoner, he arrested "the prophet Elias, who wandered the fields and isolated quarters of Paris."[55]

A more dramatic episode occurred early in November in the mountainous region of the Forez, west of Lyons. Local authorities reported to the Committee of General Security that they had arrested some eighty men, women, and children found wandering in the forest. These people told their interrogators that they had gone into "the desert" to do penance before going to Jerusalem.[56] The great majority of the wanderers were local peasants, but there were indications that the movement was more widespread. When asked to give their names, almost all replied "Bonjour." This, coupled with the fact that some of the suspects came from the Bonjour brothers' former parish of Fareins, led the authorities to assume that these wanderers were somehow connected with the brothers and their sect, now centered in Paris. The authorities were probably correct, although there is no evidence that either the Bonjours or their associates Fialin and Drevet were directly responsible for the events in the Forez.

The Forez authorities, like those who interrogated Catherine Théot and her followers in Paris, were not interested in the religious beliefs that had led these peasants to abandon their farms and set out for Jerusalem. They were concerned instead with the threat to public order in a region that had so recently witnessed the terrible rebellion of Lyons against the Republic. Nevertheless, some indications emerge from the testimony to suggest that they, too, were imbued with an essentially traditional piety to which the revolutionary crisis had given a heightened sense of eschatological urgency.

The peasants said that by leaving their farms they had carried out the wishes of "Grand-papa, Jesus Christ," for the land was "striken with plague [pestiférée]; it was absolutely essential to abandon it." They had brought their children with them because the Holy Spirit was "on earth, hidden in the shape of a child."[57] The authorities inferred, probably rightly, that they were talking about the prophet Elias, whose birth the Bonjours had announced two years before. It was known that missionaries for this Elias had been in the region since 1792.[58]

55. *Réimpression de l'ancien Moniteur*, 21: 799; Senar, *Mémoires*, pp. 184–85.
56. Jean-Baptiste Galley, *Saint-Etienne et son district pendant la Révolution*, 3 vols. (Saint-Etienne: "La Loire républicaine," 1903–9), 2: 792–801, provides a useful collection of documents from the departmental archives. Claude Hau, *Le messie de l'an XIII et les fareinistes* (Paris: Denoël, 1955), pp. 149–56, narrates the story reliably.
57. Galley, *Saint-Etienne*, 2: 795.   58. Ibid., 1: 307.

Like the Convulsionaries, the sectaries in the Forez had a special affinity for the Old Testament. Their assumption of the name Bonjour suggests that they saw themselves as a tribe of Israel,[59] a possibility made more likely by the fact that each subgroup was led by a man who was called "Moses." There are indications in the testimony that the group saw itself as a kind of republican counterpart of the Kingdom of the New Jerusalem of millenarian tradition. They were organized, the authorities reported, into "the Republic of Jesus Christ," which was divided into a number of municipalities. They may also have been communists.[60]

The National Convention sent two representatives-on-mission to investigate. They freed many of the Bonjour tribe and sent them home, keeping only the leaders under arrest. The representatives were somewhat concerned by signs that the movement had spread beyond the Forez and by the arming of many of the men, but they were contemptuous of people they considered to be ignorant and harmless religious zealots. Both the representatives and the local authorities reported that the group was sexually promiscuous. It was said that its members cohabited "pell-mell" and called it marriage. Like the Fareinists and other Convulsionaries, they were accused of believing that nothing God commanded them to do could be evil.[61] There is some question whether these allegations were more than the usual gossip against heretics of antinomian and Free Spirit tendencies. Both before and after the Revolution, the Convulsionaries of the Lyonnais were known for their ascetic piety.

According to the abbé Grégoire, a number of Convulsionary groups persisted in the Lyons area throughout the Revolution and into the nineteenth century, all awaiting the incarnation of the Holy Spirit upon the return of the prophet Elias.[62] The largest group was associated with the *Amis de la Vérité*, Desfours de la Genetière's pre-Revolutionary agency of millenarian evangelism. Unlike the Republic of Jesus Christ or the Bonjour circle, the *Amis de la Vérité* were monarchists, uninfluenced in their beliefs by the events of the Revolution. They refrained from proselytizing, preferring instead to await the un-

59. Benoit Laurent, *Les béguins* (Saint-Etienne: "La Loire républicaine," 1944), p. 91.
60. Galley, *Saint-Etienne*, 3: 798. Galley (ibid., 1: 302) says that the Fareinist sect also practiced communism well into the nineteenth century.
61. Ibid., 2: 759, 800; Henri-Baptiste Grégoire, *Histoire des sects religieuses*, new ed., 6 vols. (Paris: Baudouin, 1828–45), 2: 175–80.
62. Robert Lerner, *The Heresy of the Free Spirit in the Later Middle Ages* (Berkeley: University of California Press, 1972), pp. 22–34; Grégoire, *Histoire des sectes religieuses*, 2: 178–79.

folding of God's plan. They did, however, scan the newspapers for news that might suggest that the conversion of the Jews was at hand.[63] The Republic of Jesus Christ soon disappeared, but other Convulsionist offshoots, including the Fareinists, persisted in the Lyons region well into the nineteenth century. The same is not true of Catherine Théot's circle. By the end of 1795, all her adherents had been released from prison. With one exception, Dom Gerle, nothing further is known of any of them. Like Pierre Pontard, Gerle had abjured his clerical vows in the fall of 1793. Two years later, at age fifty-eight, the former Carthusian prior married Rose Raffet, one of Catherine Théot's most dedicated followers. He managed to find occasional Grub Street employment in Paris: library research, work at a newspaper, and finally, in 1800, a minor appointment in the Consulate's Ministry of the Interior.[64] It is unknown whether he was in touch with Pontard, who had moved to Paris in search of the same sort of employment, or whether he saw Suzette Labrousse after her return there in 1799.

For some reason, Gerle now called himself Gerle-Chalini, adding what he said was his mother's name. A letter he wrote to Reubell in 1796 suggests that he felt shame about his past. One of the five members of the Directory, Reubell had been a colleague of Gerle's in the National Assembly in 1790. Gerle now requested a post in the Ministry of Finance, urging Reubell to consider "the person rather than the name." In another letter seeking a government post, he told another former colleague that he wanted a place "more in line with his merit than with his past."[65] Why did he change his name? Because it was associated with the notorious "Gerle motion" of 1790, or because Vadier had made it a target for jokes in the National Convention? There is no way of knowing. Gerle died in Paris in 1802.

Although he had freely admitted his belief in Théot's teachings at the time of his arrest, Gerle wrote from prison that for him the only true religion was "this ancient, true, gentle, and lovely religion, which tells me to believe in God, the sole supreme being, and to love my fellow men." Théot was just an old woman whom he had occasionally visited, and any kisses Senar had seen him give her had been no more than a friendly greeting.[66] Perhaps the collapse of his religious and

63. Grégoire, Histoire des sectes religieuses, 2: 185–93.
64. Mège, Révolution française, p. 28; Lenôtre, Robespierre et la "Mère de Dieu", pp. 327-28; and Henri d'Almeras, Les dévots de Robespierre: Catherine Théot et les mystères de la Mère de Dieu (Paris, 1905), pp. 255-56.
65. Quoted in H. F., "Notes sur Dom Gerle," Annales révolutionnaires 4 (1911): 114; and Almeras, Dévots de Robespierre, p. 256.
66. Gerle, "Mémoire," in Mège, Révolution française, pp. 31-32.

political careers, together with the humiliation of his imprisonment, led Gerle to abandon the millenarian convictions that had sustained him for so many years. It is possible, although it is at least as plausible that Gerle simply kept his beliefs to himself after 1795.

In his *Mémoires*, Senar printed a translation of a Latin manuscript he said had been found in Gerle's apartment after his arrest. The manuscript is not in Gerle's police dossier, but he may have been allowed to take such documents with him when he was released from prison. And it will be recalled that not long before his arrest, Gerle had sent Pierre Pontard a "catechism" of his beliefs.

Divided into three columns headed *signa, verba prophetae,* and *eventus,* the manuscript as presented by Senar does resemble the testimony of Théot and her followers. The eight "signs" included the rite of kisses and the sign of the cross. The "words of the prophet" included several of Mother Catherine's predictions, including the crushing of the head of the serpent and the victory of France's armies. The column headed "events" concluded:

5. The Mother will reign.
6. The prophets will govern.
7. The Supreme Being will direct all.[67]

Thanks to the vigilance of the Revolutionary police and surveillance committees, the sect of Catherine Théot made its brief appearance on the historical stage. Its importance certainly did not lie in the extent of its influence, and as in the case of Suzette Labrousse, there is no evidence that Théot had any followers after 1794. What she provides is a dimension too often missing in studies of the religious history of the French Revolution. Not only had the traditions of popular piety persisted into the Revolutionary era; they had also, in an obscure fashion, been associated by her believers with the new faith of secular revolution. More basic, perhaps, to understanding the attraction that Mother Catherine had in 1793–94 for her diverse collection of disciples was the assurance she offered them that the faithful would never die. Despite the fears and uncertainties of the present, she offered them the same assurance that the prophet Daniel and John of Patmos had offered their readers: new heavens, a new earth, and immortality for the elect of God.

67. Quoted in Senar, *Mémoires,* pp. 183–84.

CHAPTER 5

The Mystical International

WHAT little notoriety the Avignon Society achieved during the French Revolution it achieved by accident. In the spring of 1794, in the course of searching out anyone suspected of harboring aristocratic sympathies, the revolutionary security network turned its attention to the personnel of the old Parlement of Paris, which had been abolished in 1790. Some of the members, among them one Bourrée de Corberon, a member of a distinguished Burgundian noble family, had signed a protest at the dissolution of their institution. When agents of the Committee of General Security learned that Corberon had two sons living in France, one of them at Avignon, they traveled to the old papal city, arrested the son, Marie-Daniel Bourrée de Corberon, and seized some suspicious-looking letters from his home.[1]

Some of these letters had been written to Corberon by Louis-Michel Gombault. Since the abolition of the royal treasury, Gombault had been serving without salary as paymaster of a regiment of the Paris gendarmerie, while continuing in his spare time to pursue his mystical and occultist interests at Petit-Bourg. In the tense atmosphere of 1794, the letters were enough to make Gombault politically suspect. He was arrested early in May and questioned especially closely about a "Society" to which he had referred in his letters to Corberon.

Another suspicious thing about the letters, in the eyes of Gombault's interrogators, was that individuals were often identified not by name but by numbers of three digits. Gombault identified the people mentioned and explained that assigning a number to each individual was in accordance with "the customs of the Masonic lodges." As to the mysterious society, he explained that before the Revolution there had been at Avignon "a Society of men, devoted to religious speculations," whose two articles of belief had been "the

---

1. Michel Eude, "Points de vue sur l'affaire Catherine Théot," *Annales historiques de la Révolution francaise* 41 (1969): 616-18; Archives Nationales, F⁷4728, doss. Gombault.

existence of a supreme being and the immortaility of the soul."[2] The
society no longer existed; that nobody had ever heard of it was proof
that it had done no harm.

One of the individuals referred to in the letters was identified by
Gombault as a Polish count named Grabianka; in a letter written in
August 1789, Gombault had mentioned the society's excitement at
the impending arrival in Avignon of "the family of the Count." Gombault explained that he had been talking with members of the society
"about a Revolution which was to arrive first in France and then in
all the globe." This Revolution would bring about "a universal Regeneration which would lead to a purity of morals, a fraternity, and a
happiness" such as the world had not seen since the Garden of
Eden. The society believed that the glorious epoch would begin when
Count Grabianka's family arrived in Avignon from Poland.

Gombault concluded his testimony with a statement that affirmed
his absolute loyalty to the Revolution. His interrogators had probably
heard such declarations many times before, but in Gombault's case
there is no reason to doubt his absolute sincerity. "I have believed
in the Revolution from the beginning," he said; "I have been convinced of the happiness that it would procure for France and one day
for the entire world."

A few months later, in London, the Avignon Society again received
a kind of incidental prominence. Two artisans, a carpenter named
John Wright and a former printer named William Bryan, published
testimonies of their belief in the prophetic pretensions of a retired
naval officer named Richard Brothers. They both declared themselves to be members of the Avignon Society, having in 1789 made a
pilgrimage "to Avignon in France" at the prompting of the Holy
Spirit. They had spent seven months there, studying the "revealed
knowledge" that the members received from a divine spirit. John
Wright now published some of these prophecies, many of which did
indeed predict a time of troubles and revolution in which thrones
would topple and blood flow before there came "the time of the new
heavens and the new earth."[3] Robert Southey, when he learned of the
Avignon Society through reading Wright and Bryan, commented
ironically that even if the abbé Barruel's version of a Masonic and
Jacobin conspiracy to overturn governments was nothing but fiction,

2. Archives Nationales, F⁷4728, doss. Gombault. Quotations in the next two paragraphs are from this letter.
3. William Bryan, *A Testimony of the Spirit of Truth concerning Richard Brothers* . . .
(London, 1795); John Wright, *A Revealed Knowledge of Some Things That Will Be
Speedily Fulfilled in the World . . . for the Good of All Men* (London, 1794).

here was a society "whose object was to change or to influence the governments of Europe; it was well organized, and widely extended, but enthusiasm, not infidelity, was the means which it employed."[4]

The Avignon Society was only one of many shoots in the lush undergrowth of mystical Masonry in the eighteenth century. While it was an independent association, with rituals and doctrines quite distinct from those of the lodges affiliated with the Grand Orient in Paris, the society enjoyed full social and intellectual respectability. When international conferences of mystics, occultists, and alchemists met at Wilhelmsbad in 1782 and at Paris in 1784, the Avignon Society sent delegates.[5] The conferences were one result of the remarkable surge of interest in mysticism in the later eighteenth century. The tidy generalities of deism and of conventional Freemasonry were beginning to seem inadequate to many in the educated classes from which these ideologies had always drawn their support.

These eighteenth-century mystics, who often called themselves "men of desire," did not repudiate the notions of social and moral improvement which Freemasonry and the other reforming movements espoused. Nor did they reject the belief that "science" and "reason" were capable of transforming the world. The difference lay in their increasing tendency to seek true science and true reason in such unlikely places as alchemical lore, cabalistic numerology, mesmerist séances, Swedenborgian spiritualism, and (perhaps most surprising of all) the Scriptures. Many of these mystical Masons expected the sort of spiritual regeneration of the world which the Avignon Society's delegates had announced to the Paris conference in 1784: the reunion of the churches and the promulgation of a new doctrine for the entire world.[6] Only in the range of its interests and activities and in the grandiloquence of its prophecies of impending revolutionary regeneration was the Avignon Society unusual in the world of late eighteenth-century mystical masonry.

The society came into being in 1779, not at Avignon but at Berlin. Its founder was Dom Antoine Pernety, a Benedictine who had re-

---

4. Robert Southey, *Letters from England*, ed. and intro. Jack Simmons (London: Cresset, 1951), p. 415.
5. René Le Forestier, *La franc-maçonnerie templière et occultiste aux XVIII e et XIX e siècles*, published by Antoine Faivre (Paris: Aubier-Montaigne, 1970), pp. 610–48; Le Forestier, "Les Convents des Philalèthes," *Cahiers de la Tour Saint-Jacques*, no. 2 (1960), pp. 36–46.
6. Auguste Viatte, *Les sources occultes du romantisme: Illuminisme-théosophie, 1770-1820*, 2 vols. (1928; reprint ed., Paris: Champion, 1969), 1: 99. A very perceptive treatment of the whole topic is that of Robert Darnton, *Mesmerism and the End of the Enlightenment in France* (Cambridge: Harvard University Press, 1968), chap. 1.

nounced his clerical vows and fled to the hospitable court of Frederick the Great. During his monastic career, Pernety had acquired a reputation more for erudition than for piety. In the 1760s, he accompanied the explorer Bougainville as chaplain on an expedition to the Falkland Islands. Upon his return, he abruptly left his monastery, abandoned clerical dress, and set out for Avignon.[7]

Avignon in the eighteenth century was a major center of Freemasonry, including its occultist and esoteric offshoots. Although the territory belonged to the Pope, Avignon's liberal and cosmopolitan society was generally allowed to believe and to practice what it pleased. One of the first Masonic lodges in France had been founded there by Scottish Jacobite exiles. This was more than the papacy was prepared to tolerate, and in conformity with papal bulls against Freemasonry, the archbishop of Avignon in 1738 and 1751 had prohibited Masonic meetings. Nonetheless, the movement persisted.

It is not known when Dom Pernety became a Mason, but within months of his arrival in Avignon in 1765, he had inaugurated a new Masonic rite that was adopted by one of the disbanded lodges. Composed entirely of nobles, it had seceded from the parent lodge and the French Masonic network some years earlier. It now reorganized on the basis of Pernety's rite, which he said was derived from hermetic lore hidden within the myths of the Greeks and the Egyptians.

Finding Avignon too risky for a monk of his clouded status, Pernety soon accepted an invitation from Frederick to come to Berlin and serve as his librarian. At Frederick's court, he continued his researches in a variety of fields, publishing books on his trip to the Falkland Islands; on the character of America; on physiognomy, or the tracing of character through the analysis of men's faces; and on his pet theory that the bulk of ancient literature was in fact disguised hermetic lore. He also practiced alchemy.

Pernety gradually assembled a circle of followers in Berlin. At his instigation, they launched what one historian has called "a sort of religion of the occult, a mixture of casuistry, ecstasy, astrology, cabalism, and alchemy."[8] Pernety's circle acquired two protectors: an angel named Assadai, who Pernety said aided him in his work; and Prince Henry, brother of the king. Henry lived in retirement near

7. Joanny Bricaud, *Les Illuminés d'Avignon* (Paris: Nourry, 1927), pp. 20–24; Marc de Vissac, "Dom Pernety et les Illuminés d'Avignon," *Mémoires de l'Académie de Vaucluse*, 2d ser. 6 (1906): 222.

8. Bricaud, *Les Illuminés d'Avignon*, p. 36. See also Le Forestier, *Franc-maçonnerie*, p. 554.

Berlin, studying religion and metaphysics with his wife and friends. Among the followers whom Pernety now brought into the prince's circle were a financier, an actor at the prince's private theater, two English merchants named Bousie, and a French priest named Guyton de Morveau, who called himself Brumore.

It was from the actor that Pernety acquired a book that he hoped would at last make it possible to accomplish the "Great Work" of alchemy, the creation of the philosopher's stone. The book was said to be the work of "Elie Artiste," an alchemist who lived quietly near Hamburg, doing his experiments and curing the sick. The title the author gave himself was one which alchemists since the time of Paracelsus had used in reference to a supreme alchemist who would one day come and lay bare the secrets of the universe.[9] Just as the pious awaited the coming of the prophet Elias, who would herald the regeneration of the world, so they awaited the Elias Artista, who would make possible its alchemical transformation.

As Brumore explained in a letter in the *Journal encyclopédique* in 1785, Elias Artista taught that the ancient Chaldeans had possessed a science of numbers that enabled men to communicate with the heavenly powers. Men had lost this knowledge through pride; they no longer believed that something as simple as arranging numbers in a cabalistic order and then making calculations could reveal supernatural truths, "because such incomprehensible mysteries are repugnant to that pride of reasoning which wants to comprehend everything."[10]

Count Tadeusz Grabianka joined Pernety and Prince Henry's circle in 1778. He was not really a count, but he was an extremely wealthy nobleman, with extensive estates in the province of Podolia in southeastern Poland. Although he had been born at Rajkowce in Podolia in 1740,[11] Grabianka spent most of his youth in France at the court of Stanislas Leszczynski, the deposed king of Poland and father-in-law of Louis XV. At his father's death in 1759, Grabianka inherited a fortune that included three castles, fourteen estates, and a fabulous

9. Michael Roberts, *Gustavus Adolphus: A History of Sweden, 1611-1632*, 2 vols. (London: Longmans, Green & Co., 1953-58), 1: 524.

10. *Journal encyclopédique*, 1 December 1785, p. 295; Viatte, *Sources occultes du romantisme*, 1: 86-88; and Bricaud, *Les Illuminés d'Avignon*, pp. 39-42.

11. There are two recent biographical studies of Grabianka: M. L. Danilewicz, "The King of the New Israel: Thaddeus Grabianka (1740-1807)," *Oxford Slavonic Papers*, n.s. 1 (1968): 49-73; and Renzo de Felice, *Note e ricerche sugli "Illuminati" e il misticismo rivoluzionario (1789-1800)* (Rome: Edizioni di storia e letteratura, 1960), pp. 42-46, 150-51.

collection of jewels. (Two of his pseudonyms, Count Ostap and Count Sutkowski, were derived from the names of estates he owned). In 1771, he married one of the greatest heiresses in Poland.

At some time in his youth, Grabianka developed the desire to succeed to the elective Polish throne. Poland in the eighteenth century was in a condition bordering on political anarchy, as factions rose and fell, pulled this way and that by the machinations of Poland's neighbors, above all Russia. When Grabianka was a child, according to one of his biographers, a fortune teller predicted that he would become king of Poland, defeat Russia, and conquer the Turkish Empire, Asia, and part of Africa. Then "he would transfer his capital to Jerusalem, where the monarchs of the earth would come to prostrate themselves before him and learn supreme wisdom from him as from a second Solomon."[12]

Another factor may have contributed to the extravagant visions that absorbed Grabianka throughout his life. In the eighteenth century, both Poland and the Ukraine were centers of Jewish mysticism and the millenarian movement that had survived the apostasy of its prophet Sabbatai Zevi. Sabbatean prophets wandered about the region, calling upon the faithful to go to Israel to await the appearance there of their king and Messiah. In Grabianka's native province of Podolia, there existed not only congregations of Sabbatean Jews but also heretical Orthodox Christian sects and some scattered Moslem antinomians. All three groups awaited a millenarian regeneration of the world, a new earth where men would live in peace under the rule of God's anointed.[13] It is surely more than coincidental that this is the province where Tadeusz Grabianka was born and to which returned to live at intervals throughout his lifetime.

Grabianka spent most of the 1760s and 1770s on his estates in Podolia or in Warsaw. It was during a sojourn in the capital that he became involved in occultism and alchemy, through the circles of noble amateurs that flourished there.[14] In all the Baltic capitals— Berlin, Warsaw, Copenhagen, Stockholm, and St. Petersburg—these circles flourished, and seekers after mystical enlightenment moved freely between them. It was also in Warsaw that Grabianka joined the "reformed" Masonic system called the Strict Observance. Of all

12. M. Longinov, quoted in Danilewicz, "Thaddeus Grabianka," p. 50.
13. Gershon Scholem, "La métamorphose du messianisme hérétique des sabbatiens en nihilisme religieux aux 18ᵉ siècle," in *Hérésies et sociétés dans l'Europe pré-industrielle 11ᵉ-18ᵉ siècles*, ed. Jacques Le Goff (Paris and The Hague: Mouton & Co., 1968), pp. 381–93; and Scholem, "Le mouvement sabbataïste en Pologne," *Revue de l'histoire des religions* 143 (1953): 30–90, 209–32; and ibid. 144 (1953–54): 42–77.
14. Danilewicz, "Thaddeus Grabianka," pp. 51–52.

the mystical Masonic associations, the Strict Observance, commonly known as the Templars, was perhaps the most widespread. Much more structured and hierarchical than the other systems, it claimed that its organization and doctrines were based on the medieval order of the Knights Templar, suppressed early in the fourteenth century by Philip the Fair.[15]

Founded circa 1760 by the German Baron Charles Hund, the Masonic Templars spread rapidly to both the east and the west. In 1778, not long after having joined the Warsaw lodge, Grabianka came to Berlin, where the Templars were particularly numerous. He rapidly gained access to Prince Henry's court and met Pernety and Brumore. His entry into the group was of considerable significance for it; not only did he rapidly become one of its leaders but he also spent his wealth lavishly in support of its projects. As Pernety in his old age withdrew more and more into his studies and experiments, the swashbuckling count became the most influential figure in the group. It was Grabianka who was primarily responsible for shifting the society's principal concern from occultism and alchemy to a millenarian anticipation of great events in the near future that would find the enemies of the Lord destroyed and Pernety's little band established as the "new people" of the New Israel, with Grabianka as their king.

The transformation began soon after Grabianka had entered Dom Pernety's occult circle. On 21 February 1779, the "Holy Word" that was revealed by means of Elie Artiste's cabalistic number lore told Pernety that a society was to be formed that would be the nucleus of "the new people of God." Those admitted to it would undergo a ceremony called the "consecration."[16] For each of nine successive days, on a hilltop outside Berlin, the candidate was to burn incense and consecrate himself to the service of God. Having thus made "an alliance with the Eternal," he would be visited by an angel.[17] The Holy Word announced that Grabianka should be the first to be consecrated, because his heart was pure. He carried out the nine days' rite, but he saw no angel. The Holy Word assured Grabianka that everything was all right and that he should go ahead and consecrate Pernety, Brumore, and a fourth member of the circle, a financier

15. Le Forestier, *Franc-maçonnerie*, pp. 103–25; Alice Joly, *Un mystique lyonnais et les secrètes de la franc-maçonnerie, 1703–1824* (Macon: Protat, 1938), pp. 51–52.
16. Bricaud, *Les Illuminés d'Avignon*, p. 45.
17. Ibid., pp. 45–48; "Breve dettaglio della Società, o Setta scoperta nell' arresto di Ottavio Cappelli, tratto dalle carte allo stesso perquisite," printed in Felice, *Note e ricerche*, p. 221. The manuscript is in the Biblioteca Nazionale Centrale in Rome, mss Vittorio Emanuele.

named Anne de Morinval. With these consecrations accomplished, Grabianka began his reign as king of the new people. Pernety was to be their pope.

During the next several years, new members were brought into the society, including most of the members of Grabianka's family, whom he had gone to Poland to fetch at the Holy Word's command. Even Pernety, who until then had been absorbed primarily in alchemy, was caught up in the new developments. In 1781, he wrote the Swedish baron Nordenskjold concerning a "Polish gentleman" (Grabianka, surely) who told all he met of "the new reign of Jesus Christ on the earth, which he describes as very near." Pernety said that the Pole had been so informed by God himself. He added, "I have certain and very clear proofs of the truth of what is said concerning the new reign of God."[18]

In 1782, the Holy Word commanded Pernety to leave Berlin and find a new city in which to establish the "new people." His angel Assadai would guide him there; it would be a forty days' journey from Berlin, on the banks of a great river. One wonders how necessary the angel's guidance was, since Pernety had after all lived for some years at Avignon, with its famous bridge spanning the great Rhone River. By 1785, Pernety and a number of other members of the society had made their way there.[19] After quarrelling with Grabianka over the failure of some alchemical experiments during a sojourn in Poland, Brumore visited various occult centers in Switzerland and Germany before arriving at Avignon in June. In 1785, Grabianka too received a divine command to leave his estates and join the rest. It took him over a year to get there. He traveled through western Europe seeking like-minded societies that might join with his in preparing the world for the reign of God.

Avignon, when Pernety and the others arrived there in 1785, was still a haven for individuals interested in mysticism and the occult. One of them, an Avignonese nobleman named the marquis de Vaucrose de Vernetti, offered the new arrivals the use of a country chateau, near the city but outside the jurisdiction of the archbishop. Pernety called the chateau Tabor. He scattered dust from Palestine on the top of a nearby hill; this he named Mount Tabor, the site of all future consecrations. Garbianka meanwhile established himself in some splendor in a house in the city. During the succeeding years, a steady stream of visitors arrived from all over Europe, some

---

18. Quoted in Viatte, *Sources occultes du romantisme*, 2: 270.
19. Bricaud, *Les Illuminés d'Avignon*, pp. 62-63, 81-82; Vissac, "Dom Pernety," p. 228.

of whom undertook the rite of consecration and became people of the New Israel.

During the same period, Pernety and Grabianka drifted apart. There was never an outright schism in the Avignon Society, but Pernety seems to have had little to do with the millenarian doctrines and proselytizing activities that centered at Grabianka's house in the city. The former monk resided most of the time outside Avignon, working in his alchemical laboratory or instructing candidates for consecration in the doctrines of the Holy Word. Grabianka, meanwhile, was preparing for the millennium that he was increasingly convinced was at hand.

It is likely that Brumore had been Grabianka's ally in Berlin in the transformation of a circle of occultists into a religious society with millenarian tendencies. In letters seized some years later by the papal police, Grabianka called the French abbé his first guide and master, even though Brumore had died in 1786, in Rome.[20] Renzo de Felice has argued that he may have gone there in order to establish contact with an Italian mystic named Ottavio Cappelli, who was also in communication with angels. Before his death, Brumore put Cappelli in touch with the Avignon Society. In 1787, Cappelli came to Avignon, where he remained for two years. After his return to Rome, he continued to provide spiritual guidance to the society through letters, but late in 1790 he was arrested on suspicion of heresy. He was freed after recanting in 1795, but in 1798 he was arrested again. This time he was put to death, possibly because his connections with Grabianka and the Russian members of the Avignon Society made the papal authorities suspect that he was a Russian spy.[21]

After Cappelli's first arrest, the papacy had published a report claiming that he was a gardener, of the lowest social class and without education. In fact, he was of middle class origin and had studied for the priesthood. After having left holy orders, he was a merchant in the Papal States, where he came into contact with some South American Jesuits who lived in exile there after the suppression of their order. Many of them were millenarians, and it may well be that their ideas helped to shape Cappelli's conviction that he was divinely called to a religious mission.

Although Grabianka gave Cappelli the title "Man-King of the New People," and although he fully believed in Cappelli's spiritual gifts, the Polish count continued to be the dominant figure in the society.

20. "Breve dettaglio" in Felice, *Note e ricerche*, p. 221; Alice Joly, "La 'Sainte Parole' des Illuminés d'Avignon," in *Cahiers de la Tour Saint-Jacques*, no. 2 (1960), pp. 105-9.
21. Felice, *Note e ricerche*, pp. 125-27, 150-54.

There is no indication what Cappelli's role in the group would have become had he not been arrested. It is clear that he was regarded by the membership as a prophet, whose counsel was sought on everything from the weather to the end of the world, and that he was preparing to make the society's rituals more conventionally Roman Catholic. Gombault, in a letter written in 1792, referred to him as "our dear victim," who must obtain "his deliverance" from imprisonment before he could complete "his mission" so that "the promises may be accomplished"[22]—but it is not clear what "promises" were meant.

The papal inquisitors questioned Cappelli closely about the Avignon Society and the letters he had received from its members. They learned that it consisted of "men and women, Laymen, Priests, Monks and Nuns, and also girls of tender age." There were "Poles, Germans, Swedes, Frenchmen, Russians, Genevans, Dutch, Irish, and Italians of both sexes." Their aim was "to form a new People of God, a new Reign of Christ, to reform Religion, to restore the law, and to expand the Faith."[23] Despite the peculiarity of some of its doctrines and the extravagant prophecies of its leaders, the papal report shows clearly that the Avignon Society was definitely part of the strong current that was moving, on the eve of the French Revolution, toward the conviction that the renewal of the church and the spiritual and moral regeneration of the faithful was imminent.

Bourrée de Corberon may or may not have been typical of the individuals affiliated with the Avignon Society on the eve of the Revolution. He is of particular interest, however, because he left a detailed account of the spiritual odyssey that finally brought him to Avignon in 1790. He came, as he wrote to another member at the time, in order to be "without human distractions in the sublime and consoling study of the religion of nature."[24] By that time he had sampled practically everything the eighteenth century had to offer, including mystical Masonry, mesmerism, alchemy, and the doctrines of Swedenborg, Cagliostro, and a Parisian who predicted the end of the world.

Born in 1748, Corberon first pursued a career in the army. At the age of twenty-five he entered the diplomatic service, serving first in the petty state of Cassel and then at St. Petersburg for six years, the

22. Archives Nationales, F⁷4728, doss. Gombault.
23. "Breve dettaglio" in Felice, Note e ricerche, pp. 221–22, 226.
24. Antoine Faivre, "Un familier des sociétés ésotériques au xviiie siècle: Bourrée de Corberon," Revue des sciences humaines, n.s. fasc. 126 (1967): 282. Faivre's article is based on Corberon's unpublished journal in the Musée Calvet in Avignon.

last three as chargé d'affaires. Then, finding that Foreign Minister Vergennes was not favorable to him, he retired, at the age of thirty-two. With the exception of a brief diplomatic stint at Zweibrücken, he never worked again.

It was during his years in Russia that Corberon became interested in occultism and mystical religion. In company with the marquis de Thomé, the abbé Pasquini, and the comte de Brühl, he plunged into the study and practice of alchemy. In 1775, he joined the mystical order called the Elus Coens. Two years later, he joined Brühl in the Masonic Templars.

Corberon had met Cagliostro in Russia and been impressed by his abilities as a healer. They met again in 1781 in Paris, where the Sicilian made an impressive entry into society under the patronage of the Cardinal de Rohan, until the affair of the Diamond Necklace destroyed the reputations of both men and forced Cagliostro to flee to England. It was while dining with the Sicilian "Great Copt" that Corberon met Bousie and resumed his friendship with the marquis de Thomé. Bousie had already been consecrated into Pernety's Avignon Society, but there is no evidence that Corberon learned of the group at this time. Instead, he, Bousie, and the marquis de Thomé began an intensive study of the writings of Emmanuel Swedenborg. Corberon took up Swedenborg with the same intensity he had given in St. Petersburg to the transmutation of metals. He continued this study during his diplomatic service at Zweibrücken in 1782–83. He also made inquiries at Hamburg concerning the alchemist and healer Elie Artiste, who was reputed to have been a close friend of Swedenborg's.[25]

In 1784 Corberon abandoned his earlier deism and became a Christian. In his private journal, Corberon gave the credit for his conversion to some of the pious noblemen he had met in the occult and Masonic circles of St. Petersburg and to the reading of Swedenborg. It was at this point in his spiritual pilgrimage that an old acquaintance took him to see Jean-Baptiste Ruer, an impressive Parisian gentleman of fifty who received heavenly communications each night.[26] Ruer predicted great events—kingdoms would fall, revolutions would break out, the Jews would be called back to the Holy Land, Jerusalem would be rebuilt. Jesus would return to earth and launch the Third Age. Ruer assured Corberon that he, his father, and possibly his wife were among the elect and would be spared in the terrible times ahead. Ruer read aloud from the divine messages that he

25. Ibid., p. 285.   26. Ibid., pp. 273–81.

received and transcribed nightly. Corberon exclaimed in his own journal: "Nothing is so simple and so beautiful as what I have heard. It is the style of Scripture, for it is Jesus Christ who speaks and dictates to Ruer."[27]

In a striking anticipation of what Richard Brothers was to announce in England ten years later, Ruer declared that he was the descendant of David, destined to rule as king in Jerusalem. Also like Brothers, Ruer described his future kingdom in great detail, including the religious services that would be conducted in the rebuilt temple. He also asserted that St. John the Divine had lived near Paris when he wrote the book of Revelation.

Apparently Corberon was himself a little startled at how abruptly he dropped Swedenborg for the very different emphasis of Ruer. Thomé remonstrated with him at the time, but by 1787 both he and Bousie were also followers of the strange prophet. It is a pattern we shall see repeated in England in 1794 among similar "men of desire" during the brief vogue for Richard Brothers.

Ruer predicted that the end of the world would come in 1786, and the believers prepared themselves. A house was secured and stocked with food to sustain them when disaster struck. Corberon and the others contributed money to Ruer so that he might complete the preparations needed to preserve the elect. Madame Corberon, a Protestant, joined the Roman Catholic church in order to be included among them. As the year of doom progressed with none of the predicted events, Corberon began to grow restive. Ruer's constant demands for money made him suspect that the prophet was at least in part a charlatan. For one thing, it seemed to Corberon that Ruer had adopted some of Cagliostro's visions as his own.

It was during this period of progressive disenchantment that Corberon met Count Grabianka, early in 1787. For three hours, the count told him about the Avignon Society; but his involvement with Ruer had made Corberon wary. Grabianka wrote to him, but he waited for over a year before replying. He then asked Grabianka's advice concerning Ruer, and the count inexplicably told him to remain loyal to the prophet. Possibly, Grabianka saw Ruer's group as another member of his international millenarian "Union." Corberon nonetheless began to disengage himself from Ruer. He also began to move toward the Avignon Society. Two members of the society, Bousie and Gombault, frequented the same Paris circles that he did, and he now began also to correspond with some of the members who

27. Ibid., p. 274.

resided in Avignon. Finally, he wrote requesting admission.[28] After all of his spiritual adventures, the society (alchemy, angels, and all) must have indeed seemed to Corberon to represent a calm and reasonable "religion of nature."

Grabianka's refusal to urge Corberon to leave Ruer for the fellowship of Avignon may seem surprising, considering that the count was the society's most active propagandist. The explanation lies in the fact that Grabianka's evangelism was directed less at winning candidates for the particular fellowship of Avignon than at the creation of some sort of millenarian international. The clearest indication that this was what he had in mind is seen in his behavior during the year he spent in London among groups dedicated to the study of the teachings of Swedenborg. One man who knew Grabianka there recalled that he was a "frequent and welcome" visitor, whose "conversation was always interesting and animated: and when he communicated the religious sentiments of his Society, he seemed to speak the very language of the New Church."[29] After he had left for Avignon, he wrote his English friends, thanking them for their hospitality and for the gift of several works of Swedenborg "as a pledge of the union, which the Lord is about to form between us." There were several other societies, he told them, "who, like you, walk in the paths of Christ and we hasten to fulfill them also in obedience to the command." The divine command had not yet come, but it was expected soon; "for, very dear brethren, the angel that stands before the face of the Lamb, is already sent to sound his trumpet on the mountains of Babylon, and give notice to the nations that the God of heaven will soon come to the gates of the earth, to change the face of the world, and to manifest his power and glory."[30] The London Swedenborgians did not reply.

Several members of the Avignon Society had been deeply interested in Swedenborg, but the interest was not reciprocated by those whose primary allegiance was to the Swedish prophet. While still in Berlin, Pernety had published a very free French translation of one of Swedenborg's works which evoked the displeasure of both the marquis de Thomé and Benedict Chastanier, the French emigré surgeon who was one of the founding members of the Church of the

---

28. Ibid., pp. 279–81; Bricaud, Les Illuminés d'Avignon, p. 87.
29. Robert Hindmarsh, The Rise and Progress of the New Jerusalem Church in England, America, and Other Parts, ed. Edward Madeley (London: Hodson, 1861), pp. 41–42.
30. Printed in ibid., pp. 46–47. Dated 12 February 1787, the letter was addressed "To the Children of the New Kingdom in London."

New Jerusalem in London. Thomé went so far as to try to prevent its publication.[31]

Swedenborg's theology seems to have had no lasting influence on the Avignon Society. Doctrinally, the society's leaders saw themselves as orthodox Roman Catholics, with a special veneration for the Virgin Mary. One member said that the society believed that Swedenborg had been "divinely taught" at first but had introduced many of his own fantasies into his published work.[32]

As far as the London Swedenborgians were concerned, no union with the Avignon Society was possible. In 1790, the *New-Jerusalem Magazine* denounced the society as "the *Antipodes* of the New Church, erected on the very borders of Babylon."[33]

Grabianka had met a likelier prospective recruit for the work of the Avignon Society in the person of Tiemann von Berend, a Saxon who said he was a major in the Russian army. In Masonic circles, he called himself Tieman.[34] Like Corberon, Tieman had investigated practically all the mystical and occult doctrines current in the eighteenth century. He traveled all over Europe, acting as companion to a succession of Livonian and Russian noblemen. Tieman was a good friend of Jean-Baptiste Willermoz, the Lyons silk merchant who was perhaps the most influential and respected figure in French mystical Masonry.

Grabianka's revelations concerning the Avignon Society and the Holy Word were hardly news to Tieman. The same sorts of predictions of crisis and regeneration were in rather general currency in the 1780s. What particularly attracted Tieman to the Avignon group, however, was Grabianka's statement that it formed the core of an international alliance of watchers for the Second Coming. He wrote Willermoz that while "the first place for the first assembly of this singular Society" was at Avignon, they would move farther south, to Florence, where "all the brothers dispersed in Europe were to go."[35] That the Florentine site derived from that city's role as the focus of the millenarian hopes of the Fraticelli and of Savonarola is a tempting but unprovable hypothesis.

31. Thomé-Nordenskjold, 11 August 1783 and 27 March 1784, Swedenborg Society, London; James Hyde, "Benedict Chastanier and the Illuminati of Avignon," *New Church Review* 14 (1907): 181–205.

32. "Friday, December 9th 1791, at the Rev. Mr. Smiths Fitzroy Street Tottenham Court Road," ms JT 35, Friends' Reference Library, London. The member who spoke at the meeting was William Bryan.

33. *New-Jerusalem Magazine*, April 1790, p. 176.

34. Joly, "La 'Sainte Parole'," p. 110; Le Forestier, *Franc-maçonnerie*, p. 620 n 20.

35. Quoted in Le Forestier, *Franc-maçonnerie*, p. 1003.

Willermoz's refusal to go to Avignon, despite the urgings of his friends Tieman and Gombault, is explained by the complete absorption that mesmerist somnambulism had for Willermoz and his circle on the eve of the French Revolution. They had certainly examined doctrines that were at least as bizarre before. Initially, Willermoz and his group of mystical Masons in Lyons had concentrated, like Mesmer himself, on mesmerism as a healing technique. In the summer of 1784, they had even secured the cooperation of some teachers at the local veterinary school for experiments on animals. By the fall, however, this activity had been supplanted by an enthusiasm for the Puységur brothers' technique of inducing hypnotic trances. Willermoz and his associates took up what in the next century would be called séances, aided by a succession of ladies who prophesied and brought news from the spirit world. In addition, in 1785 Willermoz organized a group called the Workers of the Eleventh Hour, a select band of mystics who dedicated themselves to studying the messages that a noblewoman of Willermoz's acquaintance received from heaven and transmitted by automatic writing.[36]

For some, mesmerism became a new religion, a third revelation, with clearly millenarian implications.[37] Like so many religious currents in the 1780s, it promised an imminent regeneration, a new golden age that was at once mystical and scientific. While Willermoz was both too cautious and too eclectic to go that far, it is clear that for him the Avignon Society's Holy Word, however interesting a phenomenon, offered nothing that Willermoz could not (or so he believed) attain elsewhere.

Of all the visitors to Avignon, the most untypical were surely the two English artisans, William Bryan and John Wright. All evidence indicates that the Avignon Society consisted entirely of members of the nobility, the clergy, and the wealthy bourgeoisie. Yet both Wright and Bryan testified to the kind and generous treatment they received from the society at Avignon when they turned up there in January 1789. It was William Bryan, a Quaker printer with a restless intellect and prophetic pretensions, who had learned of the society; he does not say where. He told his fellow seeker John Wright about it. Toward the end of 1788, both men felt themselves inwardly compelled to go to Avignon. They accordingly set out with just enough money to get them across the English Channel, leaving their wives and children

36. Alice Joly and Robert Amadou, *De l'agent inconnu au philosophe inconnu: Essais "La Tour Saint-Jacques"* (Paris: Denoël, 1962), pp. 50–51; Joly, *Mystique lyonnais*, pp. 215–18; and Viatte, *Sources occultes*, 1: 144.
37. Darnton, *Mesmerism*, chaps. 1–3; Viatte, *Sources occultes du romantisme*, 1: 230.

at home. Wright wrote that as he left London he "interceded with the *great* and *merciful* GOD" to care for his family, since it was "for his sake they were going to be left without any outward dependence. . . . I did not know whether I ever should see them any more; for although our first Journey was to *Avignon*, we did not know it would end there."[38]

They walked to Paris, where they went to the home of William Bousie, whom Bryan had met in London. Bousie made them welcome, and the next morning he gave them money for the rest of their trip. Wright worried that no one at Avignon spoke English, but Bryan assured him that Major Tieman, whom he had seen in England two years before, would be there and would serve as their translator. At Avignon, they found that Tieman was indeed there and that the society had been expecting them; Chastanier had written from London that they were coming. Bryan wrote: "Nothing could exceed the brotherly kindness shown by these men, who told us we were welcome to the house provided by the Lord for those of his children whom he might be pleased to send to the reunion from all parts of the earth."[39] A week later Bousie arrived and was commanded by the Holy Word to remain. He served as their translator after Tieman's departure.

Wright and Bryan stayed for seven months, reading, copying extracts from the volumes of communications from the Holy Word, and worshiping with the society. Wright wrote that "we met every evening at seven o'clock to commemorate the *death* of our LORD and SAVIOUR JESUS CHRIST, by eating bread and drinking wine. Very often when we have been sitting together, the furniture in the room has been shook, as though it was all coming to pieces . . . we were told that it announced the presence of angels."[40]

The prophecies that John Wright published in 1794 show that in addition to providing spiritual guidance and advice on topics ranging from health to the weather, the Holy Word described with some precision the political events that would precede the coming of the Lord. Some of these prophecies had long been standard in the Christian tradition—the Turkish empire would fall, Christianity would return to the Middle East, and the Jews would be converted and restored to their homeland. All people would acknowledge one God, be united in one faith, and be governed by "one sole master."[41]

38. Wright, *Revealed Knowledge*, pp. 8–10.
39. Bryan, *Testimony of the Spirit of Truth*, p. 27.
40. Wright, *Revealed Knowledge*, p. 19.   41. Ibid., p. 28.

"This is the time that we must believe all those who announce the new reign of the LORD, for his spirit is with them," the Holy Word declared. God would soon announce "the new reign" by "terror" and by "prodigies," for "this is the time of the new heavens and the new earth."[42]

Returning to London at the end of 1789, Wright and Bryan rejoined their families and more or less resumed the lives they had led before the Lord called them to Avignon. Wright returned to carpentry. The more flamboyant Bryan, excluded from Quakers meetings and from work as a printer, was unemployed much of the time before he became a pharmacist and herbal doctor. Both men testified, when they could find listeners, to the revelations they had received. Both awaited the fulfillment of the promised time of new heavens and new earth. And both men believed that the predictions of the Holy Word at Avignon had come to pass in the French Revolution. Late in 1794, they found the divinely appointed prophet of the New Age in the person of a retired naval officer who called himself the Revealed Prince of the Hebrews: Richard Brothers.

Wright and Bryan were the first of many visitors whom the Avignon Society received in 1789. For a brief time, the papal city rivaled Paris and Lyons as a mecca for those seeking occult and mystical enlightenment.[43] In the climate of "revolutionary mysticism,"[44] which awakened a sense of impending religious and political regeneration in the late 1780s and drew attention to such diverse prophets as Mesmer, Cagliostro, Swedenborg, and Ruer, the rites and revelations of the Avignon Society had considerable appeal.

People came from all over Europe. The duchess of Württemburg arrived with her two sons. Others came from Russia, Poland, and Italy, and one lady was said to have traveled from the Turkish Empire.[45] At the end of 1789, two Swedish nobles arrived. Count Gustaf Adolf Reuterholm was the friend and advisor of King Gustavus III's brother, Duke Charles of Sudermania. His companion was Karl Göran Silfverhjelm, nephew of Swedenborg himself and later Swedish ambassador to London. Both men were Templars; their

42. Ibid., pp. 30–31.
43. Joly, *Mystique lyonnais*, p. 279; Le Forestier, *Franc-maçonnerie*, p. 878; and Felice, *Note e ricerche*, p. 51.
44. Philippe Sagnac, *La formation de la société française moderne*, 2 vols. (Paris: Presses universitaires de France, 1946), 2: 450; Louis Trénard, *Lyon, de l'Encyclopédie au préromantisme: Histoire sociale des idées*, 2 vols. (Paris: Presses universitaires de France, 1958), 1: 303; and especially Darnton, *Mesmerism*, chap. 4.
45. Viatte, *Sources occultes du romantisme*, 1: 99; "Breve dettaglio" in Felice, *Note e ricerche*, pp. 216–17; and ms JT 35, Friends' Reference Library.

friend Duke Charles was the head of the order. Their travels were at least in part a search for the sort of mystical enlightenment that was a particular preoccupation of the Swedish intelligentsia throughout the eighteenth century.[46]

Before setting out for Avignon, Reuterholm and Silfverhjelm stayed in Paris with the Swedish ambassador, Baron Eric de Staël, like them a mystical Mason. Among the people they met during their stay were two members of the Avignon Society, Gombault and Bousie, and also Willermoz's friend and disciple Périsse-Duluc, one of Lyons's deputies to the National Assembly. Périsse reported to Willermoz that the two Swedes "knew all about what is called secret science, spiritual communications, visions." He added that, unlike Bousie, they were "more preoccupied with Truth than with marvels."[47]

After having left Paris, the two Swedes stopped to visit Willermoz in Lyons and then proceeded to Avignon, where they remained for a month. If there were a division within the society between Pernety and Grabianka, it was a very informal one. Reuterholm recorded in his journal daily visits both to the brothers' lodge outside the town where Pernety was staying and to Grabianka's house in the city.

On 1 December Reuterholm began the ceremony of consecration that the Holy Word had ordained a decade earlier in Berlin. Accompanied by the "pontiff," Pernety, he walked for some distance along the Rhone, then ascended the hill the brothers called Mount Tabor. "There I made with the most high the most holy of all unions," he wrote in his journal. "God give me his grace never to forget my promises!!!" He returned to town at sunset and called on Count Grabianka at his home before returning to his own lodgings. It was, he wrote, "one of the most remarkable days of my life. God has brought me all the way here from the North."[48] He ascended the hill for nine successive days, each day performing the same ceremonies. On the ninth day, Pernety again joined him. Returning to town, Reuterholm called at Grabianka's home, where for the first time he was allowed to participate in the evening worship service.

46. B. J. Hovde, *The Scandinavian Countries, 1720–1865: The Rise of the Middle Classes*, 2 vols. (Ithaca: Cornell University Press, 1948), 1: 304–7; J. Christopher Herold, *Mistress to an Age* (Indianapolis: Bobbs-Merrill, 1958; reprint ed., New York, Time-Life Books, 1964), pp. 117–18.

47. G. A. Reuterholm, "Resejournaler, 14, 16, 25, 26, and 30 November 1789, Riksarkivet, Stockholm; Perisse-Duluc letters, 16 November 1789, ms 5430, Bibliothèque de la ville de Lyon.

48. Reuterholm, "Resejournaler," 1–9 December 1789. I am grateful to Birgitta Angiolillo for her help in translating Reuterholm's manuscript. There is also a description of the rite in "Breve dettaglio" in Felice, *Note e ricerche*, p. 223.

Reuterholm and Silfverhjelm remained in Avignon for the rest of December, visiting with members of the society and seeing the local sights. Reuterholm even climbed another mountain, Petrarch's Mont Ventose. They left for Italy at the end of the month and traveled by easy stages to Rome. Reuterholm immediately sought out Ottavio Cappelli, bringing him letters from Paris and Avignon. Reuterholm wrote Duke Charles that Cappelli was "a man filled with the blessings of God, an initiate who has more enlightenment in himself alone than all the Brothers of Avignon together; who is, indeed, the source from which they draw their enlightenment."[49]

After spending three months in Rome and Naples, visiting the points of historic and artistic interest with a thoroughness that would have pleased Baedecker, the two Swedes left for home. They again stopped at Paris on their leisurely way back, but not at Avignon. Reuterholm was to have been the agent for bringing others of his countrymen into the Avignon Society, but he does not seem to have done so. He gradually abandoned mysticism as he became more deeply involved in Swedish politics.

Six months after Reuterholm and Silfverhjelm had left Rome, Ottavio Cappelli was arrested by the papal police. They seized fifty letters he had received from various members of the society at Avignon. On the basis of these letters, the police drew up a report which described the doctrines and structure of the society. In addition, the report shows that prophecies in circulation among the members had a decidedly political tone.

The year 1790 was to be an "auspicious, happy, and fortunate year," in which great events would take place, notably in Rome. Several letters mentioned imminent "confusion" there, to be followed by the sounding of the bells on the Capitoline Hill and "the drum on Mount Marius." John Wright and William Bryan had read and copied down similar prophecies the year before. Wright recorded the Holy Word as having declared that "ROME will be the theatre of great events, the sound of the drum will be heard on the *Mount Marius*, . . . and the *Capital* of the world will experience great calamities." Bryan reported that there was an eleven-year-old boy in Rome who, under the tutelage of "Spiritual and Angelic Agents," was being prepared for the great mission of destroying the Turkish Empire.[50]

49. Reuterholm, "Resejournaler," December 1789 and January 1790; Letters quoted in Viatte, *Sources occultes du romantisme*, 1: 100, and in Le Forestier, *Franc-maçonnerie*, p. 880.
50. "Breve dettaglio" in Felice, *Note e ricerche*, pp. 227-28; Wright, *Revealed Knowledge*, p. 25; ms JT 35, Friends' Reference Library.

Perhaps the drums mentioned by Wright and the Avignon letters belonged to the armies of the Turkish Antichrist. The assumption that the last great battle before the millennium would be fought against the Turks was six centuries old by 1790, and there is at least one indication that the Avignon Society shared it. One member had written Cappelli in July that peace with the Turk could not last long; soon they would reenter the Campagna, as "Dear King 1.3.9."—Grabianka—had predicted in 1783. When that moment came, the members of the society too would "receive the order to get [their] boots ready."[51]

Ready for what? Possibly to follow Grabianka to the Holy Land. In September, Tieman reported that the "Avignon oracle" predicted that "Pius VI will be the last Pope; soon the Turks will leave Europe, and the Jews will rebuild their capital."[52] Similarly, William Bryan described a prophecy that closely parallels those in the thirteenth- and fourteenth-century literature of the Fraticelli concerning an angelic Pope. Bryan had learned at Avignon that Pius VI did not have long to live. At his death, two would contend for his throne and fail. A third candidate would then be elected, "who will close the scene of Papal Tyranny and Authority."[53] One of the letters seized by the papal police in the fall of 1790 told Cappelli that the angel Raphael had described the duchess of Württemberg's son Ferdinand as "the Savior of the World," the man who would accomplish "the new reform of the corrupted Earth."[54] These terms, it might be noted, recall those applied in medieval prophecy to the secular ally of the angelic Pope, the great prince who would defeat the forces of Antichrist and inaugurate the millennium. Renzo de Felice has argued that in 1790 the Avignon Society actually contemplated some sort of military expedition, aided by Ferdinand of Württemberg and perhaps also by Prince Henry of Prussia, against the Turks. Any such plans must have involved Grabianka, who still dreamed of ascending the Polish throne and also, according to one Polish biographer, hoped to conquer Syria, Palestine, and North Africa.[55]

Two letters Reuterholm received in 1791 indicate that the millenarian hopes of the Avignon Society did not fade after Cappelli's arrest. Gombault wrote him that "everything announces to us a universal regeneration which, in achieving the good of all, will neces-

51. "Breve dettaglio" in Felice, *Note e ricerche*, pp. 226–27.
52. Quoted in Viatte, *Sources occultes du romantisme*, 1: 99.
53. Ms JT 35, Friends' Reference Library. Cf. Marjorie Reeves, *The Influence of Prophecy in the Later Middle Ages* (Oxford: Clarendon Press, 1969), pp. 322, 401–17.
54. "Breve dettaglio" in Felice, *Note e ricerche*, p. 226.
55. Felice, *Note e ricerche*, pp. 43–45.

sarily bring the happiness of each." In December, a former member of the society reported the death of one of the brothers. What was remarkable, he wrote, was that "they could never persuade him that he could die, because he was convinced that he was destined to see all the great things that were promised to him."[56]

Cappelli's arrest and the resulting investigation of the Avignon Society led the papal authorities to decide that the society was a sect with heretical tendencies. It might have been formally condemned and suppressed, but the events of the French Revolution intervened; Avignon was annexed to France at the end of 1791. Ironically, it was that same Revolution, anticipated for so long in the prophecies of the society and so sincerely welcomed when it did arrive, that effectively brought its activities to a halt.

The Avignon Society gave up its own religious rites and participated instead in the municipal patriotic celebrations. The brothers accepted all the duties of citizens in the new French Republic, but a group that consisted to such a great extent of foreigners, ex-nobles, ex-priests, and former royal officials must have invited the suspicions of the authorities. In 1793 and 1794, Pernety, Corberon, Gombault, Bousie, and Grabianka were all arrested. Other members fled Avignon, and the society dissolved for the time being. By 1800, only fifteen members were left in Avignon.[57]

Pernety died in 1796. According to his Polish biographers, Grabianka remained in Avignon for most of the decade, except for visits to London and Paris, where he was briefly imprisoned. He returned to Avignon after his release, and then, in 1799, he went to Poland to face a family council called to discuss his continued financial extravangance. His wife and sons refused to provide any more money for his religious activities. Grabianka returned to Avignon once again; then, sometime in 1802 he left, moving eastward by easy stages until he reached St. Petersburg three years later.

The reports on the last four years of Grabianka's life are vague and contradictory. He seems to have continued propagating the doctrines of the Avignon Society. He was said to have enjoyed considerable notoriety in the Russian capital in occult and Masonic circles, both as a bearer of secret wisdom and as a healer. He died in prison in 1807 after being arrested on suspicion of plotting against the czar.[58]

A few members of the Avignon Society continued on in St. Petersburg for another decade, but practically nothing is known

56. Quoted in Viatte, *Sources occultes du romantisme*, 1: 233, 238.
57. Bricaud, *Les Illuminés d'Avignon*, pp. 94–100.
58. Danilewicz, "Thaddeus Grabianka," pp. 69–72; Felice, *Note e ricerche*, pp. 42–43.

about them. Not much more is known of the brothers who remained in Avignon or who drifted back there when it was again safe to do so. A letter in the Bibliothèque de la ville de Lyon indicates that the society's millenarian expectations changed little over the years. Its writer told Willermoz that the society had been predicting *"great events very soon"* for several months. He added: "What puts me the most on my guard against this association is the promise that it makes to all its proselytes of being surely preserved at the great day of the Lord which is to precede or coincide with the second coming and the return of the Jews."[59]

When the abbé Grégoire was compiling his *Histoire des sectes religieuses* some fifteen years later, his principal informant concerning the Avignon Society was Gombault, still a frequenter of all the mystical circles in Paris. Gombault said there was only a handful of brothers left by 1804.[60] One was a former priest named Guillaume Chais de Sourcesol, who later emigrated to Wilmington, Delaware. In his *Livre des manifestes*, published in 1800, he had predicted that when Jesus Christ returned to earth, there would come "the perfect restoration of the *People of God*"[61]—the term the Avignon Society's members had long used to describe themselves.

The Avignon Society had one more moment of public notoriety before it disappeared. In 1800, a member of the Irish House of Commons named Francis Dobbs delivered a speech in that chamber in which he denounced the contemplated Act of Union between England and Ireland as inexpedient and impious, citing the books of Daniel and Revelation to prove the latter point. The speech received considerable public favor. Dobbs was encouraged by the response to publish both a nine-volume summary of world history and, in one volume, *A Concise View, from History and Prophecy, of the Great Predictions in the Sacred Writings, That Have Been Fulfilled.*

It was in the latter work that Dobbs wrote about the Avignon Society. A Swedenborgian, it may be that he had heard of the group during Grabianka's long sojourn in London in 1786. It was not long after this that Dobbs abandoned his political career temporarily in order to study the fulfillment of millenarian prophecy in history. By the time he resumed political activity in 1797, his religious convic-

59. Quoted in Le Forestier, *Franc-maçonnerie*, pp. 516, 999.
60. Henri-Baptiste Grégoire, *Histoire des sectes religieuses*, new ed., 6 vols. (Paris: Baudouin, 1828–45), 2: 194–99.
61. Guillaume Chais de Sourcesol, *Le livre des manifestes* (n.p., 1800), pt. 2, p. 77 n 1. The Library of Congress's copy has the manuscript inscription: "Gift of the author to Thomas Jefferson."

tions and his Irish patriotism had combined to produce the conviction that the Second Coming was imminent and would occur in Ireland. He had said that much in his speech in the Irish House of Commons. In his *Concise View*, he went much further. The Messiah would come either that year (1800) or the next—soon enough to prevent the Act of Union.[62]

One group of men was particularly called to follow Christ and prepare for his Second Coming: the Avignon Society. Dobbs told his readers that its members declared that "these are the glorious times when the Messiah is personally to appear and restore all things. . . . They affirm that all the old prophets, apostles, and martyrs are now upon the earth, and have been literally born again."[63] The society's directing council of seven said that Antichrist was on earth, and they knew him. Their own leader was a Polish nobleman whom they believed to be Moses; another of the seven was Aaron.

The Act of Union was passed and put into effect; Christ did not come to Ireland. Francis Dobbs, a man of charm, poetic talent, and political ability, was quickly forgotten. He died, mad and impoverished, in 1811.

The Avignon Society seems simply to have dispersed. Some of its members are said to have turned to the other-worldly mysticism of their old acquaintance Saint-Martin. One of the society's founding members, William Bousie, became a Swedenborgian.[64] The mysticism and occultism of the post-Revolutionary era was quite different from that of the 1780s; one of the casualties was the Avignon Society. In England in the period after 1800, it is not difficult to trace the trend of the millenarian followers of Richard Brothers away from his message of political-religious renovation. It may well be that the same thing happened among the Avignon brotherhood, but the same kinds of source materials do not exist. It may also be that the absence of the remarkable Count Grabianka from Avignon produced a vacuum that nobody else could fill.

The last of the faithful was the marquis de Vaucrose, whose country house had been the society's headquarters since Pernety's arrival in Avignon. In 1804, after Grabianka's departure, he attempted to

---

62. *Monthly Review* 35 (1801): 291–93; *Dictionary of National Biography*, 1921–22 ed., s.v. "Dobbs, Francis," by Henry Merse Stevens; David V. Erdman, *Blake: Prophet against Empire*, rev. ed. (Princeton: Princeton University Press, 1969), pp. 430 n 15, 483 n 16.
63. Quoted in *Monthly Review* 35 (1801): 293.
64. Carl Theophilus Odhner, *Annals of the New Church*, 2 vols. (Bryn Athyn, Pa.: Academy of the New Church, 1904), 1: 258.

reconstitute the society, but without success. Two years later, he contacted Willermoz in Lyons, saying that he wanted to associate "with the masonic Regime of Lyons," but he refused Willermoz's suggestion that he found an affiliated lodge.[65] He and his associates would submit only when it was God's will to do so—a time that apparently never came. A decade later, the marquis was still waiting. In 1816, he wrote a friend that he continued to believe, as he had done for thirty years, "that we are on the eve of extraordinary times, that they will come soon, and will be at last miraculously terminated by the justification of the good and by the destruction of the wicked."[66]

Although the Avignon Society was on the periphery of the world of mystical and occultist sectarianism that flourished in the late eighteenth century, it is important as one of the conduits by means of which the sense of imminent political and spiritual regeneration that characterized the period was transmitted to the nineteenth century. The positive, man-centered mysticism of Saint-Martin was one heir to the kind of socioreligious faith that the French Revolution had in part affirmed and in part destroyed. Swedenborg's theology, which expressed a similar confidence in man's capacity to transcend himself and a similar conviction that the spiritual world was both accessible and comprehensible, had an equally impressive revival throughout the Atlantic world. Thus the world of mystical Masonry did not disappear with the lodges that had been its center; and the sense of imminent, transcendental regeneration of man and his world would again play an important part in the climate of opinion that preceded the revolutions of 1848.[67]

65. Le Forestier, Franc-maçonnerie, pp. 881–84.
66. Quoted in Viatte, Sources occultes du romantisme, 2: 248.
67. Darnton, Mesmerism, chap. 5; Colin Wilson, The Occult: A History (London: Hodder & Stoughton, 1971), chap. 6; and Auguste Viatte, Victor Hugo et les Illuminés de son temps (Montréal: Editions de l'Arbre, 1942), pt. 1.

CHAPTER 6

The Millenarian Tradition in English Dissent

WHEN Pierre Pontard said that Suzette Labrousse's pilgrimage to Rome was a "respectable folly," part of his meaning was that the aims and assumptions that inspired it were derived from ancient and accepted Christian tradition. In the *Journal prophétique*, Pontard tried, in his disjointed and obtuse way, to show that Labrousse's "mission" conformed to the teachings of the Scriptures, the church fathers, and the theologians and "saints" of the eighteenth century. With the exception of the Jansenist theologian Duguet, however, none of Pontard's authorities was completely and unequivocally millenarian. The millenarian tradition had a great deal of vitality in eighteenth century France, as we have seen. It was even marginally respectable. It had a kind of backstairs existence, accepted but unrecognized, within both Jansenism and Freemasonry.

In England, the situation was very different. The seventeenth century had seen a lush flowering of millenarian doctrines of all kinds,[1] and in the eighteenth century, millenarianism still enjoyed a currency and respectability, even in intellectual circles, that it never

---

1. The literature on seventeenth-century English millenarianism is vast. Among the recent and divergent interpretations are Hugh Trevor Roper, "Three Foreigners: The Philosophers of the Puritan Revolution," in Trevor Roper, *The Crisis of the Seventeenth Century: Religion, the Reformation, and Social Change* (New York: Harper & Row, 1968), pp. 246–93; Christopher Hill, *Antichrist in Seventeenth-Century England* (Oxford: Oxford University Press, 1971); William Lamont, *Godly Rule: Politics and Religion, 1603–60* (New York: St. Martin's Press, 1969); Keith Thomas, *Religion and the Decline of Magic* (New York: Charles Scribner's Sons, 1971), pp. 128–46; Peter Toon, ed., *Puritans, the Millennium, and the Future of Israel: Puritan Eschatology, 1600–1660* (Cambridge: James Clarke, 1970); Bernard Capp, *The Fifth Monarchy Men: A Study in Seventeenth-Century English Millenarianism* (Totowa, N.J.: Rowman & Littlefield, 1972); and Alan Macfarlane, *The Family Life of Ralph Josselin* (Cambridge: At the University Press, 1970), pp. 185–90.

received in France. The more flamboyant sects like the Ranters and the Fifth Monarchy Men might have disappeared; the times might never again seem so portentous of the Second Coming as they had between 1640 and 1660; but the *assumptions* on which seventeenth-century English millenarianism had rested were not repudiated in the more placid times that followed. Biblical scholars and learned divines continued to approach the prophecies concerning Christ's Second Coming as a worthy subject for study and rational analysis.

The foundations of what might be called the scholarly tradition of English millenarianism were laid early in the seventeenth century. There had been a substantial development of interest in eschatology in Protestant circles since the time of Luther, nourished in part by the growth of Hebrew studies in Protestant universities. Learned Christians came to know and in some cases to accept the Jewish belief that God would at some future time literally restore the Jews to their homeland in Palestine. They also tended to interpret references in the New Testament to the future of "Israel" as referring to the Jewish people, which must be converted to Christianity before Christ could come again. Three influential works published late in the sixteenth century—the *Geneva Bible*, John Foxe's *Actes and Monuments*, and John Napier's *A Plaine Discussion of the Whole Revelation of Saint John*—suggested that the Protestant Reformation had an eschatological significance within Divine Providence at least as great as that of events in St. Paul's time. All three were important in guiding English Puritan writers toward the conviction that they, their country, and their age were specially ordained to accomplish great things in the work of the Lord.[2] Some of these Puritan writers began to look at the prophetic books of the Bible, which had fascinated believers for so long, and to see, particularly in Daniel and in Revelation, their own times foretold.

Two men were especially influential in disseminating these ideas in the tense and expectant decades of the Puritan Revolution. The first was Thomas Brightman, a graduate of Queen's College, Cambridge, and rector at Hawnes in Bedfordshire until his death in 1607. Both a convinced Puritan and a noted preacher, Brightman wrote on the prophecies in part to answer the Catholic theologians who denied that the Pope could be the Beast described in the thirteenth chapter of Revelation. Brightman's several works, all published posthumously, were primarily concerned with biblical prophecies about the climactic struggle against Antichrist, whom Brightman identified unequivocally with the Pope. Brightman was not, strictly speaking, a mil-

2. Toon, "The Latter-Day Glory," in Toon, ed., *Puritan Eschatology*, pp. 23-25.

lenarian, since he believed that Christ would come only at the end of a thousand-year struggle against the forces of evil, a struggle that had begun in about 1300. The millennium was thus not for him the sort of sudden, miraculous, collective salvation of the elect that it was for others later in the seventeenth century. Brightman did believe that the events predicted in Revelation were taking place in his own times. The angels' pouring of the vials of wrath, which was to follow the opening of the seventh seal and the blowing of the seventh trumpet, had already occurred, manifest in part in the actions of Elizabeth and her ministers against the Roman Catholics. The pouring of the last four vials would see the spread of the word of God, the destruction of Rome, the papacy, and the Turks, and the conversion of the Jews to Christianity, after which they would return to their homeland.[3]

The second founder of scholarly millenarianism was Joseph Mede, scientist, philosopher, biblical scholar, and fellow of Christ's College, Cambridge. He too believed that some of the vials of wrath had already been poured. Unlike Brightman, however, Mede worked out a precise chronology for the remaining vials. The fourth vial was being poured while he was writing in the 1620s. It had caused the Thirty Years' War and would lead ultimately to the destruction of the House of Austria. The fifth and sixth vials would produce the final events that must occur before Christ's Second Coming: the destruction of the Roman Catholic church, the conversion of the Jews, and the destruction of the Turks. Only then would the seventh vial be poured, bringing the millennium itself.[4]

Almost certainly, the principal influence on Mede in his adoption of the doctrine of a literal, terrestrial millenarianism, in place of St. Augustine's spiritualized interpretation, which had been the accepted one among biblical scholars for so long, was the German Calvinist theologian Johann Heinrich Alsted. The Thirty Years' War had forced Alsted to leave his Rhineland home for a life of exile in Transylvania, and it was that event that had led him to adopt a millenarian interpretation of current events, in a book published in 1627 called *Diatribe de mille annis apocalypticis*.[5] Five years later, Mede adopted a similar

---

3. Ibid., pp. 27-30; Lamont, *Godly Rule*, pp. 49-50, 95-104.
4. *Dictionary of National Biography*, 1921-22 ed., s.v. "Mead, or Mede, Joseph," by Alexander Gordon; R. G. Clouse, "The Rebirth of Millenarianism," in Toon, ed., *Puritan Eschatology*, pp. 56-62; Ernest Tuveson, *Millennium and Utopia: A Study in the Background of the Idea of Progress* (Berkeley: University of California Press, 1949), pp. 76-84, 229 n 8; and Michael Walzer, *The Revolution of the Saints: A Study in the Origins of Radical Politics* (Cambridge: Harvard University Press, 1965), pp. 291-92.
5. Clouse, "Rebirth of Millenarianism," in Toon, ed., *Puritan Eschatology*, pp. 42-54; Trevor Roper, "Three Foreigners," p. 247.

view in a "historical application" appended to his treatise on prophetic chronology called *Clavis Apocalyptica*. The book had had three Latin editions when Parliament, in 1643, ordered its translation into English under the grandiloquent title, *The Key to Revelation Searched and Demonstrated.*

Brightman and Mede were not as influential in seventeenth-century England as some of their contemporaries claimed, nor was their message as original as some recent scholars have believed. William Lamont has argued persuasively, however, that what their books did achieve was the continuation and elaboration of a theme developed in John Foxe's *Book of Martyrs.* England and her rulers had a divinely ordained role to play in the culminating epoch of human history, which was soon to begin. Beginning with Brightman, the crucial eschatological function in England shifted from the prince to the people, thus giving a kind of divine assurance to the Puritans in their struggle with the king in the 1640s.[6]

Mede's scholarly researches tended to support the same kind of view. And while neither he nor Brightman looked for Christ's appearance at any time in the near future, a great many of their readers did. It was a simple step for them to take. If the struggles of the godly against the unrighteous were being fought out in the 1640s, both in England and on the battlefields of central Europe, and if these times of troubles had been foretold by Daniel and by St. John the Divine, then surely the culminating events before the Second Coming were near at hand. The notion that England was the second Israel, which for Elizabeth and her contemporaries had been at least half metaphorical, became a literal identification for those Puritans who saw their civil wars in prophetic terms. Mede himself wrote an entire treatise on the question of the conversion and restoration of the Jews.[7] Throughout the seventeenth and eighteenth centuries, numerous Puritans and their dissenting descendants examined the question of the Jews' role in the fulfillment of prophecy and England's special role in its accomplishment.

We must be careful not to claim too much for Mede and the other English millenarian writers of the seventeenth century. Ernest Tuveson, for example, in his influential *Millennium and Utopia*, has made Mede the founder of the modern ideology of progress. Michael Walzer,

6. Lamont, *Godly Rule*, p. 95. See also William Haller, *Foxe's Book of Martyrs and the Elect Nation* (London: Cape, 1963), esp. chap. 7.
7. Toon, "The Question of Jewish Immigration," in Toon, ed., *Puritan Eschatology*, pp. 117–25. On the significance of Mede and Brightman, I have followed Lamont, *Godly Rule*, p. 104 n 51; and Lamont, "Richard Baxter, the Apocalypse, and the Mad Major," *Past and Present*, no. 55 (1972), pp. 70–72.

in *The Revolution of the Saints,* credited the system of "historical reference and prophecy" developed in the 1640s with enabling the Puritans to become political revolutionaries by persuading themselves that they were bringing history to its millenarian climax.[8]

All of this is too neat and too simple. It is certainly true that Mede and Brightman affirmed the tone of optimism, the assurance that all would be well in the time of the new heavens and the new earth, that had always been part of the millenarian tradition. It is also true, as Lamont and others have recently shown, that belief in the millennium was much more pervasive in the 1640s than had previously been supposed.[9]

The intensity of English millenarianism during the Puritan Revolution should not obscure how much in the doctrines that were being promulgated was very old. There had always been a psychological ambivalence to the convictions of those who awaited the Second Coming. The same mixture of anxiety and hope, of Apocalypse and millennium, that characterized the Spiritual Franciscans, the Taborites and Lollards of the fifteenth century, and the sermons of Savonarola also affected the Puritans. What made English millenarianism unusual was the rapidity with which its doctrines could be disseminated within England's "printing culture" and also the widespread acceptance of these ideas by the educated and respectable classes.[10] In seventeenth-century England, the interpenetration of popular and institutional, or "official," religious ideas and attitudes was unusually extensive.

All the participants in the several-sided debate on Puritan millenarianism assume that it faded into oblivion after the Restoration. Hugh Trevor Roper has put it baldly: "Instead of a spiritual union for the overthrow of Antichrist, the new society would be so deliberately neutral in religion that it could even be accused of a plan to 'reduce England to popery.'" Not having experienced the tensions and disasters of the 1620s, the new generation in the 1680s was "exempt from its peculiar metaphysics: they would not waste their time on the Millennium, the Messiah or the number of the Beast."[11]

It is true that millenarianism would never again enjoy the wide public acceptance it had had in the 1640s, but the legacy of Mede and Brightman was more lasting than historians have realized. Mede was

8. Tuveson, *Millennium and Utopia,* p. 76; Walzer, *Revolution of the Saints,* p. 291.
9. Bernard Capp, "Godly Rule and English Millenarianism," *Past and Present,* no. 52 (1971), pp. 115–16.
10. Elizabeth Eisenstein, "L'avènement de l'imprimérie et la Réforme," *Annales: économies sociétés civilisations* 26 (1971): 1356.
11. Trevor-Roper, "Three Foreigners," p. 50.

given continued attention by theologians for over a century and was still being cited in the 1790s. His attempt to demonstrate that biblical prophecy was being fulfilled in current events, particularly in that the struggle of Protestantism against its enemies, was continued by a distinguished line of scholars that included Sir Isaac Newton; Newton's successor in the chair of mathematics at Cambridge, William Whiston; the Lockean psychological philosopher David Hartley; and Joseph Priestley.

The young Priestley did not expect to publish works devoted to millenarian speculations. Like Isaac Newton eighty years before, he regarded the study of the prophecies as both an opportunity for rational men to see how God's plan unfolded in history and as a worthy pastime for Christians. One could say of both Priestley and Newton what Edmund Gosse wrote in 1907 of the pious scientist who was his father—that for him the book of Revelation consisted of a series of statements on events that were to happen "and could be recognized when they did happen." Priestley and Newton also sought "the explanation, the perfect prosaic and positive explanation, of all these wonders."[12] Gosse's father was an anachronism in the English intellectual community of his day. Isaac Newton was not; as Frank Manuel has shown in his recent biography, millenarian speculations were common among scientists of Newton's generation.[13] Nor was Priestley an anachronism; his millenarianism was, at the least, a thoroughly consistent product of his ideas and experiences.

In his study of the millennium, Priestley was continuing one of the most frequently elaborated lines of argument used by the "rational Christians" in their controversies with the deists in the first decades of the eighteenth century. In order to demonstrate that reason and revelation did not conflict, these Christian apologists had persistently emphasized that prophecy was a demonstration of God's power that could be verified by human experience. John Jackson had declared in 1744 that "miracles and prophecies are the two main pillars on which revelation is built. . . . They are evidences of the truth of it which are infallible, and cannot fail to have effect."[14] To show, therefore, that biblical prophecies had been fulfilled or were being fulfilled in the world's history would prove that God's power was real and that the Bible was true. This kind of proof was especially attractive to a man of Priestley's temperament. Deeply religious, despite what his enemies

---

12. Edmund Gosse, *Father and Son* (Harmondsworth: Penguin Books, 1949), p. 50.
13. Frank E. Manuel, *A Portrait of Isaac Newton* (Cambridge: Harvard University Press, 1968), pp. 363–80.
14. Quoted in G. R. Cragg, *Reason and Authority in the Eighteenth Century* (Cambridge: At the University Press, 1964), p. 54.

said of him, he was at the same time utterly without any sense of mysticism and distrustful of appeals to religious feeling. Prosaic and industrious, he tried in his numerous theological writings to provide the same kinds of tangible and coherent proofs for his religious doctrines that he sought in his chemical experiments.

It was perhaps this cast of mind that drew Priestley so strongly to David Hartley. Hartley is best remembered today as the formulator of an associationist psychology that is the ancestor of modern behaviorism. His principal aim, however, was to develop a Christian apologetic in which religious and moral "facts" would be demonstrated to be as tangible and scientific as physical "facts." His *Observations on Man* first appeared in 1749. On the basis of Newtonian physics and on the related psychological ideas of Locke and the Reverend John Gay, Hartley contended that sense impressions were received by means of vibrations in the ether, transmitted to the brain, and there, by the principle of association, organized into ideas. He then moved to what he considered the core of his work: the empirical explanation of the moral and religious sense. "All the pleasures and pains of sensation, imagination, ambition, self-interest, sympathy, and theopathy," he wrote, "beget in us a moral sense, and lead us to the love and approbation of virtue, and to the fear, hatred, and abhorrence of vice." He continued: "It appears also, that the moral sense carries us perpetually to the pure love of God, as our highest and ultimate perfection, our end, centre, and only resting-place, to which yet we can never attain."[15]

In the second part of his book, Hartley proceeded to show that the Christian revelation was in full conformity with the theory of the mind and the demonstration of natural religion that he had expounded in the first volume. He then gave considerable attention to prophecy and to the millennium. He wanted to show that God's providence was good, that "he who has brought us into this state, will conduct us through it," and that the end of God's plan was "the ultimate happiness of all."[16] The culmination would be the Second Coming of Jesus Christ, signs of which Hartley saw in contemporary events. He pre-

15. David Hartley, *Observations on Man, his Frame, his Duty, and his Expectations*, 16th ed. (London: Tegg, 1834), pp. 311-12. On Hartley, see Cragg, *Reason and Authority*, pp. 216-29; Richard Haven, "Coleridge, Hartley, and the Mystics," *Journal of the History of Ideas* 20 (Oct.-Dec. 1959): 477-94; Robert Marsh, "The Second Part of Hartley's System," *Journal of the History of Ideas* 20 (Apr. 1959): 264-73; Hoxie Fairchild, "Hartley, Pistorius, and Coleridge, *PMLA* 69 (Dec. 1947): 1010-21; and Donald J. D'Elia, "Benjamin Rush, David Hartley, and the Revolutionary Uses of Psychology," *Proceedings of the American Philosophical Society* 114 (Apr. 1970): 109-18.
16. Hartley, *Observations on Man*, pp. 322, 593.

dicted "temporal evils and woes" in "these western parts, the Christian Babylon, before the great revolution predicted in the Scriptures, before the kingdoms of this world become the kingdoms of our lord, and of his Christ." He refused to set a time for the realization of these events, but his conclusion implied that the time would be soon: "The present circumstances of the world are extraordinary and critical, beyond what has ever yet happened."[17]

Priestley first heard about Hartley's *Observations on Man* while a student at Daventry Academy from 1752 to 1755. He recalled forty years later in his memoirs that the book "immediately engaged my closest attention, and produced the greatest, and in my opinion the most favourable effect on my general turn of thinking through life."[18]

The book continued to be both a basis of his theories and a source of spiritual comfort throughout his life. In 1800, depressed by a series of disappointments that included the deaths of his wife and his youngest son, the normally buoyant Priestley wrote his friend Theophilus Lindsey: "It is nothing but a firm faith in a good Providence that is my support at present; . . . I read the introduction to the second volume of Hartley, and his conclusion, when I am most pressed."[19] For Priestley, the attraction of Hartley was that he provided a scientific foundation for the religious convictions that were under attack from the advocates of unbelief. What were unbelievers like Hume and Voltaire, Priestley asked rhetorically, "compared with *Newton, Locke,* or *Hartley,* who were equally eminent as divines, and as philosophers?"[20]

There were some points, however, on which Priestley disagreed with his mentor. Priestley united psychology and physiology even more closely than Hartley did, and he advanced a materialism that was even more radical. Matter for him was not the little billiard balls which Newton hypothesized and which many scientists in the eighteenth century took for granted. Priestley adopted the very different matter-theory of the Serbian Jesuit Roger Boscovich. He argued that matter consisted of unextended points that possessed inertia and were surrounded by shells of force that alternated between repulsion and attraction throughout space. Thus, when Priestley contended in his 1777 *Disquisition on Matter and Spirit* that everything, including

17. Ibid., pp. 594, 604.
18. John Towill Rutt, *The Life and Correspondence of Joseph Priestley,* which is vol. 1, pts. 1 and 2, of Joseph Priestley, *The Theological and Miscellaneous Works of Joseph Priestley,* ed. John Towill Rutt, 25 vols. (London: Smallfield, 1817–32), 1, pt. 1: 24 (hereafter cited as *Works*).
19. Priestley, *Works*, 1, pt. 2: 437.
20. Priestley, *Observations on the Increase of Infidelity,* in *Works*, 16: 10.

thought, sensation, and soul, was material, he was in fact speaking of a sort of divinely impelled life force very different from the mechanistic billiard balls.[21] Priestley believed that his materialism was biblical; Paul, he said, had the same idea when he spoke of the resurrection of the dead. As Priestley explained it: "Whatever is *decomposed* may certainly be *recomposed*, by the same almighty power that first composed it, with whatever change in its constitution, advantageous or disadvantageous, he shall think proper: and then the powers of thinking, and whatever depended upon them, will return of course, and the man will be in the proper sense, *the same* being that he was *before*."[22] When Priestley began to speculate on the millennium, his materialism was not an obstacle but rather a confirmation. The reign of Jesus Christ over the resurrected dead was both reasonable and "scientific." As he wrote in the preface to the second edition of his *Disquisition*, he hoped that materialism would become "the favourite tenet of *Rational* Christians; being perfectly consonant to the appearances of nature, and giving a peculiar value to the scheme of revelation."[23]

The corollary to Priestley's materialism was his principle of "philosophic necessity." Man was bound by fixed laws of causation, but a good God had created the universe and was directing it toward a termination that would be the ultimate good of all. In developing his doctrine of philosophical necessity, which like his materialism underlies all his religious and metaphysical ideas, he drew on the ideas of a diverse group of men, including Hartley, David Hume, Jonathan Edwards, Lord Kames, and Thomas Hobbes. He cited as particularly apt a paragraph in the *Leviathan* in which Hobbes described the chain of causes that traces back to God himself as first cause, who alone can see "the connexion of these causes, the *necessity* of all men's voluntary actions." Thus "God, that seeth also that *liberty* of man, in doing what he will, is accompanied with the necessity of doing that which God wills, and no more or less."[24] Given his conviction of the benevolence of the divine purpose, the doctrine provided Priestley with considerable comfort throughout his life, even when wars abroad and political persecutions at home indicated that the accomplishment of God's plan would not be so simple and rapid as he would have liked. As he wrote in one of his last letters: "The

21. Robert Schofield, "Joseph Priestley, the Theory of Oxidation, and the Nature of Matter," *Journal of the History of Ideas* 25 (1965): 285–94.
22. Priestley, *Disquisition on Matter and Spirit,* in *Works,* 3: 333.
23. Ibid., p. 210.
24. Cited in Priestley, *The Doctrine of Philosophic Necessity Illustrated,* in *Works,* 3: 456.

more I contemplate the great system, the more satisfaction I find in it; and the *structure* being so perfect, there cannot be a doubt but that the *end* and use of it, in promoting happiness, will correspond to it."[25]

There is no evidence that Priestley ever doubted that this "end" would be the millennium about which English scholars had been speculating since the 1620s. Nor did he question the premises advanced by Mede, Henry More, Isaac Newton, Whiston, Lowman, Lowth, and all the rest. Like most of them, he refused to set a precise date for the millennium; prophecy could be confirmed as it was fulfilled, not before. Like Brightman and so many later scholars, it was axiomatic for Priestley that Antichrist in the book he always called "the Revelation" was the Pope, symbol of the disastrous departures from biblical Christianity taken by all churches, but above all by the Roman Catholic church.

Priestley's religious notoriety in his own lifetime and the virulence with which he was attacked both by divines of the Church of England and by other English Dissenters derived only in part from his complete and unequivocal denial of the divinity of Jesus. It was also inspired by his equally outspoken rejection of the compromise between established church and tolerated Dissenters which most people, including Dissenters, believed had brought religious peace and freedom after the troubles of the preceding century.[26] Just as Priestley's philosophy of materialism and necessity provided an explanation of how God would accomplish the purification and regeneration of Christianity, so his conception of the millennium always had a political context derived in part from his hostility to all state churches.

Priestley first touched on the millennium in 1772 in his *Institutes of Natural and Revealed Religion*, probably his most widely read theological work. A letter written the year before indicates that the developing crisis in the American colonies was leading him to think that the end of the world was at hand: ". . . Every thing looks like the approach of that dismal catastrophe described, I may say predicted, by Dr. Hartley. I shall be looking for the downfall of Church and State together. I am really expecting some very calamitous, but finally glorious, events."[27]

In the section of the *Institutes* titled "Of the Future Condition of the World in General," he argued that the final destruction of Antichrist would come during the period "which is often denominated in

25. Priestley, *Works*, 1, pt. 2: 493.
26. Anthony Lincoln, *Some Political and Social Ideas of English Dissent, 1763–1800* (Cambridge: At the University Press, 1938), pp. 212–36.
27. Priestley, *Works*, 1, pt. 2: 146.

the Scriptures by *the coming of Christ.*" This destruction would probably not be "literal," but "figurative." During that time, Christianity would prevail in its original purity "for a space which, in the prophetic languages, is called *a thousand years.*" However, given the relative backwardness of the world, when "even the best policied states abound with so many absurd institutions, by which *the many* are miserably enslaved by the few," a thousand years would hardly suffice for the necessary political, scientific, and cultural "improvements." Thus it might take as many as 360,000 years for the world to attain its perfection.[28]

Priestley had abandoned these views before the French Revolution. Writing in 1788 in the *Theological Repository*, which he edited, he suggested that the millennium might constitute a literal earthly kingdom ruled over by Christ himself and peopled by the dead, who would rise, "not perhaps all together, but in succession, according to some law or rule at present unknown to us."[29] Having shifted to this more conventional notion of a sudden and tangible advent of Christ, it is not surprising that he ceased to speculate on the duration of the millennium.

The essays contributed by a young Cambridge fellow named Robert Edward Garnham to the *Theological Repository* may have influenced Priestley to adopt the traditional idea of an earthly kingdom ruled for a thousand years by Jesus himself. Like his and Priestley's mutual friend Theophilus Lindsey, Garnham was a Church of England clergyman who had become a unitarian in theology. Unlike Lindsey, Garnham managed to remain within the Church of England, perhaps because he was of a retiring disposition and because he published his controversial theological essays anonymously.[30] Fittingly, for a unitarian scholar and a millenarian, Garnham had attended Isaac Newton's own college, Trinity. Later, in 1793, he was elected its college preacher. An exponent of the religious radicalism that was endemic to Cambridge in the eighteenth century, Garnham also joined in the widespread support which the French Revolution received there; and like Joseph Priestley, he interpreted it in millenarian terms.

Garnham's essays in the *Theological Repository* appeared in 1786 and 1788 under the rather surprising pseudonym "Idiota." His central argument concerning the millennium was that it could only be heralded by the sudden, literal, miraculous advent of Jesus, who would descend from the clouds to rule over the whole earth. Joseph

---

28. Priestley, *Institutes of Natural and Revealed Religion*, in *Works*, 2: 365–67.
29. Priestley, *Works*, 7: 448.   30. *Monthly Repository* 10 (1802): 13–14.

Mede had been wrong in speaking of two future kingdoms. There would be only one kingdom of heaven, the one "which the God of heaven will set up on the earth . . . by means of a Son of man, coming in the clouds of heaven, an idea very different from that of a government over spirits, in regions above the atmosphere!" This other belief, Garnham held, "our present disquisitions on matter and spirit, and our improved Astronomy, render daily more improbable."[31]

Jesus, he continued, had lived and died a man, whose only proper title up to the present time was "Jesus of Nazareth, the prophet of the most High God." In fact, he argued in another essay, Jesus was the second Elias foretold by the prophet Malachi. Jesus had been *mistaken* when he said John the Baptist was that Elias. Garnham's rationally Christian but rather surprising conclusion was that trivial mistakes, such as Jesus's not knowing who he himself was, proved that scriptural events were not part of human design: "Here, then, is the finger of God."[32] The proof would come when Jesus came again, this time as the Messiah, to inaugurate the millennium.

Priestley's adoption of the same literal and miraculous millennium came shortly after Garnham's articles had appeared. In two letters, one to Lindsey and one to another Cambridge unitarian, William Frend, Priestley specifically praised Garnham's argument that Jesus was, albeit unknowingly, the second Elias.[33]

Priestley had written in the *Institutes* that the restoration of the Jews to their homeland in Palestine would *precede* both their conversion to Christianity and the coming of Jesus and would occur under their own prince, a descendant of David.[34] He developed the idea further in a 1786 essay in the *Theological Repository* and in the first of his *Letters to the Jews*, the following year. He called upon the Jews to prepare for the time when God would gather them together and settle them in their own land. Under the rule of their own House of David, they would then become "the most illustrious . . . of all the nations of the earth."[35]

Priestley's philosemitism was hardly unique in the eighteenth century. In England as in France, it had been a continuous thread within the millenarian tradition since at least the seventeenth century. A constant stream of sermons and tracts invited the Jews to convert to Christianity so that Jesus could come again. Some tracts developed the Puritan notion that the English were specially called to aid in the Jews' conversion and return to Israel.

31. *Theological Repository* 6 (1786): 259 n 1.   32. Ibid., pp. 279.
33. Priestley, *Works*, 1, pt. 1: 403; pt. 2: 77.
34. Ibid., 2: 368; 12: 438–41; and 20: 230–31.   35. Ibid., 20: 249.

In the *Institutes*, Priestley contended that the kingdoms of eighteenth-century Europe were "unquestionably represented" in the book of Daniel "by the feet and toes of the great image which Nebuchadnezzar saw in his prophetical dream." From Daniel's interpretation of the dream, it was clear that European "forms of government, ecclesiastical and civil," would have to be "dissolved" and replaced by something "greatly superior to them, more favorable to the virtue and happiness of mankind."[36] In another era and for another man, speculation might have ended there. Instead, the French Revolution gave to Nebuchadnezzar's dream and to the book of Revelation a significance that led Priestley to see the destruction of the French monarchy as a divinely ordained part of the fulfillment of God's plan. In a letter to their mutual friend Thomas Jefferson, John Adams recalled a conversation he had had with Priestley shortly after the latter's arrival in the United States in 1794. Priestley had told Adams that the French Revolution "was opening a new era in the world and presenting a near view of the millenium [sic]." Adams asked him on what grounds he could believe that France, then in the midst of the Reign of Terror, would establish "a free democratical government." Priestley answered that his opinion was based entirely on revelation and prophecy. The ten crowned heads of Europe were the ten horns of the Beast in Revelation, and "the execution of the king of France is the falling off of the first of those horns; and . . . the nine monarchies of Europe will fall one after another in the same way."[37]

Joseph Priestley's millenarianism has been something of an embarrassment to his biographers. It should not be. We must remember, first of all, that his millenarian ideas were far more respectable and conventional than some of his other opinions. Second, Priestley's nearly total acceptance of the ideology of the French Revolution had the effect of intensifying his millenarianism. It is thus impossible to separate his political opinions from his religious convictions. Having come to the conclusion that the French Revolution was divinely ordained, he threw himself into the task of fitting its events into the scheme of biblical prophecy with the same single-minded tenacity that he brought to everything else he did.

On 29 August 1790, Priestley wrote the Reverend Richard Price to congratulate him on his address to the Revolution Society (of 1688) in praise of the French Revolution and to salute "the liberty, both of that

36. Ibid., 2: 370–71.
37. Lester J. Cappon, ed., *The Complete Correspondence between Thomas Jefferson and Abigail and John Adams*, 2 vols. (Chapel Hill: University of North Carolina Press, 1959), 2: 594–95.

country and America, and of course of all those other countries that, it is to be hoped, will follow their example."[38] Five months earlier, Priestley himself had received a letter from a former student named John Hurford Stone, who was then living in Paris. "I cannot close my letter without congratulating you on the accomplishment of those great events which have taken place in Europe, since I had last the pleasure of seeing you," Stone wrote. "And as the same causes under similar circumstances, produce the same effect, I congratulate you still more, on what must *necessarily come to pass.* . . . You seem to have viewed the revolution with a prophetic eye many years since." If the world progressed as rapidly in the next ten years as it had in the last ten, Stone concluded, Priestley would see "the accomplishment of [his] labors, the summit of [his] wishes, the empire of false-hood, religious and political, overthrown, and the world free and happy!!!"[39]

One of thirty-eight printed replies to Burke's *Reflections*, an attack on the French Revolution and its English supporters, was made by Priestley. The two men had been friendly and politically allied during the American Revolution, but no longer. The French Revolution was "in many respects unparalleled in all history," Priestley wrote. It was, "to adopt your own rhetorical style, a change from darkness to light, from superstition to sound knowledge, and from a most debasing servitude to a state of the most exalted freedom." The outcome of the revolution would be the separation of church and state that Dissenters had sought for so long in England, "an end to national prejudice and a reign of universal peace, end to Empires and civil war."[40] In a letter to Price written the same month (January 1791), Priestley's millenarian hopes intruded more clearly. "I rejoice with you that the French Revolution goes on, to all appearance, so well," he wrote. "I also rejoice that the Russians are so near Constantinople. That is the only war that I *wish* to go on."[41]

In July 1791, rioters in Birmingham destroyed Priestley's house, his laboratory, and most of his library and manuscripts. He came to London, where he replaced his recently deceased friend Price as pastor to the Gravel-Pit Meeting at Hackney.

A year later, the French Legislative Assembly took time out from the tense political situation that accompanied the fall of the monarchy to confer citizenship upon a mixed bag of foreigners. The moment had arrived for "a national convention . . . to fix the destinies of

38. Priestley, *Works*, 1, pt. 2: 79.
39. The John Hurford Stone letter is quoted in a hostile pamphlet, *New Light on Jacobinism* (Birmingham, 1789), pp. 54-55. Despite the dubious source, I am inclined to accept the letter as authentic.
40. Priestley, *Letters to Burke* (January 1791), in *Works*, 22: 236, 238.
41. Priestley, *Works*, 1, pt. 2: 100.

France, perhaps to prepare that of the human race," the Legislative Assembly declared, sounding a trifle millenarian itself. A free people should seek out those who "by their sentiments, their writings, and their courage, have shown themselves worthy."[42] The first name on the list of new citizens was that of Joseph Priestley.

Three of these so honored were subsequently elected to the National Convention. Thomas Paine and Anacharsis Clootz accepted, but Priestley declined. He gladly accepted French citizenship, he wrote the assembly, and he did not believe that it conflicted with his English citizenship. Yet he was totally unqualified to be a deputy. His French was poor, and he had little knowledge of local conditions in the department of the Orne, which had elected him. However, he said that he would communicate his views on matters of concern to the assembly: "As a citizen of the world, I have the right, and as a French citizen, I have the duty to do so. . . . I consider your recent revolution as the most important era in the history of the human race; its happiness depends on you."[43]

Two weeks later, Priestley's old friend and present adversary, Burke, wrote to Lord Fitzwilliam that he had seen letters from Priestley "to others of the Murderers in which he censures some *excesses*; or indeed rather laments them for no other reason than as tending to hurt so good a Cause."[44] Burke was probably referring primarily to a letter to Roland, the minister of the interior, which had been read aloud in the Legislative Assembly on 20 September 1792. In it, Priestley praised Roland's conduct in "the recent troubles"—meaning, presumably, the September Massacres in which some 1,300 persons had died. "You cannot conceive the sadness these irregular and illegal actions have spread among all the friends of your revolution in this country, and how much your enemies triumph from it."[45] In a letter to Rabaut Saint-Etienne, the Protestant minister who, like himself, had been elected a deputy to the Convention from the department of the Orne, Priestley wrote at the same time: "As a minister of religion, the object of my most ardent desire in your happiness. I sincerely pray that the Supreme Being . . . may destroy the machinations of your enemies, and put an end to the troubles with which you are now agitated."[46]

42. *Réimpression de l'ancien Moniteur*, 32 vols. (Paris: Bureau Central, 1840-54), 13: 541.
43. Ibid., 14: 75.
44. Edmund Burke, *The Correspondence of Edmund Burke*, ed. P. J. Marshall and John A. Woods, 9 vols. (Chicago: University of Chicago Press, 1958-70), 7: 234.
45. *Réimpression de l'ancien Moniteur*, 14: 75. The letter does not appear in Priestley's *Works*, but it is paraphrased in 1, pt. 2: 191.
46. Priestley, *Works*, 1, pt. 2: 191.

By April of 1793, however, Priestley was less sanguine. To one friend he wrote, "The prospect is very melancholy. The conduct of the French has been such as their best friends cannot approve."[47] To another, "You will see my apprehensions in my sermon. Every thing indicates a beginning of troubles in Europe. I wish my friends, especially my young ones, safely out of it."[48]

The sermon to which Priestley referred was the first of two Fast Sermons in which he developed his millenarian convictions to their fullest extent. The Fasts were proclaimed in order to secure divine sanction for the war with the French that had begun in February, but Priestley's words to his Hackney congregation were not what George III and Pitt had in mind. And although Priestley had a weak voice and was plagued by a stammer, at least one auditor recalled that he was an effective speaker. The Quaker diarist John Jenkins wrote that "his mode of preaching was, with but little action, his delivery in short sentences, distinct, fluent, and impressive."[49]

The war, Priestley declared in the 1793 Fast Sermon, was "the work of God." Like all evils, it was "calculated to produce many good effects." For several reasons, this war was uniquely significant. In the first place, it was "a war respecting *the principles of government*," which would inspire discussion of the subject and therefore lead to knowledge of it. "Real knowledge" always leads to "improvement," and therefore the war was bound to result in "the melioration of the condition of men, as members of civil society." Equally important, the French had launched the great "experiment" of separation of church and state, and surely "a friend to real Christianity must be an enemy to the civil establishment of it."[50]

Finally, three great events that were "pretty clearly announced" in scriptural prophecy were in preparation in the French Revolution: the fall of Antichrist, the fall of the Turkish Empire, and the return of the Jews to their homeland. Daniel had prophesied that the Jews' return would be preceded by a time of troubles; the Pope was definitely in decline; the other rulers of Europe had given "their power and strength to the beast. . . . The Turkish empire also seems to be shaking to its base, so that it will probably soon fall." All these events would lead to "a state of great improvement in knowledge, virtue, and happi-

47. Joseph Priestley, *Scientific Correspondence*, ed. Henry C. Bolton (New York: Privately printed, 1892), p. 135.
48. Priestley, *Works*, 1, pt. 2: 199.
49. John Jenkins, "Records and Recollections" (compiled 1821–22) (typescript copy in the Friends' Reference Library, London, ss. 355–56).
50. Priestley, *Works*, 15: 512–13, 514–15, 517–18, 543.

ness." The culmination would be the true kingdom of God prophesied in Nebuchadnezzar's dream, and the resurrection of the saints, who "will *live* and reign *with Christ for a thousand years.*"

Priestley's 1794 Fast Day Sermon bore the title *The Present State of Europe compared with Ancient Prophecies.* Delivered shortly before Priestley and his wife sailed to America to join their sons in Northumberland, Pennsylvania, it went through three editions in England and was printed in the United States, too. In addition to David Hartley, whose views he said were the principal influence on the sermon, Priestley cited two preachers whose sentiments on the French Revolution as herald of the millennium were close to his own. One was the American evangelist Elhanan Winchester, who in two sermons titled *The Three Woe Trumpets* had declared that the earthquake prophesied in the eleventh chapter of Revelation meant the fall of the French monarchy; and the "slaughter of the names of men," the destruction of the prerogatives of the privileged orders in France. Priestley cited Winchester's views with approval and called the sermons "deserving of serious consideration of all Christians, who are attentive to the *signs of the times.*"[51]

It is not at all surprising that Priestley should have interested himself in Elhanan Winchester, who, like Priestley, had been a Calvinist in his youth. Around 1780, Winchester had been persuaded by a German religious tract that at the end of time there would be a "universal restoration" when all men, even the most notorious sinners, would be saved. When he began to preach this doctrine openly, he was excluded from his Baptist church in Philadelphia, but he found a new meeting place at the University of Pennsylvania's University Hall. A gifted preacher, Winchester attracted large audiences, which included some of the more distinguished residents of Philadelphia.[52]

Six years later, Winchester felt called to go to England, where for nearly seven years he preached the universal restoration and its corollary, the millennium. In London in 1788, he delivered a series of *Lectures on the Prophecies that Remain to be Fulfilled,* which was published in four volumes in 1790. He also wrote a very long and very bad poem on the millennium, the time when Jesus would come again to bring an end to misery and sin, and salvation to all men. Despite

51. Ibid., p. 538 n.
52. Edward Martin Stone, *Biography of the Rev. Elhanan Winchester* (Boston: Brewster, 1836), pp. 34–41; Elhanan Winchester, preface to G. P. Siegvolk [pseud.], *The Everlasting Gospel . . .* (London, 1792); and *Dictionary of American Biography,* 1936 ed., s.v. "Winchester, Elhanan," by Elwood Starr.

the hostility of many English Dissenters to his views, Winchester's literate and dynamic preaching drew large crowds.[53]

Joseph Priestley was sympathetic to the doctrine of universal restoration, even though he never fully accepted it. Also, Winchester's approach to biblical prophecy was very much like his own. In *Lectures on the Prophecies*, which Priestley does not seem to have read, Winchester wrote that "these prophecies must be fulfilled in a plain literal manner or (for the conviction of the world) they might as well not be fulfilled at all."[54]

In *The Three Woe Trumpets*, Winchester attempted, like Mede and so many others, to show that certain events were the effects of the pouring of the vials of wrath predicted in the book of Revelation. According to Winchester, the first three vials were being poured as he wrote. The wars of the French Republic against her enemies were, in effect, God's punishment of the Roman Catholic powers. He followed Mede concerning the last four vials. These would result, first, in the destruction of Rome and the papacy, then in the destruction of the Turks, the restoration of the Jews, and the coming of the millennium.[55] Priestley agreed with Winchester that when the Lord said in the book of Haggai, "I will shake all nations, and the desire of all nations shall come," he meant that the wars of the French Revolution were a necessary chastisement of the western world that must precede the millennium. "That those great troubles . . . are now commencing," Priestley wrote, "I do own I strongly suspect . . . and the events of the last year have contributed to strengthen that suspicion."[56]

Another sign of the times that Priestley noted in his 1794 Fast Sermon was the "great prevalence of infidelity," particularly evident in countries like France and England, where established churches had made "unbelievers much faster than all rational Christians can unmake them."[57] To support his contention that the spread of unbelief was a sign of the approaching millennium, he cited Isaac Newton, William Whiston, and a sermon that had recently been delivered at Cambridge. Although Priestley did not name him, the author of the sermon was Robert Garnham, then college preacher at Trinity. In his

53. Stone, *Elhanan Winchester*, pp. 104-6; Geoffrey Rowell, "The Origins and History of the Universalist Societies in Britain, 1750-1850," *Journal of Ecclesiastical History* 22 (1971): 38-42.

54. Elhanan Winchester, *A Course of Lectures on the Prophecies That Remain to Be Fulfilled*, 4 vols. (London, 1789-90), 2: 366.

55. Elhanan Winchester, *The Three Woe Trumpets . . . Being the Substance of Two Discourses from Revelation xi. 14-18*, 2d ed. (London, 1793), pp. 46-56.

56. Ibid., pp. 37-38; Priestley, *Works*, 15: 535-36, 538, 543.

57. Priestley, ibid., p. 547.

sermon, Garnham said that it was in the best interests of Christianity, which henceforth would become a religion of the heart, that the leaders of the French Convention were deists. There would be an end to "superstition," and instead, the recognition of Christianity's "miraculous credentials of prophecies [would be] completed in our times."[58] Apparently Priestley believed that this was happening in France, for late in 1794 he wrote: "I have read with pleasure, and even with enthusiasm, the admirable Report of *Robespierre* on the subject of *morals* and *religion*, and I rejoice to find by it, that so great and happy a change has taken place in the sentiments of the leading men of France."[59] Priestley's and Garnham's sentiments were echoed in the radical journal titled *Politics for the People*, where an anonymous "Vindex" (Garnham himself?) wrote that France would soon be "not only the most delightful country in the world for the productions of nature, but we shall see RELIGION SHINE in its TRUE COLORS: for it never can shine in its resplendent lustre if it be obliged to bow its head to *any kind of religious test or establishment.*"[60]

Shortly before his departure for America, Priestley had talked of the Second Coming with Thomas Belsham, his successor at Hackney. "You may probably live to see it. I shall not. It cannot, I think be more than twenty years."[61] After his arrival, he wrote Lindsey that "the present state of things, confounds all speculation. A new state of things is certainly about to take place." Some important prophecies would soon be fulfilled. Recent events, he continued, "make me see this in a stronger light than I did when I wrote my Fast Sermon. Many more of the prophecies than I was then aware of indicate the great destruction that will be made of mankind before the restoration of the Jews. . . . The destruction of *kings* seems to be particularly mentioned."[62]

Priestley's last ten years in America were just as productive as the first sixty in England had been. He resumed his chemical experiments, he continued to write in defense of Christianity as he understood it, and he took up the study of natural history and of oriental religion. He continued to embroil himself in controversies because of

58. Robert Edward Garnham, *A Sermon Preached in the Chapel of Trinity College Cambridge, on Thursday, Dec. XIX, M.DCC.XCIII* (n.p., n.d.), pp. 16, 18–19. Priestley printed the sermon as an appendix to his 1794 Fast Sermon (*Works*, 15: 575–80).
59. Priestley, *A Continuation of Letters to the Philosophers and Politicians of France on the Subject of Religion* (1794), in *Works*, 21: 113–14.
60. *Politics for the People; or, A Salmagundi for Swine*, pt. 2, 2 (1794): 3.
61. Thomas Belsham, *Memoirs of Theophilus Lindsey* (London: Williams & Nargate, 1873), 248 n.
62. Priestley, *Works*, 1, pt. 2: 280.

his political and religious opinions. As he declared in a letter in 1799, "I am not used to secrecy or caution, and I cannot adopt a new system of conduct now."[63]

Prophecy and the millennium appeared intermittently in Priestley's published writings of those last years, but his tone was the cautious one of the *Institutes*, not the bold one of the two Fast Sermons. His letters, however, reveal that the "signs of the times" continued to be a central preoccupation. He confided to one correspondent that he intended to write no more on prophecy until certain points in scripture, particularly in Daniel, were clearer in his mind. Meanwhile, he read everything his friends could supply on the millennium, even the pamphlets by and about Richard Brothers, the self-proclaimed Revealed Prince of the Hebrews—although these last he dismissed as "Brothers, and other curiosities."[64] Priestley continued in his letters to allude to events in Europe as the fulfillment of prophecy, but one senses that he found developments during the period of the French Directory less encouraging than those of the heady days of 1792–94.

A new work by Robert Garnham, an *Outline of a Commentary on Revelations xi. 1–14*, came to Priestley's attention. In it, Garnham identified the ten horns of the Beast of the Apocalypse with the ten rulers who were "most wonderfully and unexpectedly combined" against the French Revolution. Because of their actions France was presently (and temporarily) undergoing a period of military dictatorship and religious intolerance. Garnham apologized for the sketchiness of his *Outline*; but he was "anxious to add even one grain to the mass of evidence in favour of our most holy religion, which from infidelity on the one hand, and ecclesiasticism on the other, seems in danger, without some divine interposition, such as the completion of ancient prophecies in our day, of falling under entire misconception and neglect." Priestley liked the new work less well than Garnham's earlier studies. He wrote Thomas Belsham that "Antichrist and the beasts, &c., &c. must be visible powers or governments, and not opinions or superstitious practices."[65] He preferred a long treatise by an English Baptist named James Bicheno titled *The Signs of the Times*, the second edition of which appeared in 1794. Bicheno's political opinions and his interpretation of Revelation were close to Priestley's own, and he offered the kind of concrete insight into prophecy Priest-

63. Joseph Priestley, "Letters to George Thatcher," *Massachusetts Historical Society Proceedings*, ser. 2, 3 (1886–87): 18–19.
64. Priestley, *Works*, 1, pt. 2: 312.
65. Ibid., pp. 290, 313; Robert Edward Garnham, *Outline of a Commentary on Revelations xi. 1–14* (London, 1794), pp. 4, 12, 19.

ley liked when he held that the seven thunders predicted in Revelation were the seven periods of warfare in eighteenth-century Europe before the wars of the Revolution.[66]

It is clear that the events of the 1797–98 French surge across Europe encouraged both Priestley's political hopes and the millenarian convictions that were so interconnected with his perception of the French Revolution. He considered, not for the first time, the possibility of settling in France, hoping to advance the cause of rational Christianity there. He continued to believe that revolution in England and the fall of her monarchy were part of God's plan as foreseen by St. John the Divine. "I really think the present war will not end without the downfall of all the European monarchies, that of England (one of the horns of the Beast) included,"[67] he wrote a friend in the spring of 1798. It is surely not a coincidence that two weeks later he wrote another friend of his decision to add to an exposition of the New Testament on which he had resumed work, "what I had not before attempted, an Exposition of the Revelation."[68] A month later, he had completed it and begun to study the prophecies of Daniel.

When the publication that same year of several letters to Priestley from his old pupil, John Hurford Stone, and Stone's companion, the novelist Helen Maria Williams, caused considerable commotion in Pennsylvania,[69] Priestley defended his own and Stone's views in a series of *Letters to the Inhabitants of Northumberland*. He wrote that both he and Stone had initially wanted simply the "reform of abuses to prevent revolution" in England, but now they were inclined to agree that a revolution there was "absolutely necessary for the good of the people." The French National Assembly, during the early years of the Revolution, had similarly intended only reform of the monarchy; "but God has given them a government purely republican and representative, like that of America . . . and the same benefit, I doubt not, with my correspondent, is intended for all those countries whose kings are at present confederated against France and universal liberty."[70]

66. James Bicheno, *The Signs of the Times; or, The Overthrow of the Papal Tyranny in France, the Prelude of Destruction to Popery and Despotism; but of Peace to Mankind*, 2d ed. (London, 1794), p. 93; Priestley, *Works*, 1, pt. 2: 284.
67. Priestley, "Letters to George Thatcher," pp. 18–19.
68. Priestley, *Works*, 1, pt. 2: 398.
69. [John Hurford Stone and Helen Maria Williams], *Copies of Original Letters Recently Written by Persons in Paris to Dr. Priestley in America* (London, 1798).
70. Priestley, *Letters to the Inhabitants of Northumberland* (1799), in *Works*, 1, pt. 2: 394–96.

Similarly, in 1799, Priestley wrote in the last of his series of addresses to the Jews that Nebuchadnezzar's dream indicated that the fall of the European monarchies would be "with violence, and not by peaceable revolutions."[71] He wrote Benjamin Rush that the European monarchies "will all fall *together* and with violence." Doctor Rush has been absorbed in the study of biblical prophecy since he had read Winchester's *Lectures on the Prophecies* in 1791. Like his friends Jefferson and Adams, he became a friend and admirer of Priestley. Unlike them, he disapproved of Priestley's unitarianism, but he approved of his speculations on the millennium. Priestley told him that Napoleon Bonaparte might be "only the *precursor* to the *great* deliverer. I think it more probable that the French nation will be the great instrument in the hands of God to effect these great things."[72]

Priestley's absorption in the present unfolding of events foretold in prophecy continued to the very end of his life. In one of his last letters, he referred to Napoleon's 1803 campaign with a mixture of hope and fear. "I dread the approaching contest, which may throw everything into confusion," he wrote. "It has probably taken place before this time. But there is a Sovereign Ruler, and he, we cannot doubt, will bring good out of all evil."[73]

Priestley died in 1804. Benjamin Rush, who had attended him in his last illness, wrote John Adams that while he had never approved of Priestley's peculiar religious principles," "they produced in him in his last sickness uncommon resignation, peace, and composure of mind. He died in a full belief of a happy immortality."[74]

This same kind of resignation characterized Priestley's treatment of the millennium in his last published writings. In a general essay on the prophecies in his *Notes on All the Books of Scripture*, he warned his readers not to "affect to be wiser than those who have gone before us." They should look forward to the millennium with the "most joyful expectation; but of the particulars we must be content to remain ignorant till the great event shall take place. . . . When it shall take place, it may excite our surprise, as well as our admiration and joy." The fall of the papacy and the monarchies of Europe seemed near, and these events might be followed by the restoration of the Jews—but these are mere conjectures."[75] And in a sermon that he did

71. Priestley, *Address to the Jews* (1799), in *Works*, 20: 284.
72. Priestley, *Scientific Correspondence*, p. 156.
73. Priestley, *Works*, 1, pt. 2: 520.
74. Benjamin Rush, *Letters of Benjamin Rush*, ed. Lyman H. Butterfield, 2 vols. (Princeton: Princeton University Press, 1951), 2: 927.
75. Priestley, *Notes on All the Books of Scripture, for the Use of Pulpit and Private Families* (1804), in *Works*, 12: 308, 343.

not live to deliver, he wrote: "Let us then be ever *looking for*, as we are *hastening unto*, the *coming of this great day of God*. . . . That greatest of all events is not less certain for being delayed beyond our expectations."[76]

In 1796, in the intensely millenarian final pages of his *Religious Musings*, Samuel Coleridge had written of Priestley, "patriot, and saint, and sage,"

> . . . Calm, pitying he retired,
> And mused expectant on these promised years.[77]

The "years" of the millennium had not come, as Priestley and Coleridge in 1796 had both believed they would. It must have been difficult for Priestley to see in the Corsican military adventurer who ruled France after 1799 an agent either of democracy or of God's plan. The point to be emphasized, however, is that Priestley's belief in the millennium was as strong as ever, nor is there any evidence that he ever doubted that it would come "soon." Priestley's convictions had not changed, nor had his understanding of the divine process upon which all his ideas were based. It was simply that men were fallible; they might guess at the sequence of events that would culminate in the Second Coming, but until that great event had taken place, they would be speculations and nothing more.

76. Joseph Priestley, *Memoirs . . . to Which Are Added, Four Posthumous Discourses*, 2 vols. (London, 1806-7), 2: 43.
77. Samuel Taylor Coleridge, *The Complete Poetical Works of Samuel Taylor Coleridge*, 2 vols. (Oxford: Clarendon Press, 1912; reprint ed., 1968), 1: 123.

CHAPTER 7

The Land
of the
Learned Pig

IN FRANCE, millenarianism during the French Revolution derived from a variety of sources. Some were old traditions of popular piety, some had grown up in the preceding century within the more militant offshoots of Jansenism, and some were related to the eighteenth century's search for spiritual enlightenment in such diverse areas as occultism, the rituals of Freemasonry, and pseudo-sciences like mesmerism.

In England, millenarian doctrines were both more widely accepted and more publicly asserted than in France. They derived from a continuous body of religious tradition, manifested ever since the days of the English Revolution in a steady stream of learned treatises, sermons, and popular tracts. English and French millenarians differed in several significant respects. For example, the English accorded no great importance to the coming of Elias. Instead, probably because they based their speculations more directly on the Bible, they concentrated on the prophetic statements of Daniel and St. John the Divine, giving detailed and loving attention to every nuance of their thought. The English millenarians tended to be literal in their interpretations—this event was foretold in this verse, that event in that verse. Only among Huguenots like Pierre Jurieu did France see the kind of biblical reflections that were commonplace in England.

Equally important, there existed in England a mystical tradition as persistent as the biblical one. Mysticism survived among the Quakers, and in the eighteenth century it received new impetus from the influence of the Moravians and the early Methodists. John Wesley himself had been a pupil of William Law, a mystic who retained a considerable body of readers long after his death.

And that brings us to the most important difference between the two millenarian traditions. In England, the public circulation of all kinds of literature, even the most theologically bizarre, meant that millenarian ideas could be disseminated (and can now be examined by the historian) with far greater ease than in France. Between 1793 and 1795, in a revolutionary crisis produced by war with the French and hard times at home, all these ideas, preserved and elaborated in a flood of sermons and religious tracts, converged in the dramatic emergence of Richard Brothers as a prophet of a revolutionary millennium. His moment of glory was as brief as Suzette Labrousse's; his ended, as hers had done, with his incarceration as a madman. Yet, before the government intervened and placed him in confinement, Brothers had helped to generate, throughout England and in all social classes, an intensive examination of prophecies of the millennium, the likes of which had not been seen since the days of the Commonwealth.

This chapter will examine the cultural climate that made possible the emergence of a prophet as unlikely as Brothers, by tracing the various paths that led a diverse group of Englishmen to the conviction that the retired navy man was a prophet of the millennium.

In England, wrote Robert Southey under the pseudonym of a Spanish traveler named Don Espriella, anything that was strange or was called strange would attract a crowd, "no matter what the wonder [were] and no matter how monstrous, or how disgusting." He wrote of a woman born without arms who made a good living writing and cutting paper with her toes, and of a family who traveled around the countryside living in and exhibiting a cart shaped like a teakettle. In London, in Saint George's Fields south of the Thames, he had seen exhibited (for sixpence) a woman with a painted face and a feather in her hair who claimed to be an American Indian. He had also seen "the surprising Large Child"—really a stupid four-year-old. The situation was even worse in the provinces. A friend there had seen "a shaved monkey exhibited for a Fairy" and a shaved bear, dressed in a checked waistcoat and trousers, sitting in an armchair. Its keeper claimed that the bear was an Ethiopian savage. The "friend" was in fact Southey himself; as he noted in his *Common-Place Book*, he had seen the Fairy and the Ethiopian at a fair in Bristol in the 1790s.[1] Southey also saw Toby, the famous Learned Pig, who "was in his day a far greater object of admiration to the English Nation than ever was Sir Isaac Newton." The talented pig was never beaten. If Toby did not perform his tricks well, his trainer

1. Robert Southey, *Letters from England*, ed. and intro. Jack Simmons (London: Cresset, 1951), pp. 338–40; Southey, *Southey's Common-Place Book*, ed. J. W. Warter, 4 vols. (London: Longmans & Co., 1849–51), 4: 359.

would simply threaten to remove the pig's red waistcoat, of which Toby was very fond.

Southey was not the only poet who wrote of the Learned Pig. In William Blake's manuscript notebooks are the lines:

> Give pensions to the Learned Pig
> Or the Hare playing the Tabor
> Anglus can never see Perfection
> But in the Journeyman's Labour.[2]

For Southey, Toby epitomized the credulity and superficiality of the English. For Blake, he represented instead England's indifference to the hardships to which Blake's own artisan class was subjected in the period of the Revolutionary and Napoleonic wars.

The fascination with the odd, the mysterious, and the prophetic that permeated English culture in the era of the French Revolution is striking. William Blake was not the only man of his generation who saw angels, nor were Richard Brothers and Joanna Southcott the only prophets to whom God spoke. Indeed, the English, unlike the French, have always taken pride in their own eccentrics. The greatest flowering of this dimension of English genius occurred during the English Revolution, but, as one writer noted in 1795, there had been numerous examples of it since Cromwell. For example, the eighteenth century had seen the "French Prophets," then "the affair of the *Rabbit Woman* and the *Life Guard Man* and *Fanny Fanny.*"[3]

The three French prophets—Elie Marion, Jean Cavalier, and Durand Fage—arrived in London in 1707 from the mountainous Cévennes region in southeastern France, where the protestant Huguenots had been in rebellion against Louis XIV's religious repression for over twenty years. Thanks in part to the sermons and writings of the Huguenot pastor Pierre Jurieu, the Protestant rebels saw their struggle in apocalyptic terms, with the French monarchy and its armies cast in the role of servants of the Beast of Revelation. The religious excitement produced a wave of prophesying, in which the prophets, many of whom were children, assured the beleaguered Huguenots that God would soon destroy their enemies. The crown's ruthless suppression of the revolt drove many of the rebels into exile, some of them to England. The three prophets

---

2. William Blake, *Complete Writings*, ed. Geoffrey Keynes, new ed. (London: Oxford University Press, 1966), p. 548.
3. Joseph Moser, *Anecdotes of Richard Brothers, in the Years 1791 and 1792, with Some Thoughts on Credulity* . . . (London, 1795), pp. 11-12.

preached in the streets of London and published their predictions of an imminent millenium, to be preceded by the destruction of the wicked by famine, pestilence, and earthquake. They attracted considerable attention and won some converts to their views before they departed for the Continent six years later. The Rabbit Woman claimed to give birth to rabbits; George I's physicians went to examine her. The Life Guard Man was a crazed soldier who predicted the destruction of London by earthquake in 1750. I have been unable to trace the delightfully named Fanny Fanny.

The absence of censorship and the wide availability of printed matter of all kinds provides another explanation for the seeming abundance of curiosities in eighteenth-century England. England had a "print culture" to a far greater extent than France in the same period. Newspapers, magazines, and pamphlets contained all sorts of scraps of unlikely information. At one end of the spectrum, there was that sedate compendium of odds and ends, the *Gentleman's Magazine*, and its several imitators. At the other, there were fugitive periodicals like the *Wonderful Magazine* and the *Conjuror's Magazine*. In 1792, the latter stated that "Sir Isaac Newton may keep his nonsense of vacuum and attraction out of the way, for we are not indebted to mythology and superstition for life and presiding genii in the sun, planets, and all creation, but to sound reason, genuine theosophy, and the oracles of GOD."[4] William Blake would surely have approved of these sentiments.

On the eve of the French Revolution, when Paris had no more than a handful of newspapers, devoted almost entirely to court gossip and literature, London had fourteen daily newspapers, offering a fairly extensive variety of information and opinion.[5] Possibly as revealing as the news items as indications of public opinion were the advertisements that filled at least a quarter of each issue. A characteristic advertisement announced an "exhibition of live and moveable stones, a surprising Prodigy of Nature." It cost half a guinea to look at the stones, and ten guineas to buy one. In addition, two courses of lectures were offered: one on animal magnetism, the other on "Experimental Philosophy, in which [would] be performed the most curious Experiments, many of these entirely new."[6] A

4. *Conjuror's Magazine*, March 1792, p. 340.
5. Raymond Williams, *The Long Revolution* (New York: Columbia University Press, 1961), p. 185; Lucile Werkmeister, *A Newspaper History of England, 1792-1793* (Lincoln: University of Nebraska Press, 1967), pp. 19-41.
6. Quoted in Hester Thrale Piozzi, *Thraliana: The Diary of Mrs. Hester Lynch Thrale, 1776-1809*, ed. Katherine C. Balderston, 2d ed., 2 vols. (Oxford: Clarendon Press, 1951), 2: 911.

London daily newspaper that catered to popular tastes, the *Oracle*, reported the discovery in a field at Hooten Roberts of two "nondescript animals" with green scales, heads like lions, and fourteen legs each.[7]

In addition to newspapers and magazines, there was an extensive trade in cheap pamphlets. Throughout England, but concentrated in the City of London, there were booksellers who, despite occasional prosecutions, specialized in these pamphlets, which were astonishingly wide-ranging in their presentation of opinions of all kinds on every conceivable subject, including religion. There are many indications that religious tracts were easy both to procure and to have published. Cornelius Cayley, who gave up a sinecure in a noble household to become an itinerant preacher, recalled wandering among the bookstalls in the streets of London, where, under signs that invited readers to *"Pick and chuse for Two-pence or Three-pence,"* he found books that gave his soul "the most comfort and spiritual edification . . . poor old shabby-looking books, quite despicable to appearance, and the authors chiefly persons of low estate in life." Similarly, the Quaker diarist John Jenkins recalled how "book stalls, and Jews-stands with cutlery, and toys, . . . contributed to crowd the streets."[8] He remembered a landlord of his who had received "visions of the night" and "sounded his 'Ram's Horns' through pamphlets which few read." A mystic in Bristol wrote a friend concerning a young woman who had communicated her visions of heaven in a small pamphlet. "There were numbers of them sold in this City; but the second edition [did] not go off."[9]

In France, the prophecies of Labrousse circulated in print, but only incidentally. In England, as we shall see, it was primarily through the medium of print, above all cheap pamphlets, that the notoriety of both Richard Brothers and Joanna Southcott was spread.

It is impossible to be precise, but it seems certain that the importance in popular culture of printed literature of all kinds was much greater on the English side of the channel than on the French. It is not difficult to guess why this should have been so. The dissemina-

7. *Oracle*, 18 August 1794, p. 4.
8. Cornelius Cayley, *The Riches of God's Free Grace Displayed in the Life and Conversion of Cornelius Cayley*, 5th ed. (Leeds, 1813), p. 34; John Jenkins, "Records and Recollections" (compiled 1821–22) (typescript copy in the Friends' Reference Library, London); Southey, *Letters from England*, p. 416; Richard D. Altick, *The English Common Reader* (Chicago: University of Chicago Press, 1959), pp. 47–48.
9. Jenkins, "Records and Recollections," s/57; Thomas Langcake to R. Tighe, Northampton, 27 April 1782, "The Correspondence of Henry Brooke; Copies by his Son-in-Law," Dr. Williams's Library, London.

tion of the printed word had been of central importance in the Protestant Reformation and in the succeeding centuries of the Protestant tradition. Not only the Bible but also the *Book of Common Prayer*, *Pilgrim's Progress*, and Foxe's *Actes and Monuments* were part of the common experience of Englishmen in a way that no book can be said to have been part of the common experience of Frenchmen.[10] In the eighteenth century, the shared concerns and presuppositions of an English print culture that was primarily protestant and puritan can be discerned in the books, pamphlets, and sermons that played such an important part in preserving and disseminating the beliefs that fed into the great burst of popular interest in millenarian prophecy during the 1790s.[11]

Another important factor in explaining the character of English culture in the eighteenth century was a religious toleration unique in Europe. Dissenters like Joseph Priestley could justifiably complain of the political and professional disabilities to which they were subjected, but to a remarkable degree they were permitted both to believe as they chose and to make their views known in whatever manner they deemed suitable.

As E. P. Thompson demonstrates in the chapter "Christ and Apollyon" in *The Making of the English Working Class*, the dissenting tradition contained a current of political radicalism dating from the time of the English Revolution.[12] In the 1790s, this radicalism found an outlet in the millenarian excitement that attended the French Revolution. In 1800, an ex-radical named William Reid, in denouncing his former allies, linked them to their "straggling auxiliaries. . . . These consisted of Mystics, Muggletonians, Millenaries, and a variety of eccentric characters of different denominations." He singled out "a pretty numerous circle" of "Ancient Deists" who met near Hoxton and included the dissatisfied of all sects and all classes. There, "human learning was declaimed against . . . and dreams, visions, and immediate revelations were recommended as a substitute!" The group believed that future events could be foretold

10. William Lamont, *Godly Rule: Politics and Religion, 1603–60* (New York: St. Martin's Press, 1969), pp. 23–25; Elizabeth Eisenstein, "Some Conjectures about the Impact of Printing on Western Society and Thought: A Preliminary Report," *Journal of Modern History* 40 (1968): 38–39.
11. Elizabeth Eisenstein, "L'avènement de l'imprimérie et la Réforme," *Annales: economies sociétés civilisations* 26 (1971): 1355–82; Altick, *Common Reader*, chap. 2.
12. E. P. Thompson, *The Making of the English Working Class*, rev. ed. (Harmondsworth: Penguin Books, 1968), chap. 2.

and that they could converse with the dead. When the French Revolution came, Reid wrote, the members were converted into *"politicians and inquirers after news."*[13] As we shall see, Hoxton was not the only place in England where "mystics and millenaries" were transformed by the Revolutionary crisis.

Even the Ranters, the most notorious of the Commonwealth sectarians, seem to have survived into the 1780s. Robert Hindmarsh, one of the organizers of the Swedenborgian Church of the New Jerusalem in that period, recalled meeting a man from Shoreditch in the East End who told him "that there was *no God in the universe but man*"; that there was *"a society,"* of which he was a member, "of such as professed themselves to be God"; and "that he himself was *a God.*"[14]

William Reid complained that there was a growing number of uneducated preachers in England, especially "field-preachers." Many of them had been apprentices, including one "who fancied he was sent to call the Jews" and who sold old clothes in Duke's Place. Even the London workhouses, he added, "have been used as places of training and exercise, for some years past, by these fanatical adventurers."[15]

The most famous of those "adventurers" was an inmate of the Shoreditch workhouse who called himself Poor-Helps. By all indications, he was a prophet of some renown on the eve of the French Revolution. The noted Quaker physician Dr. John Lettsom recalled that "he was thought to be inspired, and was much followed. . . . Crowds followed him to know their fate, and what was going on in the future world." Dr. Lettsom said Poor-Helps was a thief who had become a prophet to avoid prosecution, but the attendants at the workhouse said he was a former Spitalfields weaver named Samuel Best, who had broken with his family and chosen to live in the workhouse. The bishop of Norwich had visited him, and the king was said to have called upon him incognito. The mystical philosopher Claude de Saint-Martin, who was to meet and disapprove of both Suzette Labrousse and Catherine Théot, visited Poor-Helps when he was in England in 1787. He was impressed with the old man's ability to

13. William Hamilton Reid, *The Rise and Dissolution of the Infidel Societies of the Metropolis* (London, 1800), pp. 18-19, 91-92.
14. Robert Hindmarsh, *The Rise and Progress of the New Jerusalem Church in England, America, and Other Parts*, ed. Edward Madeley (London: Hodson, 1861), p. 44 n.
15. Reid, *Rise and Dissolution*, p. 42; *Dictionary of National Biography*, 1921-22 ed., s.v. "Best, Samuel," by Thomas Finlayson Henderson.

quote to his visitors scriptural passages that foretold their future. Poor-Helps's predictions concerning him, Saint-Martin claimed, had been fulfilled within two weeks.[16]

The prophet's room was decorated with biblical scenes made ot straw. Upon entering the room, wrote a correspondent in the *Gentleman's Magazine*, one is "struck with an awful solemnity: stars and celestial figures are marked on the floor with chalk, also on [Poor-Helps's] shoes: and his companions are a little dirty boy, whom he calls Lord Cadogan, and a Bantam cock." The prophet's habit was to take each visitor by the hand and then, staring at the visitor's thumb, to repeat whatever Bible verses he thought "apt and particularly interesting" to the visitor's own situation, past, present, and future. The writer concluded: "He so struck me with truth, that, were I required to relate every incident in my life, I could not deliver it more minutely or faithfully than he did to me."[17]

In a second letter, the same correspondent reported that Poor-Helps lived on a diet of "bread and cheese, and gin mixed with the tincture of rhubarb." He claimed to be visited nightly by celestial powers, including the angel Gabriel. The writer urged those with "any curiosity" to visit Poor-Helps, who also predicted that the world would come to an end in 163 years.[18]

There is no question that belief in the millennium was far more widespread in England than in France on the eve of the French Revolution. Even among the Methodists, who discouraged belief in an earthly millennium, there was a "millenarial instability," in E. P. Thompson's phrase. John F. C. Harrison suggests that England and America possessed a millenarian "culture" in the 1780-1860 period with which popular reformist movements like Owenism had to come to terms.[19] Millenarianism took various forms, but in general there were two currents, both of which can be traced back at least to the seventeenth century. One was the "scholarly, respectable study and interpretation of prophecy," which continued the tradition of Foxe, Brightman, Mede, Isaac Newton, and so many others. The

---

16. *Gentleman's Magazine* 60 (1786): 1106; 61 (1787): 116, 309-10; 63 (1789): 1031; John Lettsom, *Memoires of the Life and Writings of the Late John Coakley Lettsom . . . with a Selection from His Correspondence*, ed. Thomas Joseph Pettigrew, 3 vols. (London, 1817), 3: 146-47; Louis-Claude de Saint-Martin, *Mon portrait historique et philosophique (1789-1802)*, published by Robert Amadou (Paris: Juilliard, 1961), pp. 69-70.

17. *Gentleman's Magazine* 60 (1786): 1162.   18. Ibid. 61 (1787): 309.

19. Thompson, *Making of the English Working Class*, pp. 51-55; John F. C. Harrison, *The Quest for a New Moral World: Robert Owen and the Owenites in Britain and America* (New York: Charles Scribner's Sons, 1969), pp. 94-97.

other was a "popular, adventist millenarianism." As Harrison points out, however, there was no precise division between the two. The followers of Richard Brothers, for example, included a surprising number of respectable and scholarly individuals who were persuaded that Brothers had been foretold in the Bible, while Mrs. Hester Thrale Piozzi, Samuel Johnson's confidante, who despised Brothers as a fanatic and a Jacobin, was entirely credulous concerning a variety of millenarian omens and portents, especially when they were connected with unusual weather or the movements of the stars and planets.

The fascination with meteorological omens of divine displeasure was a continuing feature of eighteenth-century millenarianism. The three French prophets, in the course of their preaching, had declared that the millennium would be preceded by the destruction of London. "A terrible Tempest [will] be poured out upon thee, O London," they declared. "God Almighty [will send] his Battering pieces against this city."[20] They and their English disciples traveled through England and Scotland proclaiming a message of imminent doom and destruction. At Cambridge, they met with William Whiston, Isaac Newton's successor as professor of mathematics and, like Newton, a millenarian. Since his dismissal for rejecting the doctrine of the Trinity, Whiston had spent his time working for the restoration of the pure, primitive Christianity that would spread to all the earth when Christ came again. He did not accept the French prophets' version of the Last Days, but in 1712 he did predict that a comet would soon destroy the world.[21]

Interest in the French prophets waned fairly rapidly after their departure from England, but the kinds of predictions they had promulgated continued to be a staple of English popular religion. Their memory may have been revived in 1750 when London was shaken by two earthquakes precisely four weeks apart. After the second cataclysm, John Wesley noted in his *Journal*: "To-day God gave the people a second warning."[22] The Right Reverend Prelate of the Church of Ireland declared that "earthquakes are evidently placed

20. Quoted in Serge Hutin, *Les disciples anglais de Jacob Boehme aux* xviie *et* xviiie *siècles* (Paris: Denoël, 1960), p. 95. On the French Prophets in England, see also John Symonds, *Thomas Brown and the Angels* (London: Hutchinson & Co., 1961), pp. 15-41; and D. P. Walker, *The Decline of Hell: Seventeenth-Century Discussions of Eternal Torment* (Chicago: University of Chicago Press, 1964), pp. 96, 253-57.
21. Southey, *Common-Place Book*, 4: 396; Perry Miller, "The End of the World," *William and Mary Quarterly*, 3d ser. 8 (1951): 181-84.
22. John Wesley, *The Journal of the Rev. John Wesley*, ed. Nehemiah Curnock, 8 vols. (London: Epworth Press, 1938), 6: 456.

among those methods, by which God punishes a rebellious and wicked people,"[23] and an anonymous poet contributed these lines to the *Gentleman's Magazine*:

> Yet while we live, what *gratitude* we owe!
> God, tho' provok'd, witholds the *final blow*,
> That *dreadful shock*, which felt thro' ev'ry vein,
> Shall back to *chaos* give this earth again
>
> . . . .
>
> They speak, *earth, ocean, air*; I hear them say
> "*Awake, repent*, 'ere we dissolve away!"[24]

On 4 April, the magazine reported that "incredible numbers of people," fearing a third and final earthquake four weeks after the second, an event predicted by the "crazy lifeguardsman," walked in the fields, sat in boats in the river all night, or thronged the roads out of London.[25]

The third earthquake did not occur, but the first two were not forgotten. In November, a correspondent noted that the third volume of Whiston's memoirs had appeared. Whiston listed ninety-nine signs that would precede the restoration of the Jews to the Holy Land in 1766. These included the fall of the tenth part of the city and the killing of 7,000 "names of men," as predicted in the eleventh chapter of Revelation. London was clearly the city of the prophecy, the writer contended, because of her "enormous wickedness." A tenth of London would be destroyed in an earthquake, and the deaths of the 7,000 noted men would frighten the rest of the residents into giving "glory to the god of heaven" as God's divine plan unfolded.[26] Five years later, a far more terrible earthquake struck Lisbon. In 1773, in one of the period's many tracts that discussed the imminent end of the world, a mystic who described himself as "*almost* the only Witness to the great Dispensation approaching" warned that there had recently been nine hundred more earthquakes around the world: "Christ has been speaking to the World since, and will continue to speak in Earthquakes and other Signs in Times and Nature too."[27]

In London, as on the Continent, the last decades of the eighteenth century saw the growth of various circles devoted to the study of the occult and to the acquisition of mystical enlightenment. Sometimes these groups were in direct contact with mystical developments elsewhere. For example, Silfverhjelm, the Swedish ambassador to Great

23. *Gentleman's Magazine* 20 (1750): 169.
24. Ibid., p. 182.   25. Ibid., p. 178. See also pp. 89, 125.   26. Ibid., p. 486.
27. Richard Clarke, *Signs of the Times; or, A Voice to Babylon, the Great City of the World; and to the Jews in Particular* (London, 1773), pp. viii, 8.

Britain, who in 1789 would accompany Count Reuterholm to Paris and Avignon, founded a society devoted to the study of hermetic wisdom and animal magnetism. And in 1786, Cagliostro returned to London after a twenty year absence and attempted to renew his connections with the Freemasons. Failing in that, he ran an advertisement in a newspaper inviting "all true Masons in the name of Jehovah to assemble at O'Reilly's Hotel to form a plan for the reconstruction of the New Temple of Jerusalem."[28] Again failing to generate much interest, Cagliostro departed alone for Switzerland.

Cagliostro had failed to win many converts to his blend of occult wisdom, magic, and spiritual therapy, but his presence had nonetheless attracted a certain amount of attention. In London, as in Paris, "spiritual" healing of all kinds was widespread. Mesmerism enjoyed a brief vogue.[29] Cagliostro's somewhat similar techniques also had practitioners, the most noted of whom were the distinguished painter Philip de Loutherbourg and his wife. In many ways, Loutherbourg's spiritual odyssey resembles that of French "men of desire" like Baron Corberon. Loutherbourg had dabbled in alchemy until his wife, in an excess of religious fervor, smashed his crucible. Having given up alchemy, he began to attend Baptist meetings, listen to revivalist preachers, and read the works of Emmanuel Swedenborg. In 1784, Loutherbourg was one of the founding members (together with, among others, two more painters and two engravers) of the Theosophical Society, dedicated to the dissemination of the doctrines of the Swedish visionary.[30] Then, following his association with Cagliostro, he and his wife advertised themselves in the newspapers as faith healers. It is said that they treated as many as three thousand people a day, for no charge, at their home on the Thames in Hammersmith. They gave up this work in 1789, after a mob of disappointed patients stormed their house. Loutherbourg abandoned neither his therapeutic labors nor his spiritual quest, and five years later he became one of the followers of the prophet Richard Brothers.[31]

Among all the eighteenth-century religious movements that generated a millenarian sensibility on the eve of the French Revolution, the most important was probably the Church of the New Jeru-

28. Auguste Viatte, *Les sources occultes du romantisme: Illuminisme-théosophie, 1770-1820*, 2 vols. (1938; reprint ed., Paris: Champion, 1969), 1: 39; W. R. H. Trowbridge, *Cagliostro* (1910; reprint ed., London: G. Allen & Unwin, 1926), pp. 276-79.
29. Jenkins, "Records and Recollections," s/292; Piozzi, *Thraliana*, 2: 878.
30. Hindmarsh, *Rise and Progress*, p. 23 n.
31. Trowbridge, *Cagliostro*, pp. 280-82; Austin Dobson, *At Prior Park and Other Papers* (London: Chatto & Windus, 1912), pp. 94-127; and [Mary Pratt], *A List of a Few Cures Performed by Mr. and Mrs. De Loutherbourg, of Hammersmith Terrace, without Medicine, by a Lover of the Lamb of God* (London, [1789]).

salem, an outgrowth of the Theosophical Society and other groups dedicated to the study of the writings of Swedenborg. The connection is not a direct one, since the orthodox Swedenborgian doctrine was that the millennium had already come and was entirely spiritual—precisely the opposite of the conception held by the millenarians of the Revolutionary era. The leading Swedenborgian preachers, both within the Church of England and in the New Church, specifically repudiated the notion of a literal, earthly, millenarian kingdom.

Swedenborg's doctrines did not attract much public notice until the 1780s, but they had been quietly winning adherents for some years prior to that time. Swedenborg himself had lived in London until his death in 1772. In England's tolerant and open religious climate, Swedenborg's affirmation of the possibility of spiritual regeneration and his detailed descriptions of supernatural entities attracted interest, especially among Methodists, Quakers, and mystically inclined members of the Church of England. Judging from the amount of attention they received at the end of the century in newspapers, books, letters, and memoirs, the influence of the Swedenborgians was greater than their numbers might suggest. Although they subsequently became a small and prosperous denomination, they initially attracted much interest among the working classes in manufacturing towns like Birmingham, Manchester, and London.[32]

One of the first to preach the new doctrines was the Reverend John Clowes, for sixty-two years the rector of St. John's Church in Manchester. St. John's had been endowed by a wealthy benefactor interested in the promulgation of the mystical teachings of William Law. While still at Oxford, Clowes had been selected to be St. John's first rector, because he was known to be a student of Law, Boehme, Mme. Guyon, and other mystical writers. None of these writers had completely satisfied him, writes Clowes's biographer, because they "failed in practical application to the common business of the world." In 1773, Clowes visited a wealthy gentleman in Liverpool, a friend of John Wesley and the executor of the estate of the deceased benefactor of Clowes's church. The man had been reading Swedenborg in Latin for several years. He told Clowes that an Anglican clergyman named Thomas Hartley had translated some of

32. Thompson, *Making of the English Working Classes*, p. 53; John Evans, *Sketch of the Various Denominations of the Christian World*, corrected and brought down to the present day by J. H. Bransby, 18th ed. (London: Longman & Co., 1842), p. 267.

his works. He claimed further that Wesley had told him that "in the writings of Swedenborg we might learn all that there is necessary for us to know."[33]

Clowes returned to Manchester, read several of Swedenborg's books, and began to correspond with the aged Hartley. Hartley encouraged him to help in the translation of Swedenborg's writings and to preach his doctrines. Clowes's preaching led in turn to the formation of study groups in and around Manchester. He rode out regularly to the nearby manufacturing villages, where the factory owners often permitted their workers to leave work in order to hear him talk about Swedenborg.

In the nearby cotton-milling town of Bolton, where the Shakers had had their beginnings some thirty years before, a group met to study the writings of Boehme and Law. Clowes's translation of Swedenborg's *Universal Theology*, further elaborated by Clowes himself, led the members to adopt the Swedish visionary as their sole spiritual guide. When Clowes's other activities and responsibilities made it impossible for him to visit Bolton regularly, he encouraged one of his parishioners, a young farmer and part-time botanical healer named Samuel Dawson, to go in his stead. For thirty years, Dawson led the Bolton congregation while supporting himself by his practice of herbal medicine.[34] Among his converts was Samuel Crompton, inventor of the spinning mule; many members of the Bolton society were associated with the burgeoning cotton industry, as weavers, spinners, managers, and manufacturers. Thanks to Clowes and the converts he made, Lancashire remained the area in which Swedenborgians were most numerous through the nineteenth century.

In London, Swedenborg's teachings first attracted the attention of members of the colony of Swedes resident there. By the 1780s, a group of English followers was meeting regularly to study his writings. They met for worship at the chapel of the Asylum for Female Orphans, across the river in Lambeth, near St. George's Fields, where Southey and Blake had seen the Learned Pig. The chaplain of the Orphans' Asylum was Jacob Duché, like Clowes, an Anglican follower of Swedenborg. A native of Philadelphia, Duché had been

---

33. Theodore Compton, ed., *The Life and Correspondence of the Reverend John Clowes* . . . (London: Longman & Co., 1874), pp. 14–19; *Intellectual Repository* 6 (1823): 474.
34. Compton, *John Clowes*, p. 22; James Daheyne, *History of the Bolton New Church Society from 1781 to 1888* (Bolton: Speirs, 1888), pp. 1–10; Dawson's obituary is in *Intellectual Repository* 6 (1823): 474–79.

chaplain to the Continental Congress until he despaired of the American cause in 1777 and fled in disgrace to England. He had long been mystically inclined. Ten years before his exile, he had written John Paine, Samuel Johnson's publisher and a writer and translator of mystical tracts, telling him of the great effect that William Law's writings had had upon him. "My mind, which had hitherto been unsettled, dark, doubting, and yet anxious to find the Truth, became serene calm and sweetly composed," Duché wrote.[35] He had acquired Swedenborg's works in the original Latin on an earlier visit to England, but it was only after his exile that he was converted. He preached Swedenborgian theology at the asylum until his retirement in 1789. In addition, he conducted Sunday evening discussions at his home. It was to Duché's group that Count Grabiańka made his dramatic pronouncements concerning the Avignon Society and the millennium.

We know a great deal about Duché's circle, largely because William Blake may have been one of the mystically inclined artists and engravers who attended its meetings.[36] Although Duché never left the Church of England and never evangelized with the zeal of Clowes, his intellectual distinction, preaching skill, and wide contacts in English society made him one of the most important disseminators of the doctrines of the New Church.[37]

One of those who had attended the Sunday evening sessions at Duché's house was a young printer named Robert Hindmarsh. In his lively and informative history of *The Rise and Progress of the New Jerusalem Church*, Hindmarsh described his own introduction to Swedenborg. He had first heard of him in 1779, from members of the family of the printer to whom he was apprenticed. A few years later, while Hindmarsh was visiting his family in Canterbury, his father, a Methodist preacher, told him of a Quaker gentleman who owned some of Swedenborg's writings that Hindmarsh might borrow. "From that time," he wrote, "I began to search out other readers of the same Writings in London, in order to form a society for the purpose of spreading the knowledge contained in them."[38] Hindmarsh was then twenty-four years old.

35. Duché-John Paine, 18 December 1767, "Correspondence of Henry Brooke."
36. Desirée Hirst, *Hidden Riches: Traditional Symbolism from the Renaissance to Blake* (New York: Barnes & Noble, 1964), pp. 207–8; David V. Erdman, *Blake: Prophet against Empire*, rev. ed. (Princeton: Princeton University Press, 1969), pp. 12 n 19, 240 n 18; and Erdman, "Blake's Early Swedenborgianism: A Twentieth Century Legend," *Comparative Literature* 5 (1953): 257 n 27.
37. Charles Higham, "Jacob Duché, M.A.," *New Church Review* 22 (1915): 210–25, 408, 417.
38. Hindmarsh, *Rise and Progress*, p. 13; Marguerite Beach Block, *The New Church in the New World* (New York: Henry Holt & Co., 1932), pp. 62–72.

He invited three or four individuals he knew to be interested in Swedenborg to meet at his house. At the end of 1783, the group advertised its first public meeting, at a coffee house on Ludgate Hill. The response was far from promising at first, but by the following year Hindmarsh and his friends were sufficiently sanguine to organize themselves as "the Theosophical Society, Instituted for the Purpose of Promoting the Heavenly Doctrines of the New Jerusalem, by Translating, Printing, and Publishing the Theological Writings of the Honorable Emanuel Swedenborg." At about the same time, some of Clowes's parishioners in Manchester also began to print and circulate Swedenborg's writings.

It was Hindmarsh's society that proposed to the English Swedenborgians that they form a sect separate from the Church of England. The proposal was voted down "on the ground that the proper time for separating from the old Establishment had not yet come,"[39] but Hindmarsh and those who agreed with him went ahead and in 1788 built their first temple in Great Eastcheap. England had rapidly become the leading center of the Swedenborgian movement. The initial surge did not last long, but the impact on Churchmen, Dissenters, and Methodists was nonetheless considerable.

In general, the New Church confined itself to preaching the new doctrines in its own churches or in those of adherents like Clowes and to publishing tracts by and about Swedenborg. Two converts, however, took it upon themselves to utilize the old Methodist institution of "field preaching" to announce the arrival of the spiritual millennium. In 1786 and for several years thereafter, they made a wide circuit across England, preaching and organizing societies in many towns.[40]

The two field preachers were named Joseph Salmon and Ralph Mather. Both had been Methodists; Salmon had been introduced to Swedenborg's writings by Wesley's close friend, the Reverend John Fletcher of Maddeley. Mather, a native of Bolton, had worked closely with Wesley himself in the West of England before he left the Methodists in order to pursue an independent quest for spiritual regeneration. Wesley had described him as "a devoted young man, but almost driven out of his senses by Mystic Divinity."[41] Mather's own correspondence abundantly confirms Wesley's judgement. Despite the peculiarity of some of Mather's ideas and the flamboyance of his personality, he was an effective agent of the new doctrines of Swedenborg. At the end of his tour of England, he served as minister of

39. Quoted in Compton, *John Clowes*, p. 47.
40. Hindmarsh, *Rise and Progress*, pp. 64–65.
41. *Wesley, Journal*, 6: 10 (29 January 1774); "Correspondence of Henry Brooke."

the first Swedenborgian church in Liverpool. After quarreling with his congregation, he emigrated to the United States, where he led Swedenborgian congregations at Germantown near Philadelphia and at Baltimore.[42]

One of those who heard of Swedenborg from the two missionaries was John Wright of Leeds. In April 1788, the Holy Spirit told Wright to go to London to find "a *sect* of people that belong to the *New* Jerusalem Church, to which *Salmon* and *Mather* belonged, who came to *Leeds* as Preachers, who cried it up for some great and wonderful light, such as never appeared before." Wright therefore saved some money; then, taking his carpenter's tools with him, he went to London, where he found employment and lodgings on Tottenham Court Road. One of his fellow workers told him of the new temple in Great Eastcheap, but when he went there he found only "old *forms* of worship established by man's will." Wright expressed his disappointment in the Swedenborgians to a converted Jew whom he had met at the service. He told him that the true New Jerusalem Church "would be established by the *Spirit* and power of Elias," and its ministers would be sent "with the mighty power of GOD, in signs and wonders," as at Pentecost.[43] The Jew told Wright of a young printer named William Bryan who had similar convictions about the New Jerusalem.

The two young artisans met in October 1788. Bryan, as he wrote later, told Wright "of a Society at *Avignon* who were favoured with divine commissions." Bryan had met Major Tieman "two years before," when the latter had been in London.[44] Bryan does not say where a printer encountered a companion of Russian princes, but the likeliest possibility is one of the Sunday evening meetings at the home of Jacob Duché.

Early in 1789, Wright and Bryan both found themselves mysteriously compelled to go to Avignon, hoping to find in the society that called itself the New Israel the church for the age of the spirit they believed was at hand. They therefore left their jobs, wives, and children, crossed the channel, and set out on foot for Avignon, where, as we saw in chapter 5, they spent nine months in communication with the Holy Word.

---

42. Block, *New Church in the New World*, pp. 79, 91.
43. John Wright, *A Revealed Knowledge of Some Things That Will Be Speedily Fulfilled in the World . . . for the Good of All Men* (London, 1794), pp. 3-4, 21-22.
44. William Bryan, *A Testimony of the Spirit of Truth concerning Richard Brothers . . .* (London, 1795), pp. 20, 27.

After his return, John Wright continued to believe in spiritual and millennial doctrines that had much in common with those of the Swedenborgians, the Avignon Society, and also William Blake. Like Blake, Wright fought the evil influences of Locke's and Newton's empirical rationalism. He continued to expect, as Blake would express it, the building of Jerusalem on earth.

On 14 July 1794, the son of Wright's shop foreman told him he had been "reading a book of a Prophet that was then in *London*." Wright read a page or two of Richard Brothers's prophecies, and he recorded what happened then: "I went at night to see him, and as soon as he had spoke two or three words, I said, I have seen many, but never saw any, that I was so well satisfied with before, and the testimony of the HOLY SPIRIT was to me, *this* is *him*, of whom MOSES and the *prophets* and *John* in the *Revelations* spoke of as . . . the *son* of DAVID the KING OF THE JEWS, the *rod* that comes out of the *stem* of JESSE."[45]

John Wright disappeared into obscurity after 1795, but another leading Brothers disciple who is known to have come to millenarianism by way of Swedenborg, William Sharp, died a famous man, hailed by the *Edinburgh Review* as "the greatest engraver this country (perhaps Europe) has ever produced."[46]

Sharp was born in London in 1749. His father, a gunmaker, recognized the boy's skill at drawing and encouraged him to learn engraving so that he could decorate firearms. After a brief apprenticeship, William went into business for himself. Unlike Blake, he prospered. Those who knew him agreed that he was genial, intelligent, and hardworking, not at all the stereotype of the millenarian adept. The playwright Thomas Holcroft called him "a worthy and excellent man," who, "in spite of his insanity, had an acute, strong, and inquiring mind."[47]

Sharp was never intimate with William Blake, but, sharing as they did a profession, an interest in millenarian religion, and in the years around 1792 an involvement in English Jacobinism, they must have seen quite a bit of each other. Sharp probably tried to interest Blake in Richard Brothers and, a decade or so later, Joanna Southcott. He failed completely. According to H. Crabb Robinson, who

---

45. Wright, *Revealed Knowledge*, p. 23.
46. *Scot's Magazine* (later *Edinburgh Review*) 94 (1824): 383; W. S. Baker, *William Sharp, Engraver* (Philadelphia: Gebbie & Barrie, 1875); and *Gentleman's Magazine* 94, pt. 2 (1824): 471–72.
47. Thomas Holcroft, *The Life of Thomas Holcroft*, ed. Elbridge Colby, 2 vols. (London, 1925), 2: 246.

knew them both, "Blake himself a seer of visions and a dreamer of dreams would not do homage to a rival claimant of the privilege of prophecy." Blake, Robinson felt, was guilty of "excessive pride," but Sharp seemed "of a quieter and more amiable turn of mind."[48]

Long after Sharp had left Swedenborg, first for Brothers and then for Joanna Southcott, he evidently retained some Swedenborgian notions. In the introduction to a Southcott pamphlet in 1803, Sharp wrote that Christ invited men "to stand like Gods to claim their own, and then command the earth—GOD AT FIRST CREATED MAN TO BE IMMORTAL; AND MADE HIM AN IMAGE OF HIS OWN ETERNITY." The same pamphlet contained Sharp's answer to an Anglican clergyman who hesitated to accept the prophetic claims of Joanna Southcott because he had been led to believe from reading the writings of Swedenborg "that this world was to be regenerated, without any particular character to come forth." Swedenborg had written thirty years before Joanna had received *her* revelation, Sharp said, and hers could not have been known "before an *appointed time*."[49]

Sharp had also been associated with the therapeutic activities of Philip de Loutherbourg, although he never, apparently, showed the same skill as a healer. By 1792, he had joined the Society for Constitutional Information, whose membership included Richard Sheridan, John Horne Tooke, and Tom Paine. He was called before the Privy Council in 1794 in connection with the treason trial of Horne Tooke. There, so the story goes, he nonplussed the members by inviting them to subscribe to an engraving of the Polish patriot Kosciusko that he planned to execute.[50] When he took up the cause of Richard Brothers, he simply raised his political radicalism to a more spiritual plane. In 1799, he told Holcroft that "he himself had been absolutely favored with a revelation" concerning revolutions that were to take place immediately, and later that same year he claimed that it had been communicated to him one night "by authority" that Bonaparte was safe after a battle that had occurred in Germany the previous day.[51]

On the eve of the French Revolution, it was not only mystical wayfarers like Sharp, Blake, and John Wright who experienced a

48. Henry Crabb Robinson, *Diary, Reminiscences, and Correspondence of Henry Crabb Robinson*, quoted in G. E. Bentley, Jr., ed., *Blake Records* (Oxford: Clarendon Press, 1969), p. 235; Erdman, "Swedenborgianism," pp. 256–57.
49. William Sharp in Joanna Southcott, *Divine and Spiritual Communications* (London, 1803), pp. x, 27.
50. "Biographical Memoir of the Late Mr. Sharp," *European Magazine* 86 (1824): 194.
51. Holcroft, *Life*, 2: 246.

sense of millenarian expectancy. Those barometers of opinion, the *European Magazine* and the *Gentleman's Magazine*, included respectively a two part "Essay on the End of the World" and a long letter on "Signs of the Times," both of which indicated that God might be preparing to bring human history to an end. In the essay in the *European Magazine*, the author dismissed the conventional belief that the Messiah should not be expected until the year 2000 as "evidently false." The interpretation of the book of Revelation was at present extremely difficult, but since the book was intended for "the *use* of all ranks of christians" and not for "the *amusement* of the wise and learned," we should expect that its prophecies would be fulfilled, perhaps very soon. ". . . Even the *men of this generation* will see plainly many of them accomplished. Are the *vials of wrath* yet poured out? or is *Antichrist* yet destroyed? Are not the spirits of *Infidelity* and of *Heresy* broke loose upon us; and with a rapid violence do not they threaten the most dismal effects?"[52]

In a letter to the *Gentleman's Magazine* published late in 1789, a correspondent contended that there were three kinds of "signs of the times" by which God would warn men that the end was near: political developments, "natural circumstances," and the "temper" of men. He called attention to the great number of earthquakes that had taken place, "beginning with Lima and Lisbon, and ending with Calabria and Sicily." He recalled the political disturbances that America, Holland, France—even "our happy island"—had experienced. Holland had been restored to order, but perhaps "America, the seat of Discord and Discontent," never would be. And perhaps France would pay for having intervened in British affairs during the American Revolution and "be itself involved in civil war or anarchy." The most evident sign of God's impending judgment of mankind was the prevalence of sins and excesses of all kinds: "Was there any period in which the old world was so generally wicked?"[53]

A similar tone had been adopted by William Jones, F.R.S., in a sermon delivered in Canterbury in September. In France, he said, the masses had rejected "the doctrine of divine authority." Should French principles triumph in England as well, the result would be the overthrow of "our constitution in church and state; with such . . . *distress*, and perplexity, and terror, as can be conceived only by those who have been witnesses to such disorders." Yet we should not be distressed by the signs of the times, "but should rather pray . . . that

52. *European Magazine* 14 (1788): 405–8; 15 (1789): 12–15.
53. *Gentleman's Magazine* 66 (1789): 993–94.

God would *shortly accomplish the number of his elect, and hasten his kingdom.*"[54]

The same disquiet is reflected in Mrs. Piozzi's private compendium of thoughts and incidental information, *Thraliana*. One of the more remarkable women of her generation, Mrs. Piozzi read and wrote Hebrew, Greek, and Latin. For sixty years, until her death in 1821, she devoted much of her time to the study of the Bible, especially in connection with prophecy and the end of the world. The *Thraliana* also reveals her fascination with obscure books and prophecies of all kinds and with strange astronomical or meteorological phenomena that might be interpreted as warnings from God. As the deputies assembled at Versailles for the first session of the Estates General, Mrs. Piozzi felt a sense of foreboding: "The French struggling to obtain that Liberty they will not know how to use; the Rage for emancipating Negro Slaves, and the Number of Jews lately baptized into Protestant Churches: The expected Comet, and the propagation of the Gospel in so many newly discover'd Countries, make one think the end of the World approaches."[55]

Mrs. Piozzi's expectations at this point could be described as apocalyptical rather than millenarian. Her dislike of the French, already strong as a result of two earlier visits, deepened as the Revolution progressed. Like many others in England, she concluded that events precipitated by the Revolution were among those prophetically announced to be the heralds of the end. Not surprisingly, she was later to be particularly excited by the French occupation of Rome, the supposed seat of the Beast, and by the emergence of Napoleon. Her antipathy toward the French and her distrust of the popular classes guaranteed that she would never find in the French Revolution anything that resembled the millennium of prophecy.

In England, as in France, there were those who in the French Revolution's early years did see events ushering in a "closing scene" that would be happy and glorious—even if it were not precisely the millennium. Typical of that kind of response was the message sent to the French National Assembly in November 1789 by the Revolution Society (of 1688), whose membership included many leading politicians and some of the most distinguished religious Dissenters in England. Having received a friendly reply, Earl Stanhope responded

54. William Jones, *Popular Commotions Considered as Signs of the Approaching End of the World* (London, 1789), pp. 11, 14.
55. Piozzi, *Thraliana*, 2: 744. See also Edward Mangin, *Piozziana: or, Recollections of the Late Mrs. Piozzi, with Remarks* (London: Moxon, 1833), pp. 7, 223–24.

in the name of the society that it hoped the time would soon come when the principles of civil and religious liberty would "possess every human heart [so] as to put an end to all jealousies between nations, exterminate oppression and slavery, and cause wars, those dreadful errors of governments, to cease in all the earth."[56]

The same confidence in an imminent regeneration of mankind is seen in one of the replies to Burke's *Reflections on the Revolution in France*. "I, of course, live in the hope of better things," the author declared; "a millennium (not a fifth monarchy, Sir, of enthusiasts and fanatics), but a new heaven and a new earth in which dwelleth righteousness; or, to drop the eastern figure and use a more philosophic language, a state of equal liberty and justice for all men."[57]

Dissenting ministers who were sympathetic to a Revolution that seemed to them to signify the end of the clerical establishment they so deplored and also members of the Church of England who leaned toward Joseph Priestley's brand of Unitarian Christianity employed "a more philosophic language" without repudiating the "eastern figures" of Daniel and St. John. We saw in the previous chapter how some English millenarians sought to demonstrate, through an analysis of prophecy in the great tradition of Joseph Mede and Isaac Newton, that the French Revolution represented the unfolding of the Last Days before the glorious millennium. An example was the letter that young John Hurford Stone sent from Paris to his former minister and teacher, Joseph Priestley. Going farther than Priestley would probably have gone in 1790, Stone congratulated him for having foreseen what was now taking place in France, adding that Great Britain, too, should anticipate a revolution: "It requires no uncommon degree of sagacity to foresee, that an *Ideot King*, a *slavish Hierarchy*, a *corrupt administration*, and the *delusion of the people*, will melt like snow before the sun of truth." Should the world advance as rapidly for the next ten years, Priestley would live to see "*the empire of falsehood, religious and political, overthrown, and the world free and happy*!!!"[58] This interpretation of the French Revolution survived among some Englishmen, particularly among the Dissenters, for the entire period. As late as 1807, a pamphleteer declared, in reference to the acquisition of religious and political liberty by Jews and Protestants in France, that "all those beneficial changes have arisen from

56. Quoted in *New Annual Register* (1789), pp. (128)–(129).
57. Quoted in Anthony Lincoln, *Some Social and Political Ideas of English Dissent, 1763–1800* (Cambridge: At the University Press, 1938), p. 3.
58. Printed in *New Light on Jacobinism* (Birmingham, 1789), pp. 54–55.

the French Revolution as the beginning of the fulfillment of the sacred predictions relative to the Millennium state."[59]

If Joseph Priestley and John Hurford Stone were led by their political and religious beliefs and by study of the Bible to relate the French Revolution to the millennium, others came to that position by more direct routes. A merchant in Hull named Coggan, for example, began in 1791 to have intimations that "GOD has employed the French to accomplish great things," particularly in striking blows against the Whore of Revelation, which was the Church of Rome. He began sending letters to prominent persons warning them that England would be cursed if she supported Rome and opposed the French: "That crowns will fall, kingdoms be overturned, and this country be visited with a dreadful scourge, is what I have anticipated, and long beheld hastily approaching. . . . Whatever support Popery has had from this country, GOD will repay us as a nation."[60]

In *The Making of the English Working Class*, E. P. Thompson wrote of the "sudden emergence of millenarial fantasies" in 1793 and 1794.[61] It would be more correct to describe the phenomenon as an intensification of a long tradition of piety that depended heavily on the literal interpretation of Scripture and on the conviction that even its most obscure passages would be understood when the course of events brought their fulfillment. For over a century, the millenarian and prophetic traditions had flourished in England as they had never done in France. They inspired continual speculations concerning the unfolding of divine Providence in political events and natural phenomena. Those who did contemplate the revelation of the hand of God in events, as predicted in the Bible, tended to make no distinction between natural and political cataclysms. The predicted "earthquakes" of Revelation could be either actual earthquakes (as in 1750), or the figurative earthquakes of political revolution, or both at once.

It is important to remember that in the first years of the French Revolution, support for it was widespread in England. It was not initially a politically divisive issue. The prime minister, William Pitt, said that he expected the present disorders to end with the emergence of France as one of the most brilliant powers of Europe. "She will enjoy that kind of liberty which I venerate." His bitterest rival,

59. *Causes and Consequences of the French Emperor's Conduct towards the Jews . . . by an Advocate for the House of Israel* (London, 1807), pp. 128–29.
60. G. Coggan, *A Testimony of Richard Brothers* (London, 1795), pp. iii, 4, 36, 43.
61. Thompson, *Making of the English Working Classes*, p. 127.

Charles James Fox, called the French Constitution of 1791 "the most stupendous and glorious edifice of liberty which has been created on the foundations of human integrity in any time or country."[62]

As we saw in the second chapter, the events of 1790 produced a crucial shift of opinion in France concerning the Revolution. By the end of that year, confidence in the possibility of national regeneration, which initially had helped to unite public opinion in support of the Revolution, had evaporated, never to return. A similar shift began to occur in England in 1791. One factor was certainly the publication of Edmund Burke's *Reflections on the Revolution in France* at the beginning of the year. The Baptist historians David Bogue and James Bennett, writing some twenty years later, held that from the publication of this book, "a melancholy change took place in the public temper."[63] The change was not so abrupt as Bogue and Bennett believed, but it is certainly true that the toleration of religious and political dissent that had characterized eighteenth-century England was giving way to a hostility that sometimes, as in the Priestley Riots, burst out in violence. Priestley received "numberless insulting and threatening letters" in the aftermath of the riots; one asserted that "a Wretch that denies his Saviour as Divinity and wod Whet the ax for decapetation ought to be Blasted here and Stond to Death." It was signed, "A Believer in Christ."[64]

By the end of 1792, with France at war with half of Europe, the French monarchy overthrown, and French orators proclaiming a policy of expansion and the liberation of oppressed peoples, Pitt's government began to prepare the country for war. One form that this preparation seems to have taken was the utilization of England's tradition of biblical exegesis for the interpretation of prophecy for patriotic purposes. Under the government's covert sponsorship, prophecies were disseminated in newspapers and pamphlets that cast the French Republic in the role of the Beast of Revelation. Such an interpretation involved a momentous change in the traditional Protestant interpretation, which cast the church of Rome in that role. Yet not only had the international crisis of 1792 brought England into tacit alliance with the Catholic powers; it had also made her a

62. Quoted in Asa Briggs, *The Making of Modern England, 1783-1867: The Age of Improvement* (New York: David McKay Co., 1960; reprint ed., New York: Harper Torchbooks, 1965), p. 130.
63. David Bogue and James Bennett, *History of Dissenters, from the Revolution in 1688 to the Year 1806*, 4 vols. (London: By the authors, 1809-12), 4: 195-97.
64. Joseph Priestley, *The Theological and Miscellaneous Works of Joseph Priestley*, ed. John Towill Rutt, 25 vols. (London: Smallfield, 1817-32), 15: 528 n.

haven for refugee priests. Events and prophecy had combined to produce a confusing situation for English millenarians, one which they met in a variety of ways in tracts and sermons.

Mrs. Piozzi was quick to note this new interpretation of prophecy in her *Thraliana*: "Here is an odd Idea now that the Beast of the Revelation is this French Democracy." That government was the successor to Louis XIV, who had aspired to Universal Monarchy and whose name in Latin "makes the Number 666 exactly." The French armies would go to Rome, "and if they do destroy the great City . . . we know what is coming. Meanwhile, the all-conquering Canaille carry every thing before them, and plant their Tree of Liberty in Holland, threaten Spain, ruin Austria, destroy Brabant, and declare their intention of coming to plunder Great Britain."[65]

In the next entry in *Thraliana*, Mrs. Piozzi noted a sermon "now going about from hand to hand, preached in the year 1701 . . . predictive of Events existing at this Moment," and she pasted in her book an extract from it which had appeared in the *St. James Chronicle*.[66] The sermon was by a Scottish Presbyterian minister named Robert Fleming. Its predictions about the French are similar to those of the "prophecy" Mrs. Piozzi had noted earlier.

Mrs. Piozzi was not the only one struck by the apparent relevance to current events of Fleming's ninety-year-old anti-French sermon. The day before, a correspondent had written the *Gentleman's Magazine* about it, launching a correspondence in its pages that lasted for two months. In February, a letter to the *European Magazine* expressed surprise that the magazine had not, "as most of the newspapers and some of your competitors have done," printed Fleming's prophecy, which had first appeared, according to the writer, on 15 January 1793 in the *Whitehall Evening Post*.[67]

The initial appearance of old prophecies unfavorable to the French in two newspapers that received government subsidies, on the eve of war between England and France, does create the suspicion that the ministry had a hand in reviving Fleming's speculations after ninety-odd years of oblivion. Joseph Towers, a Unitarian friend of Priestley, believed that Fleming's discourse had been distorted in the version inserted "in several *ministerial* papers," and he noted that it had been brought before the public in the first place by a member of Pitt's administration who was "a zealous advocate of the present war." As

65. Piozzi, *Thraliana*, 2: 851–52.   66. Ibid., pp. 853–54.
67. Ibid.; *Gentleman's Magazine* 63 (1793): 8, 100, 159–60, 203–4; and *European Magazine* 23 (1793): 84.

a result, the public had been led to believe that God "had manifested his displeasure against the people of France, and had signified his intention of inflicting on them the most signal punishment." Towers added that he knew for a fact that Fleming's predictions had "excited, in personages of the most elevated rank in this country, the most marked attention."[68]

The most significant of Fleming's interpretations of prophecy derived from his interpretation of Revelation 16, wherein seven vials are poured out by angels as the world moves toward the Second Coming. Fleming held that the pouring out of the fourth vial had begun in about 1648. This was the vial poured on the sun and heavenly bodies. Fleming contended that this must refer to princes and monarchs generally and to the French—the symbol of whose king was the sun—in particular. This vial would "expire" in 1794, when the French monarch consumed itself just as the Spanish monarchy had done in the seventeenth century.[69]

Fleming had been dead for over eighty years when his prophecies were rediscovered in 1793. He was the son of an exiled minister of the Church of Scotland who had settled in Holland, where he held the pastorate of an English church in Rotterdam. In Rotterdam at that time, the Huguenot preacher Pierre Jurieu was announcing the imminent destruction of the French monarchy. The younger Fleming, after succeeding to his father's pastorate, became acquainted with the stadtholder, William of Orange. After William had seized the English throne, Fleming joined him in England. Thus Fleming's interpretation of prophecy had considerable bearing on his own times and on the struggle against the French of the monarch who was his patron.

The anti-French tone of his discourse, coupled with his inclusion of the date 1794, helped to give Fleming's work its popularity during the French Revolution. Reprinted several times, it launched a far more extensive and varied rummaging-through-old-prophecies than had characterized France in 1790. It is surprising, perhaps, that these collected scraps of sermons and hearsay, many of which could only with great difficulty be tied to current political developments, managed to find readers. The chief explanation is probably that such prophecies had long been a staple of English popular literature.[70] There was in the 1790s a public eager to read prophetic utterances of

68. Joseph Towers, *Illustrations of Prophecy* (Philadelphia, 1808), pp. iv–v.
69. *European Magazine* 23 (1793): 84; Piozzi, *Thraliana*, 2: 854.
70. Altick, *The English Common Reader*, p. 38; Keith Thomas, *Religion and the Decline of Magic* (New York: Charles Schribner's Sons, 1971), pp. 128–45, 389–415.

all kinds, as the careers of Richard Brothers and Joanna Southcott would soon demonstrate.

By August, ransacking for prophecies had become so popular that the *Critical Review* complained that not even Dr. de Mainaduc, the leading exponent of animal magnetism in England, had manipulated public opinion more wantonly than had those engaged in "the discussion of pretended prophecies relating to the French Revolution." The complaint was made in connection with one of the several editions of Fleming's prophecy that appeared in 1794. The readers of the full work found that Fleming's main concern was the millennial kingdom that would follow the pouring of the seven vials, the sounding of the seven trumpets, the opening of the seven seals, the destruction of the Antichrist, and the Second Coming of Jesus Christ. Another anti-governmental periodical, the *New Annual Register*, complained of "the numerous republications of the worst trash, which disgraced the presses of the last century."[71]

A pamphlet with the splendid title *Antichrist in the French Convention* attempted to continue Fleming's work and evade the implication that hostility to France might mean support for Rome by proposing that both Rome *and* republican France represented the Beasts of Revelation. The second Beast had its "mark" in the revolutionary cockade that was worn by everyone: "Even negroes are presented with it, and are saluted with the kiss of fraternity." Perhaps the Protestant countries were the "saints of God," and England, God's "special care."[72] The English must struggle against the French or be enslaved by them, yet they must under no circumstances align themselves with the ten Roman Catholic kingdoms represented by the ten horns of the Beast in Daniel. All would be well; the papal power would fall in 1796.

A more coherent attempt to keep England out of the embrace of the Beast is found in the collection of old prophecies called *Prophetic Conjectures on the French Revolution*, which appeared in 1793. It was also successful in the United States, where it had three editions, one of them in German. Fleming's prophecy was of course included, together with ten other prophecies written between 1550 and 1750. Prophecy, the editor explained in the introduction, was intended not only to confirm the truth of the Bible by its fulfillment but also to provide comfort in "times of public distress and danger." The extracts that he offered to the public were neither a *"new* revelation"

---

71. *Critical Review*, 2d ser. 8 (1793): 645; *New Annual Register* (1793), p. 200.
72. *Antichrist in the French Convention* (London, 1795), pp. 2, 11–12.

nor were they "guesses." They represented *"rational conjectures* on the *scripture prophecies,* which form a powerful argument in favor of divine revelation."[73]

The leaders of the French Revolution had not intended to accomplish prophecy, "yet had this been their only design they could not have done it more effectually." They had freed France from the despotism of tyrants and priests, making possible, after the present troubles, the revival of "the pure spirit of religion in France." The English could expect "soon to see the day break, and the shades of antichristian darkness flee away,—when the empire of peace and good-will upon earth shall be established, and Christ the everlasting king of glory triumphantly reign in the hearts of men!"[74] One of the commentators included in *Prophetic Conjectures* was Jurieu, who, as we have seen, predicted the fall of the Roman Catholic Church through the agency of the French. Like Fleming, he expected the event to occur in the 1790s. The collection also included the Baptist preacher John Gill, whose sermons on prophecy delivered in the 1750s had been republished in 1793. Gill emphasized an event Fleming and Jurieu had ignored: the conversion of the Jews. The time of the blowing of the seventh trumpet was at hand, when the Jews would be converted, "as a body, as a nation of men." Gill refused to calculate dates, but he was sure that soon Christ would come and "make all things new; produce new heavens, and a new earth, and set up his tabernacle among his people, and dwell with them, and they reign with him."[75]

Of the prophecies in *Prophetic Conjectures,* possibly the most influential in the years 1793–95 was that attributed to the Presbyterian divine Christopher Love. Contained in a speech Love is supposed to have made shortly before his execution in 1651, it had the distinct virtues of brevity and clarity. In addition, it emphasized the special role that Divine Providence was to give to England in the Last Days. England would "wax old in wickedness," Love said, but then a bright star would arise out of her, "whose light and voice [would] make the heathen to quake and knock under with submission to the gospel of Jesus." No new prophets would arise, but rather, "the Lord by his spirit shall cause knowledge to abound among his people,

73. *Prophetic Conjectures on the French Revolution and Other Recent and Shortly Expected Events* (Philadelphia, 1794), pp. 4, 74.
74. Ibid., pp. 78, 82, 84.
75. John Gill, *The Sure Performance of Prophecy. A Sermon Preached . . . January 1, 1755* (London, 1794), pp. 30, 36.

whereby the old prophecies shall be clearly and perfectly understood."[76]

Love did calculate some of the times when the great events would occur. The final scenes were far in the future: in 1885 a worldwide earthquake would inaugurate the period when "God will be universally known by all. Then a great reformation and peace for ever, when people shall learn war no more." Yet the 1790s were great enough. Love expected the destruction of popery ("Babylon's fall") in 1790, and then a great man would appear: "God will be known to many in the year 1795; this will produce a great man."[77] It was not difficult to identify the "great man" of 1795 with the "bright star" who would arise in England.

The vials continued to distress many who contemplated prophecy. One minister identified both the fourth and fifth vials as Jacobinism, poured on the sun of monarchy and darkening the hopes inspired by the first years of the Revolution. James Bicheno, whose *Signs of the Times* was widely read both in Great Britain and in the United States, held that it was the vial poured upon the sea that was currently in force, and therefore God's judgments could "fall on maritime powers, on navies, and on insular countries."[78] Joanna Southcott, who began to receive divine communications in 1792, interpreted the vials in terms of high prices and poor harvests:

> For the *first Vial* was poured on the earth,
> In every nation you have heard a dearth,
> But yet much dearer things will surely be;
> And now comes on the other mystery.
>
> ·
>
> 'Tis on the SUN the Vial is poured out;
> And fervent heat it shall so strongly burn
> That all the earth shall feel it, and shall mourn;
> Because the Sun shall burn so very strong
> That All the Corn it surely will consume.[79]

76. Christopher Love et al., *The Strange and Wonderful Predictions . . . also Extracts from the Writings of Dr. Gill and Robert Flemming* (sic), *to Which Is Added Nixon's Cheshire Prophecy* (London, n.d.), pp. 6–8; Christopher Love, *The Remarkable Predictions of Mr. Christopher Love* (n.p., 1795), pp. 4–5.
77. Love et al., *Strange and Wonderful Predictions*, p. 8.
78. Alexander Pirie, *The French Revolution Exhibited in the Lights of the Sacred Oracles* (Perth, 1795), pp. 145, 202, 214; James Bicheno, *A Word in Season; or, A Call to the Inhabitants of Great Britain, to Stand Prepared for the Consequences of the Present War* (London, 1795), pp. 44, 77.
79. Joanna Southcott, "Communication of 1794 concerning the Vials of Revelation," in *The First Sealed Prophecies* (London, 1803), p. 81.

Even the Quakers were affected by the vogue for interpreting current events in terms of the fulfillment of prophecy. John Jenkins, who said his own faith in "gallery-prophesy" had always been weak, complained of the prophetic forebodings that were communicated at meetings he attended. These forebodings were especially prevalent among American Friends, one of whom predicted that the Roman church would surely fall in the midst of the present commotions. At that same meeting, someone else declared that great troubles were at hand and the rod would soon fall "upon friends, and others, for their sins." After the meeting, a group was discussing what they had heard. Someone asked who would carry out the punishment. The French, undoubtedly, said another. The first responded: "What, the French come *here* to punish us for our sins; the French indeed! Why *they* are as wicked as we are."[80]

Mrs. Piozzi continued to fill her *Thraliana* with prophetic snippets she had read or heard that seemed to point to the imminence of the end of the world. It is difficult to say how typical Mrs. Piozzi's fascination with prophecy was, but her journal for 1794 and 1795 reflects in a striking fashion the mingled hopes and fears that the events of those years inspired in one devout and intelligent woman. She had of course picked up Christopher Love's prophecy. With the combining of the natural and the supernatural that we have so often seen before, she wrote that " 'tis now particularly dry weather. So it was in Elijah's day, and many people have thought that a great Man would arise in the year 1795. Nous verrons."[81] She observed strange phenomena in the heavens. She wondered if Lord Macartney's embassy to China would result in the pouring of one of the vials and the effacing of the boundaries between Europe and Asia. She noted a Sybilline prophecy about Africa and asked if it did not refer to the antislavery movement: "When Africa *does* actually *recover* her *Liberty* and escape from the original Curse,—*the world will come to an End.*—She is recovering now, is she not?" Mrs. Piozzi wondered who were the two witnesses who were to be killed and reborn after three and a half years, and concluded that "old Brightman" was right: they were the Old and New Testaments.[82]

She continued to pay considerable attention to prospects for the conversion of the Jews. A friend told her that the Jews would return to Israel *before* their conversion. She was excited by a convocation of Jews in Amsterdam to investigate the truths of Christianity. Since

80. Jenkins, "Records and Recollections," ss/345, 348.
81. Piozzi, *Thraliana*, 2: 880.   82. Ibid., pp. 863, 865, 879.

"Conversion *must* follow Enquiry . . . our Saviour's *second* coming will be most surely at hand,"[83] she wrote on 25 January 1794.

Mrs. Piozzi then turned to a very different concern. "A French invasion is hourly expected and prepared for," she wrote, expressing what was then a widely held belief. She had always deplored the French Revolution and all its works, so it was not long before she was giving it apocalyptical significance. Jeremiah had mentioned that God would destroy a mountain, she wrote in April, and perhaps both that mountain and Babylon "agree typically and figuratively with what is now called *the Mtn* par Eminence, or French Convention consisting at one time of 666 people."[84] She found the 1260 year period of Daniel's prophecy coming to culmination in the French Revolution, especially in Collot d'Herbois's dechristianizing activities in Lyons and in the introduction of the revolutionary calendar. In September, she noted that the weather continued hot and dry and that "the people are gaping for Wonders of every kind, and expect Marvels in the Natural World to keep Pace with the strange Events observed in the *Civil* and *Political* world."[85]

Mrs. Piozzi perhaps reflected a very general sense of disquiet at the end of 1794 when she wrote that "the Times are sadly out of Joynt indeed, the War ruinous, and Peace a peril that I hope we shall be spared." She was conscious of the hardships and high prices that the war had caused, and she sympathized with the sufferings of the poor, but she fully supported both the prosecution of the war on the Continent and the prosecution of radicals in England. If the French and their subversive principles were not kept out of the kingdom, "they will come up like the Frogs of Egypt." At midnight on the thirty-first of December, she wrote an epitaph for that troubled year:

> After tonight then, We no more
> Must date our Letters Ninety four,
> For Time at length has shut his Door
> Against this old Year—Ninety four.
> So deep in Guilt, so stained with Gore
> Is seventeen hundred Ninety four.
>
> . . . .
> For not afflicted France has bore
> Alone the Ills of Ninety four;
>
> . . . .
> Teach us to give our Follies o'er
> And banish Vice with Ninety four.[86]

83. Ibid., pp. 860, 875, 880.   84. Ibid., pp. 880–81.
85. Ibid., p. 886.   86. Ibid., pp. 905–6.

Mrs. Sarah Flaxmer also looked at the present times with fore-boding. She had been receiving visions and dreams from God for some three years, and sometimes He would in a loud voice direct her to read biblical passages that pertained to prophecies soon to be ful-filled. Having been thus led to the eighth chapter of Revelation, she read that when the seventh seal was opened there would be "silence in Heaven about the space of half an hour." This, Mrs. Flaxmer in-formed the world in a pamphlet early in 1795, referred to the six months of relative quiet in domestic and foreign politics that was then coming to an end.[87]

Given the excitement that the belief in the imminent fulfillment of prophecy aroused in England during the French Revolution, it is surely no surprise that some individuals were inspired to see them-selves as prophets. Richard Brothers, the most impressive claimant to the prophet's mantle that the crisis produced, was by 1794 at-tracting some attention, at least in London. But before turning to Brothers, there is at least one other prophet whose career is worth recounting, if only to emphasize once again the diverse religious and cultural currents that fed into the millenarian excitement of the Revolutionary period.

In late October 1794, Robert Southey concluded a letter to a friend: "Tomorrow I am to be introduced to a prophet!!" Southey was then living in Bristol, and the prophet was almost certainly Wil-liam Bryan, whom we met in chapter 5 as a pilgrim to Avignon. In 1794, Bryan was living in Bristol, where he worked as a druggist and herbal doctor. Southey, who devoted a full chapter of his *Letters from England* to Bryan, wrote later: "I knew Bryan and heard the whole system from his own mouth."[88]

At one time or another, William Bryan was interested in prac-tically every conceivable aspect of late eighteenth-century occult, mystical, and quasi-scientific inquiry. Like Catherine Théot and Suzette Labrousse, he was conscious at an early age that he "was frequently favoured with a knowledge of the Divine Goodness in a sensible manner." At the age of sixteen he left his native Shrewsbury for London, where for a long time he lived a life of idleness and dissipation. He at last gave up his loose friends and began to read the Bible, and he attended the meetings of various dissenting sects until he rediscovered his childhood sense of God's grace among the Quakers. In 1784, Bryan married "the woman appointed for [him]

---

87. Sarah Flaxmer, *Satan Revealed; or, The Dragon Overcome . . .* (London, 1795).
88. Robert Southey, *New Letters*, ed. Kenneth Curry, 2 vols. (New York: Columbia University Press, 1965), 1: 82, 468.

by the Lord . . . , a true helpmate.''[89] For a time, he was a bookseller, specializing in religious tracts. He then found work as a copperplate printer; it was William Sharp, mystic and engraver, who arranged for his instruction in the trade and who set him up in business.[90] He and Bryan were probably introduced by a mutual friend, Thomas Duché, a talented painter and the son of the Rev. Jacob Duché. (At Avignon, one of the questions Bryan had asked the Holy Word was whether it was "the will of Heaven that he should cause his wife to come with Duché to be consecrated."[91]) Bryan was also known to Robert Hindmarsh, either as a fellow printer or a fellow student of Swedenborg or both. Hindmarsh considered Bryan something of a crackpot, who claimed to possess some rather peculiar powers: "He could, he said, blow down buildings on both sides of the street with one blast of his mouth."[92] Like Suzette Labrousse, Bryan practiced the healing techniques of animal magnetism.[93]

Unable to find work as a printer after his return from Avignon at the end of 1789, Bryan had worked for a time as a dyer before he began to earn his living by means of his therapeutic talents. He moved to Bristol a few years later, then settled at Hoddesdon. In 1820, John Jenkins, who had known Bryan since his Quaker days, could describe him as "the *celebrated* Will.m Bryan, formerly of London, Bookseller, Printer, Stationer, Dyer, etc. etc. *Cum Multis Alis,*—of Bristol, Doctor, of Avignon in France, AP, or associated prophet,—now the botanical doctor,—the Galen of Hoddesdon."[94]

Despite Bryan's peculiarities, he was a man whose considerable charm and intelligence favorably impressed people who met him. Southey wrote that his resemblance to pictures of Jesus Christ was "so striking as to truly astonish" him. Bryan was extremely handsome, almost beautiful, and had in addition "a natural eloquence."[95]

Although it is not known exactly what Bryan told Southey at their meeting in 1794, his prophecies were probably along the lines of a statement he had made three years earlier, which he repeated substantially unchanged in a pamphlet published in 1795. The Holy Word

89. Bryan, *Testimony of the Spirit of Truth*, pp. 15–18. This section of Bryan's tract has the title "A Brief Account of the Manner of the Lord's Gracious Dealings with Me."
90. John Timbs, *English Eccentrics and Eccentricities* (London: Chatto & Windus, 1898), p. 190; "Biographical Memoir of the Late Mr. Sharp," pp. 193, 197.
91. Southey, *Letters from England*, p. 424, quoting Bryan.
92. Hindmarsh, *Rise and Progress*, p. 47 n.
93. Ms JT 35, Friends' Reference Library, London.
94. Jenkins, "Records and Recollections," ss/1020–21.
95. Southey, *Letters from England*, p. 417.

had told him and his Avignon brethren that there would be great revolutions before 1800. The Turkish Empire would be destroyed through the agency of a boy then living in Rome. The Jews would be restored to the Holy Land: "It is in this generation that the whole dispensation will be accomplished." His predictions for the papacy corresponded exactly to those the spiritual Franciscans had made in 1300. There would be a disputed election after the death of the present Pope, but then a third candidate would be elected who would "close the scene of Papal Tyranny and Authority."[96]

Bryan had assured his listeners in 1791 that there would be no counterrevolution in France; the Revolutionary government would be "improved to a greater Degree of Purity and Perfection." England would have her share of troubles, but she would then emerge "as or more glorious than France." He may have been less sanguine in 1794. Living in Bristol, an important port for the traffic in slaves, made him painfully conscious of the evils of the slave trade. And during the "Bridge Riots" of 1793, a constable had fired into a crowd protesting the collection of tolls. These things came into Bryan's mind when the Lord spoke to him on 12 December 1794: "Woe to this city of BRISTOL! the cry of innocent blood is against it: it shall be shaken, and fall."[97]

When God spoke to him of Bristol, Bryan was returning from a trip to London, where he had stayed with his Avignon companion, John Wright. While in London, Bryan had visited the prophet Richard Brothers, in testimony to whom Wright had recently published a pamphlet. Bryan had first heard of Brothers from friends at Bath. Unlike Wright, he had not been impressed, and he was sorry when he learned that Wright had become a disciple.

Apparently Bryan had made his displeasure known, for early in December he received a letter from Brothers himself, informing him that he and Wright were the two witnesses predicted in Revelation, but that Bryan had forfeited that place "by speaking against [Brothers], his prophet." A battle of the prophets seemed imminent. Bryan sent Brothers a letter denouncing him. Brothers responded that God had told him to burn the letter without reading it; this reply, understandably, threw Bryan into "more doubt and reasoning."

96. Bryan, *Testimony of the Spirit of Truth*, p. 28; ms JT 35, Friends' Reference Library.

97. Ms JT 35, Friends' Reference Library; Bryan, *Testimony of the Spirit of Truth*, p. 5. On the Bridge Riots, see Samuel Taylor Coleridge, *The Collected Works I: Lectures, 1795, on Politics and Religion*, ed. Lewis Patton and Peter Mann (Princeton: Princeton University Press, 1969–), pp. 328–29.

Bryan came to London, where he contemplated "plunging my *knife* into his *heart*." But after meeting Brothers, Bryan's own prophetic pretensions seem to have collapsed. The absolute assurance that Brothers always expressed concerning his own mission must have had its effect. Brothers was no Labrousse, with her conditional phrases like "if I am not mistaken." He was too much for the more flexible, less obsessed Bryan. While Bryan was sitting in meditation at Wright's house, God delivered him "from the power and operation of the spirits of darkness."[98] He therefore published his own testimony that Richard Brothers was a prophet of God. It is to Brothers's career that we must now turn.

98. Bryan *Testimony of the Spirit of Truth*, pp. 2–5; Brothers's letter to Bryan is printed on p. 4.

CHAPTER 8

A
Methodical
Madness

R ICHARD Brothers has fared somewhat better at the hands of historians than either Suzette Labrousse or Catherine Théot.[1] The pages on Brothers in Ronald Matthews's *English Messiahs* and George M. Balleine's *Past Finding Out* are reliable and reasonably objective. Perhaps the earliest study is the best. Alexander Gordon's factually authoritative article in the *Dictionary of National Biography* is based on personal conversations with followers and on manuscript materials that have since disappeared. The reliability of the studies on Brothers is less a commentary on Brothers himself, who unlike the French prophetesses clearly *was* mad, than on differences in cultural and historiographical traditions.

Richard Brothers was born in Placentia, Newfoundland, on Christmas Day 1757. He went to England while still a boy and was educated at Woolwich. At the age of fourteen he entered the navy as a midshipman and saw some service in battle off the African coast and in the American War for Independence. At the end of that war, in 1783, he was promoted to lieutenant, then discharged at half pay the same year.

Gordon says that Brothers visited Spain, Italy, and France after his discharge. Balleine adds that he visited the New Israel Society at Avignon;[2] this is possible, but very unlikely. There is no indication of such a visit anywhere in Brothers's writings, and the group had barely established itself at Avignon by the time Brothers returned to England. Had Brothers gone to Avignon, one would expect that he, Bryan, or Wright would have mentioned the fact.

Brothers is said to have married shortly after his return to England in 1786. He could not have lived long with his wife, because he arrived

---

1. Ronald Matthews, *English Messiahs: Studies in Six English Pretenders, 1656–1927* (London: Methuen, 1936), chap. 3; George R. Balleine, *Past Finding Out: The Tragic Story of Joanna Southcott and Her Successors* (New York: Macmillan Co., 1956), pp. 27–36; and Alexander Gordon's biography of Brothers in *Dictionary of National Biography*.
2. Balleine, *Past Finding Out*, p. 28.

in London alone in September 1787 and remained there until his death in 1824. Asked by the workhouse commissioners in 1791 if he had ever been a "house-keeper," Brothers replied that he had, once, for two months "but as a very melancholy idea comes across my mind when I think of that period, I hope you will not press me further upon it."[3] In London, he lived quietly on his navy half-pay and worshipped at a Baptist chapel.

In 1789, Brothers developed scruples about the requirement of taking a "voluntary" oath of loyalty in order to receive his pay. He wrote several letters to the Admiralty, setting forth his objections in a clear and coherent prose that contrasts with his later prophetic writings. "I can pass by the oath," he wrote. "It is frequently done; the terms are low, safe, and easy; . . . but to me, the evasion would be dishonourable."[4] He wrote some years later that in 1790 the spirit of God had first begun to enlighten his understanding, although he had *"always had a presentiment of being sometime or other very great."*[5] He continued to write the Admiralty, but they refused to waive the oath and stopped his pay. In August 1791, he was placed in a workhouse.

In what was actually a testimony to her belief in his divine mission, Mrs. S. Green, Brothers's landlady, recounted his peculiar behavior.[6] Brothers had been her lodger for over two years; during the second year, he had never left the house. He had broken his sword, saying he would never draw it against his brother; nor would anyone else. Brothers had received several visions while lodging with Mrs. Green. After one, in which he was told that London would be destroyed in 1791, he had lain on his face for three days and nights without eating. After he had gone several months without paying any rent., Mrs. Green finally complained to the parish officers about her strange lodger, asking them to "take particular care of him (as he was a gentleman)."

Brothers wrote about this period of his life three years later.[7] His actions had been in response to a divine warning in January 1791,

3. Joseph Moser, *Anecdotes of Richard Brothers, in the Years 1791 and 1792, with Some Thoughts on Credulity,* . . . (London, 1795), p. 16.

4. Richard Brothers, *A Letter of Richard Brothers . . . to Philip Stephens* (London, 1795), p. 5; *Letter to N. B. Halhed, Esquire, M. P., from an Old Woman* (London, 1795), p. 29. Both the style and the information contained in the latter pamphlet suggest that Joseph Moser was its author.

5. Richard Brothers, *A Revealed Knowledge of the Prophecies and Times,* 2 vols. (London, 1795), 2: 49.

6. Mrs. S. Green, *A Letter to the Publisher of Brothers's Prophecies* (London, 1795), pp. 4–5.

7. Brothers, *Revealed Knowledge,* 1: 39–45.

which came in the form of tremendous thunder, "the loudest that ever was heard since man was created." It was the voice of the angel mentioned in Revelation 17, proclaiming the fall of Babylon the Great. Like Daniel (and William Blake, we might add), Brothers had an "attending angel," and he informed Brothers that Babylon was in fact London, which God was determined to burn immediately. Brothers begged God to let him warn London of its doom. God at first refused but finally agreed, for Richard Brothers's sake, to spare the city for a time.

It was also during the period before he was sent to the workhouse that Brothers had what was perhaps his most famous vision, which Coleridge and Southey parodied in their satirical poem of 1799, *The Devil's Thoughts.* Brothers saw "Satan walking leisurely into London: his face had a smile, but under it his looks were sly, crafty, and deceitful. On the right side of his Forehead were seven dark spots, and he was dressed in White and Scarlet Robes."[8]

A popular writer named Joseph Moser had been a member of the workhouse board that took Brothers under its care in 1791. In 1795, when the former inmate was one of the most widely discussed individuals in England, Moser recalled his impressions in a pamphlet that is remarkable for its sympathetic appraisal of the prophet. Moser said of Brothers's first interview before the board: "I must confess his appearance prejudiced me greatly in his favour. He seemed about thirty years of age, tall and well formed, and in his address and manner much mildness and gentility."[9] This impression was echoed by many others who were in no sense disciples. The only peculiarities of his appearance were unusually short hair and sober attire; all agree that he was very tall and handsome, well bred, with nothing of the "enthusiast" in his manner.

Brothers came before the board with his hat on, but he removed it after having been invited to be seated. Asked why he had resigned his naval commission, he answered: "Disgust! I conceived the military life to be totally repugnant to the duties of Christianity; and that I could not *conscientiously* receive the wages of *Plunder, Bloodshed,* and *Murder!*"[10]

It seemed to Moser and the workhouse board that Richard Brothers's was "a very methodical kind of madness." They gave him a room of his own in the workhouse, which he kept extremely (obsessively?) tidy. Moser visited him often, and found that his conversation was

8. Ibid., p. 43.
9. Moser, *Anecdotes of Richard Brothers,* p. 14.   10. Ibid., p. 15.

perfectly normal on every subject save religion. His landlady, Mrs. Green, told the board that Brothers had often said he expected a visit from a lady, but she never came. Moser, on the basis of his almost daily conversations with Brothers, found him "ever in expectation; sometimes of a lady, who was to descend from the clouds, sometimes of immense sums of money, which were, probably to be showered upon him—sometimes of a period like that foretold by the Prophet *Isaiah*, when *turbulence* & *war* should cease, and *peace*, *love*, and *happiness*, be extended to all mankind."[11]

In February 1792, after spending about six months in apparent contentment in the workhouse, Brothers was able to settle his accounts and leave. He became a healer, having decided he could restore sight. Moser said he drew large crowds, in part because he gave small sums of money to those whose eyes he touched.

Several months later, Brothers went to Moser's home to thank him and to inquire if John Pitt (the prime minister's brother and first lord of the Admiralty) had called, for Brothers had written him a letter in which he mentioned Moser. Brothers had become interested, quite suddenly, in politics. He wrote letters to the king, the queen, the prime minister, and others in the government in which he declared that "the Revolution in France proceeded from the judgment of God. Therefore all attempts to preserve the Monarchy there would be opposing God."[12] On 17 May 1792 he went to the Houses of Parliament to inform the Commons "of their own sudden fall into the Jaws of the earth by a predetermined Earthquake" should they persist in their policy of hostility to the Revolution. He was turned away at the door. God then assured him that it was not Brothers who had been insulted, "but me in our person that sent you."[13]

Once again Brothers was taken before a court for nonpayment of rent. This time he was placed in Newgate, London's most notorious prison. He spent eight weeks there, until he signed a power of attorney for the collection of his navy pay. Before signing it, he struck out a phrase referring to the king as "our sovereign lord" that he regarded as blasphemous.

The experience, as Brothers described it two years later, must have been terrible. He was placed in a room "with fourteen poor men, little air, and much crowded." He was told that that space was available because a man had died the day before *for want of proper nourishment.* Each inmate was fed a penny's worth of bread each day, with

11. Ibid., p. 28.   12. Quoted in Balleine, *Past Finding Out*, pp. 31–32.
13. Brothers, *Revealed Knowledge*, 2: 18–19.

beef once a week. Neither bed nor blankets were provided: "THE POOR ARE ENTIRELY DESTITUTE HERE," he declared with considerable justification. Newgate confirmed Brothers in his opinion that London was the Babylon of Revelation equally with Rome: "No man who had any Knowledge of God can justly say that London is without guilt, and her people are without sin; when her Streets are full of Vice, and her Prisons are full of oppression."[14]

In all probability, Brothers's experience in Newgate deepended his own grievance against those who refused to listen to his message concerning France's divine mission. *Revealed Knowledge* indicates that Brothers had predicted dark times for the English crown for some time. Thanks to the "methodical" nature of his "madness," he carefully dated all the visions he set forth in his book. In June 1791, at two o'clock in the afternoon, he saw a hand, with its forefinger extended, appear on the wall near the door of his room. That night, God informed him that this apparition signified "the speedy end of the present King of England and his Empire, like Belshazzar and Babylon, both of which would soon be destroyed."[15] In 1791, however, England's doom appears to have rested on her sinfulness and corruption. It was only in 1792 that Brothers's visions took on an increasingly political tone, and he announced that the French armies would inevitably triumph and monarchies fall all over Europe.

We know practically nothing of Brothers's life between his release from Newgate in November 1792 and his sudden emergence to prominence two years later, except in connection with the visions he described in *Revealed Knowledge* and later in *An Exposition of the Trinity*. These indicate that it was during this period that he came to believe himself called to fulfill a role that sets him apart from the other prophets of the Revolutionary era. He became convinced that his special mission was to gather the Jews, including the "Jews" who, like himself, were "hidden" among the population of Great Britain, and lead them to Palestine, where he would rule over them until the Second Coming. Brothers spent the last thirty years of his life planning the New Jerusalem and designing its flags, uniforms, and palaces. Although Brothers himself was forgotten, the idea that the English were the New Israel grew and flowered in the nineteenth century and has persisted to the present day.[16] An echo of Brothers's

---

14. Ibid., pp. 45–46.   15. Ibid., p. 73.
16. John Wilson, "British Israelism," in *Patterns of Sectarianism: Organization and Ideology in Social and Religious Movements*, ed. Bryan Wilson (London: Heinemann, 1967), pp. 345–76; Balleine, *Past Finding Out*.

notion may, perhaps, be found in William Blake's long poem of 1821, *Jerusalem*.

It is not clear how or when Brothers decided that he was to be king of the Jews and ruler of the New Jerusalem. He wrote in *Revealed Knowledge* that in November 1792 (soon after his release from Newgate), he had set out on foot toward Bristol, intending to leave England and contrary to God's command, "never to have anything to do with prophecying [*sic*] or the character of restoring the Hebrews to Jerusalem." But God forcibly turned him around some twenty-five miles from London and ordered him "to return and wait his proper time."[17] On his journey out of London, he had cast aside a staff that he had cut a few months before by divine command from a wild rosebush; he now retrieved the rod, with which he would later promise to perform miracles like Moses's, in order to convince the Jews of the world to follow him and return once again to the Promised Land.

Brothers was not the first Englishman to think that there was a special affinity between his nation and Israel, nor was he the first to proclaim himself king of the Jews. John Foxe, in his *Book of Martyrs*, had taught generations of sixteenth- and seventeenth-century Englishmen that they were God's chosen people, called to do battle with the Catholic Antichrist, and the millenarian exitement of the 1640s and 1650s produced at least two prophets who proposed to lead the Jews to the Holy Land. One was the Ranter, John Robins, who abandoned the project after Lodowick Muggleton pronounced a sentence of damnation against him. The other was a mad goldsmith named Thomas Tany. Like Brothers, Tany proclaimed himself to be a Jew; he even had himself circumcised. In 1655, he stormed the Houses of Parliament armed with a rusty sword, having been commanded in a vision to kill the members of Parliament. He was imprisoned. After his release, he built a boat and set out to assemble the Jews of Holland. He did get to Amsterdam, where he visited the celebrated mystic, Antoinette Bourignon, before disappearing without a trace.[18]

Despite the close similarity of their conceptions of themselves and their missions, Brothers had probably never heard of Thomas Tany.

---

17. Richard Brothers, *An Exposition of the Trinity* (London, 1795), p. 18.
18. On Robins and Tany, see the excellent biographies by Alexander Gordon in *Dictionary of National Biography*; Alexander Gordon, *The Origins of the Muggletonians* (Liverpool, 1869), pp. 17–19, 24–25; Bernard Capp, *The Fifth Monarchy Men: A Study in Seventeenth-Century English Millenarianism* (Totowa, N.J.: Rowman & Littlefield, 1972), pp. 43, 190; and Serge Hutin, *Les disciples anglais de Jacob Boehme aux XVIIe et XVIIIe siècles* (Paris: Denoël, 1960), pp. 233–34.

He probably knew nothing of the poet Christopher Smart, either, who in his *Jubilate Agno* of 1751 had declared that "The ENGLISH are the seed of Abraham." Smart believed himself to be a descendant of David, who would be a prince when Christ came again in 1760 and the New Jerusalem was built "in England's green and pleasant land."[19]

Philosemitism had been an integral part of English millenarian thought since the seventeenth century, when even Cromwell had for a time been deeply involved with the question of the restoration and conversion of the Jews. Most millenarians believed that before they could return to Israel, the Lost Tribes would have to be found. Brothers and his predecessors had discovered them among the English, but in the 1790s there was also widespread belief that they would be found by European explorers, perhaps among the American Indians, the Afghans, or the Negroes of Africa. To judge by their printed testimonies in his behalf, however, Brothers's followers were less interested in his discovery of the Lost Tribes among the English than he was. They appear to have been attracted to him for other reasons. Some, like William Sharp, John Wright, and William Bryan, were already deeply involved in the mystical and millenarian currents of English popular religion. They also shared the prophet's conviction of England's deep sinfulness, particularly as it was embodied in their government's support of the powers of the Old Regime against the nation of Revolutionary France. By 1794, the political crisis was accompanied by economic distress and social tensions of almost unprecedented severity. It was in this charged atmosphere that Brothers began to attract followers.

Brothers's earliest and most faithful disciple was an army captain named Hanchett, "a very respectable gentleman of large fortune."[20] He provided Brothers with much financial support, including the cost of printing his first books, which were given away to the prophet's visitors. Practically nothing is known of Hanchett save his connection with Brothers, and he wrote nothing with the possible exception of an anonymous testimonial, the author of which is described as a man "particularly mentioned by the Prophet in his Books in the warmest Terms of Gratitude and Esteem." Its arguments in support of Brothers are remarkably simple and direct; fitting, perhaps, for an army man. Brothers was the man Jeremiah

19. Quoted in A. D. Hope, "The Apocalypse of Christopher Smart," in *Studies in the Eighteenth Century: Papers Presented at the David Nichol Smith Memorial Seminar, Canberra, 1966*, ed. A. F. Brissenden (Canberra: Australian National University Press, 1968), pp. 280–81.
20. *Oracle*, 6 March 1795, p. 2.

predicted as "the Prophet which prophesieth of PEACE." Brothers had written letters to people in the government predicting certain developments, and "his prophecies coming true, absolutely prove him a true prophet."[21]

It was Hanchett who approached the Swedenborgian printer Robert Hindmarsh early in 1794 and asked him to print the first part of *Revealed Knowledge*, offering to pay two or three times the usual cost. Hindmarsh refused, because the book predicted the death of the king.[22] Hanchett then found a printer in the respected publisher and bookseller George Riebau, who, like Hanchett and a very few others, remained a faithful disciple until Brothers's death. Not long afterwards, an Anglican clergyman who had adopted Swedenborg's doctrines and "was disposed to examine every new pretension to supernatural communications" asked Hindmarsh to accompany him to see the prophet. They found Brothers installed in a comfortable apartment on Paddington Street. He told the two visitors his history and outlined "the commission he was enjoined to execute." He showed them the miraculous wild-rose rod, declaring that it was "the emblem of that power, which will shortly astonish the world." Much of Brothers's time was devoted, it appears, to giving this sort of interview to his numerous callers.

There is no evidence concerning when William Sharp became a disciple of Brothers; the likeliest guess would be in 1794, after he had dropped out of radical politics. The painter Loutherbourg, who had made the same spiritual pilgrimage from Swedenborg to faith healing as had Sharp, may have discovered Brothers at the same time. A third early disciple who arrived by way of Swedenborg was the chemist and alchemist Peter Woulfe. Brothers singled Woulfe out for divine favor in the first part of his *Revealed Knowledge*. The passage is particularly interesting because it begins, "And you PETER WOULFE—*one of the Avignon Society*,"[23] and then assures him that his property in France will be restored. It is tempting to imagine that Brothers was somehow connected with a yet undis-

21. Printed in Nathaniel Brassey Halhed, *A Calculation of the Commencement of the Millennium* (Albany, N. Y., 1796), pp. 17, 22.
22. Robert Hindmarsh, *The Rise and Progress of the New Jerusalem Church in England, America, and Other Parts*, ed. Edward Madeley (London: Hodson, 1861), pp. 122–23.
23. *Dictionary of National Biography*; 1921–22 ed., s.v. "Woulfe, Peter," by Philip Joseph Hartog; John Timbs, *English Eccentrics and Eccentricities* (London: Chatto & Windus, 1898), pp. 126–27; and Brothers, *Revealed Knowledge*, 2: 93. Woulfe's membership in the Avignon Society is also mentioned in the report of the papal investigators printed in Renzo de Felice, *Note e ricerche sugli 'Illuminati' e il misticismo rivoluzionario (1789–1800)* (Rome: Edizioni di storia e letteratura, 1960), p. 219.

covered London branch of the Avignon circle, but unfortunately the only evidence that such a group existed is found in the pamphlet *Satan Revealed*, by the singular Mrs. Flaxmer. She declared that Satan's synagogue was at Avignon and "its members are his angels," who were dispersed "into all nations." She then told how John Wright and another man, as emissaries of the Avignon Society, had called on her to talk about Richard Brothers. She had refused to see them.[24]

The disciples we have mentioned may all have learned about Richard Brothers through the same sort of circulation of news within the religious and philosophical underground as that through which Catherine Théot and Suzette Labrousse acquired their followers. But popular culture in eighteenth-century England was a "printing culture," and unquestionably, the bulk of Brothers's followers learned of his prophecies by reading them. In 1794 and 1795, Riebau published (and Hanchett, we assume, paid for) reams of literature by and about the prophet, mostly in the form of cheap pamphlets. According to several contemporary accounts, copies of Brothers's principal work were given away to visitors; one said he had given away over 8,000 copies.[25]

The Brothers circle also published collections of old prophecies that could be interpreted as pointing to Brothers as being God's prophet for the times. One such collection, which according to one journal was given away to visitors along with *Revealed Knowledge*, included the prophecies of Christopher Love. The extracts selected emphasized the emergence in 1795 of a "great man," who was, the editor explained, the descendant of David, who would lead the Jews to Israel and rule over them: in other words, Richard Brothers. The pamphlet added other prophecies, including those of the Bohemian Christopher Kotter, the German John Maximilian Daut, and the leading English follower of the three French prophets, Sir Richard Lacy. Brothers assured the readers of this pamphlet that all the prophecies printed in it "were explained to [him] through the HOLY GHOST, and by REVELATION in Visions of the night from the Lord God."[26] In 1795, Riebau issued a longer, somewhat more restrained collection of prophecies. This collection added Jacob

24. Sarah Flaxmer, *Satan Revealed: or, The Dragon Overcome* . . . (London, 1795), pp. 9-11.
25. "Convert," *The Age of Prophecy; or, Further Testimony of the Mission of Richard Brothers* (London, 1795), p. 27; Eliza Williams, *The Prophecies of Brothers Confuted, from Divine Authority* (London, 1795), p. 16; and *British Critic* 5 (1795): 436.
26. [Richard Brothers, ed.], *Extracts from the Prophecy Given to C. Love* (London, 1794), p. 8; *Prophetical Passages concerning the Present Times* (London, 1795).

Boehme to the prophets heralding the advent of Brothers. It also included a number of dreams through which believers had been led to accept the mission of "the Revealed Prince of the Hebrews," as Brothers was then calling himself.

A collection of prophecies first published in 1794 and not apparently directly connected with the Brothers circle indicated that his fame was indeed spreading. In the introduction, the editor wrote of the new prophet in terms that may help to explain the sudden notoriety of so unlikely a candidate for fame as Richard Brothers. Since the present times were "the most momentous that the history of this nation affords, some prophet may be naturally expected to arise for the guidance of man through this maze of awful, impending fatality." The person who seemed at that time to claim "the most faith and attention" was Brothers, "who in a most candid, unreserved, and interesting manner" had published his interpretation of scripture and his predictions. He had been visited by "the pious and the learned," who had come away impressed with "the unassumed modesty of the man, the placidity and benevolence of his countenance, and the temperate habits of his life."[27] There followed eight pages of paraphrases and quotations from Brothers's book, then a motley collection of other prophecies from a diverse group that included Fleming, Jurieu, Nostradamus, Christopher Love, Robert Nixon (the Cheshire Idiot), Swedenborg, Bishop Newton, and Joseph Priestley. Clearly, prophecy—any prophecy—had become a matter of deep concern to many in England in the troubling year of "ninety-four."

Even if this is granted, however, it is still difficult to understand the immense success that *A Revealed Knowledge of the Prophecies and Times* enjoyed. The British Museum has four separate editions published in London, plus one that appeared in Dublin in 1795. In the United States, there were eighteen editions, including a German translation. A translation appeared in Paris in 1795 titled *Les Prophéties de Jacques Brothers*. During the first half of 1795, the book and the pamphlet literature that it engendered were discussed in all the literary reviews, and *Monthly Review, Gentleman's Magazine,* and *Analytical Review* even set aside sections of their magazines for the subject of "prophecy."

Revealed Knowledge was initially a pamphlet, approximately sixty pages long, which Brothers had completed by the end of 1793.

---

27. *Wonderful Prophecies, Being a Dissertation on the Existence, Nature, and Extent of the Prophetic Powers in the Human Mind,* 3d ed. (London, 1795), pp. 16–17.

He made two additions to it during the next few months; then, in April 1794, he published part 2. He made five additions to this second part, the last dated 20 February 1795. In its final form, the work numbered 168 pages.

About half of the book consists of scriptural passages. Daniel and Revelation are quoted at great length, but so are many of the other Old Testament prophets, some of the Epistles, and the apocryphal (and apocalyptic) books of Esdras. Sometimes Brothers inserted parenthetical explanations of phrases in the Scriptures that had been told him "by Revelation."

The author's visions, in a roughly chronological order, are interspersed with Scripture and commentary throughout the book. Some of the visions relate to experiences in Brothers's own life or to a series of thunderstorms that he interpreted as signifying the warnings of angels preceding the destruction of London, an event averted only by Brothers's personal intervention with God. There is also a series of political visions, concentrated mostly in the second part of the book. Brothers claimed to have predicted the deaths of both Louis XVI and Gustavus III of Sweden. Interpreting the Beasts of Daniel and Revelation in much the same fashion as Joseph Priestley, he expected all monarchies to fall by 1798. Brothers had warned the king and his ministers not to join the war against the French, whose revolution was predicted by Daniel, but God "permits this opposition for Three years and a half to fulfill the determined part of this Prophecy on all that oppose it; that done, his judgments will take place, to punish man and lay waste Kingdoms."[28] George III's own life, as the prophet had told him in 1792, had been delivered by God into Brothers's own hands. When Brothers was "revealed," George would yield up his crown to the prophet.

Brothers had been informed by God that he was to leave for Constantinople by July 1795. His mission would have been finally revealed at the beginning of the preceding month. Like Moses, he would work miracles with his wild-rose rod in order to persuade the Jews, including the "hidden" Jews, "to receive the Commands of God" through him, and "to collect all their property and depart in great haste from all nations to their own land."[29] At the same time, in June 1795, London and much of the rest of the world would be destroyed by a great earthquake.

Brothers's *Revealed Knowledge* represented traditions long present in English popular religion. The calculations of the millen-

28. Brothers, *Revealed Knowledge*, 2: 7.   29. Ibid., p. 82.

nium with which the book opens, the sense of identity between Englishmen and Jews, the translation of meteorology into prophecy, and the insistence that the Bible's prophecies be literally understood all had a long history. Speculations of this kind had always been especially intense in times of crisis, and England had seldom experienced a time as filled with distress and a sense of disaster as 1795. As a result of the war, an exceptionally severe winter, and crop failures, food prices soared. Pitt's popularity, never high, was at its nadir; and there was a definite "Jacobin tinge" of political radicalism to many of the handbills and circular letters of city and countryside alike.[30] The antiwar activities of the London Corresponding Society and other radical groups was never more extensive than in 1795, following the triumphant acquittal of Thomas Hardy, John Horne Tooke, and other defendants in treason trials at the end of 1794. In Parliament, the opposition led by Charles James Fox, Richard Sheridan, and Lord Stanhope continued to attack Pitt's war policy, and their views were echoed in several of the London newspapers, notably the *Chronicle* and the *Morning Post*.

A retired soldier named John Stedman noted in his diary at the beginning of 1795: "Now the British nation petitions for peace to Parliament, while the King's speech breathes only war." In February, he wrote that "This is the hardest winter evern known. In the north the snow 12 and 18 feet deep. The poor are starving with cold and hunger, for want of trade, especially with Holland."[31]

That same month, in Bristol, young Samuel Coleridge, his hair unpowdered and uncombed in protest against the Hair-Powder Tax, delivered a lecture "On the Present War": "Our national faith has been impaired," he declared. "Our social confidence hath been weakened, or made unsafe: our liberties have suffered a perilous breach. . . . And shall we carry on this wild and priestly War against reason, against freedom, against human nature?"[32]

At the end of January, Mrs. Sarah Trimmer, one of the more egregious heralds of Victorian piety, prayed that God would spare

30. E. P. Thompson, "The Moral Economy of the English Crowd in the Eighteenth Century," *Past and Present*, no. 50 (1971), p. 218. See also E. P. Thompson, *The Making of the English Working Class*, rev. ed. (Harmondsworth: Penguin Books, 1968), pp. 148-58; and M. Dorothy George, *English Political Caricature: A Study of Opinion and Propaganda*, 2 vols. (Oxford: Clarendon Press, 1959), vol. 2.

31. John Gabriel Stedman, *The Journal of John Gabriel Stedman, 1744-1797, Soldier and Author*, ed. Stanbury Thompson (London: Mitre, 1962), pp. 368-69.

32. Samuel Taylor Coleridge, *The Collected Works I: Lectures, 1795, on Politics and Religion*, ed. Lewis Patton and Peter Mann (Princeton: Princeton University Press, 1969-), p. 74.

her nation, despite its sins, and that He would "go forth . . . with our fleets and armies; deliver us from our cruel enemies! maintain our cause, and save us from destruction for thy mercies sake."[33]

Mrs. Piozzi noted inflammatory handbills posted on the church door *"demanding*, not *requesting* relief for the lower Orders." In February, she commented on the treason trials, the emergence of Brothers, and the general state of the kingdom with her usual vigor: "They suffer all Traitors to go loose, and then wonder that there is Treachery abroad. Indeed I believe no Jury Men will condemn them, such a Spirit of Democracy is gone forth: People say openly now that 'tis no Treason to cry *George's head in a Basket*—so I suppose 'tis no Blasphemy to say that you are *God Almighty's Nephew*, as this fine Mr. Brothers makes no Scruple of doing; . . . Every Thing is worse, and every body is wickeder than I thought them to be."[34]

It was in February that Richard Brothers acquired the disciple whose support probably won him the greater part of the attention he received in the press: Nathaniel Brassey Halhed, former official of the East India Company, translator of Latin verse and Hindu laws, and member of Parliament for Lymington in 1795.

The son of a director of the Bank of England, Halhed attended Harrow and Christ Church, Oxford. He went to India to serve with the East India Company, and there, at the request of Warren Hastings, he translated the so-called Gentoo Code, a digest of Sanskrit law books, from the Persian. He returned to England in 1785 and five years later secured a seat in Parliament, which he resigned in 1795 as a result of his advocacy of Richard Brothers. He spent the last thirty-five years of his life in retirement in London, where he continued his earlier studies of Eastern language and his imitations of classical poetry.

A 1795 portrait of Halhed shows a mild, scholarly man, bald except for a fringe around the ears.[35] He was then in his mid-forties. Even those who scorned his religious ideas testified to his brilliance and personal charm, and the several pamphlets that he produced in 1795 in support of Brothers are composed in an elegant style, in marked contrast to most of the testimonies published by Brothers's

---

33. Sarah Trimmer, *Some Accounts of the Life of Mrs. Sarah Trimmer*, 2 vols. (London: Rivington, 1816), 1: 245.

34. Hester Thrale Piozzi, *Thraliana: The Diary of Mrs. Hester Lynch Thrale, 1776–1809*, ed. Katherine C. Balderston, 2d ed., 2 vols. (Oxford: Clarendon Press, 1951), 2: 909.

35. The portrait is included in the second volume of collected tracts on Brothers in the Houghton Library, Harvard University.

followers. Halhed himself affirmed that he had had no particular religious convictions before he took up Richard Brothers, and there is a wit and an ironic tone in his pamphlets that convinced some reviewers that he was not sincere in his advocacy of the prophet. Halhed, however, denied the charge vehemently. He had first heard of Brothers on 5 January 1795, he told the House of Commons; five days later, he went to see him. He then read Brothers's books, compared them with Scripture, and became a disciple. "I declare upon my honour," he said, "this is the whole and entire ground of the present bias of my thoughts, which in one sense may certainly be called my conversion."[36]

Halhed had attempted to speak in Brothers's behalf in connection with a motion in support of negotiations with the French in January. Failing to be recognized by the speaker of the House, he wrote out his testimony, had it printed, and distributed a thousand copies to members of Parliament and other "public personages," still "perfectly assured" that he would obtain "the suffrages of a very considerable majority both in and out of Parliament."[37]

That Halhed began and ended his *Testimony* with denunciations of the war suggests the central importance of that crisis in his "conversion." The war could result in "the whole world peopled with nothing but soldiers; and every established form of government in Europe, not excepting our own," destroyed.[38] The ministry said the war was just and necessary, but it was "just only because it justifies God's vengeance—and necessary, only because necessary for our punishment." The king had proclaimed another Fast Day for 25 February, "to implore success on our arms"; it should be instead "a solemn and sincere humiliation for our crimes."[39]

According to Halhed, troubled times always produced visions and prophecies, and in the present crisis, no "production" was "so general in circulation nor a thousandth part so forcible in its delineations of approaching misery" as Brothers's *Revealed Knowledge*. The forcefulness of the work rested in part on the fact that it was written "in terms precisely suited to the comprehension of the most ordinary capacity: replete with grammatical faults; destitute alike of harmony of arrangement, and elegance of diction: in the style of a peasant exalting himself above the mightiest of princes."[40]

36. William Cobbett, ed., *Parliamentary History of England*, 36 vols. (London: Hansard, 1806–20), 31: col. 1419.
37. Nathaniel Brassey Halhed, *The Whole of the Testimonies to the Authenticity of the Prophecies and Mission of Richard Brothers* (London, 1795), pp. v–vii.
38. Nathaniel Brassey Halhed, *Testimony on the Authenticity of the Prophecies of Richard Brothers* (London, 1795), p. 2.
39. Ibid., p. 40.   40. Ibid., p. 6.

Halhed confessed that he himself had been "rather negligent of our own sacred writings" but that he had studied the Hindu scriptures. He had discovered that the "Hindu triad" of Brahma, Vishnu, Shiva was "nothing more than poetical personifications of *matter, space*, and *time*." With this training in the critical study of sacred writings, Halhed was able to do as Brothers recommended and discern prophecies of modern European history in the Old and New Testaments. Brothers had come to his knowledge by the "shorter way" of divine inspiration, but Halhed would show "by scientifical proofs, and almost ocular demonstration,"[41] that Brothers's prophecies were true. There followed an interesting but hardly surprising series of identifications. Daniel, for example, promised the destruction of the British Navy in this war. The four Beasts of Daniel were (as Brothers had also said) "four kings *now*": George III, Catherine of Russia, Louis XVI, and Frederick William of Prussia. The prophetic books had predicted the destruction of the papacy, which, Halhed wrote, "is now on its deathbed, expiring in great agony."[42]

Halhed devoted some eight pages of his pamphlet to the reasons why England was the Babylon of Revelation, but here his witty and elegant style often makes what were probably genuine sentiments sound rather hollow. In a curious passage that provoked much amusement among satirical pamphleteers and reviewers, Halhed said that he himself had sold his soul in Parliament. There he sat, "crouched behind the Treasury Bench," with his soul in his hand: "and while I *did* sell my soul, it was all in the true spirit of commercial credit *that so peculiarly distinguishes this country*."[43] He referred, one gathers, to his failure to speak out against Pitt's foreign policy and the war. Brothers had seen Satan dressed in red and white robes, Halhed continued. In that costume, he must have resembled the peers going into Westminster Hall at the "diabolical Impeachment" of Halhed's former chief in the East India Company, Warren Hastings.

Halhed concluded with an argument that he reiterated in other pamphlets in 1795 and in two speeches on Brothers's behalf in the House of Commons: before the man was dismissed as either an impostor or a madman, he should receive a full hearing in order to determine whether his prophecies had in fact come true.

Unquestionably, the public declaration of belief in the claims of Richard Brothers by a member of Parliament and distinguished scholar like Halhed enhanced the prophet's reputation far more than the testimonies of the Bristol druggist William Bryan or the Leeds carpenter John Wright had done. Mrs. Piozzi noted that her friend

41. Ibid., pp. 10, 11, 13.   42. Ibid., pp. 15–22, 30.   43. Ibid., p. 33.

Lyson had written that "since the publication of Mr. Halhed's Pamphlet, numberless People even of Rank and Character run in Flocks to increase the Presumption or feed the Phrenzy of this extraordinary Man Richard Brothers."[44] *Gentleman's Magazine* summarized Halhed's *Testimony* in lengthy quotations, noting that while Halhed might seem "joined the impostor to laugh at him," yet he sat in a room "in the same house, whither so many resorted to see and consult the prophet, and ready to be seen himself—if enquired after."[45] A correspondent expressed shock that a member of the "British Senate" should support the doctrines of Richard Brothers, particularly since these were "written for the understanding, and adapted to the purchase, of the lower class, the bulk of the people, whose minds in these days do not need disquiet." The writer told of asking a friend at dinner how Brothers's two pamphlets had been received in London, whereupon a servant "stept from the sideboard, and respectfully observed to his master, that he had the books we were speaking of, and we should be welcome to see them." The servant said he had gone "more than once" to see Brothers in Paddington.[46]

Several newspapers took notice of Brothers and Halhed in February. The opposition *Post* agreed with Halhed's conclusions concerning the war but said these required "no great depth of knowledge." The *St. James Chronicle* dismissed Halhed's *Testimony* as "this criminal, as well as ridiculous production," and wondered if the soul Halhed said he held in his hand was not instead a trumpet, for "our modern Jonah is deaf, and makes use of an ear-trumpet." And the *Oracle*, in an article under the heading "BROTHERS!" gave a full account of what Brothers planned to do. The story occurs nowhere else, but since it fully conforms to Brothers's own writings, it is probably substantially correct. In May, according to the *Oracle*, "this hopeful monarch of the blind" would go to Cheapside, where he would cast down his wild-rose rod, which, like that of Moses, would become a serpent. He would then summon the Jews to depart for the Holy City, "where this bedlam is to reign over all nations." By the next day, "the *chosen*" would be clear of the city, a third part of which would then be destroyed by an earthquake.[47]

Two of England's leading caricaturists signaled the prophet's sudden prominence in cartoons that appeared in early March. Isaac

---

44. Piozzi, *Thraliana*, 2: 912 (8 February 1795).
45. *Gentleman's Magazine* 65 (1795): 227–28.   46. Ibid., p. 208.
47. *Morning Post*, 19 February 1795, p. 2; *St. James Chronicle*, 17–19 February 1795, p. 4; and *Oracle*, 2 March 1795, p. 3.

Cruikshank depicted a boxing match between a London alderman (who supported peace with the French) and his opponent in a by-election for a seat in the House of Commons. Among the books on the ground, two were particular prominent: *"Brothers Prophecy"* and *"Pain's* [sic] *Rights of Man."* James Gillray, in a cartoon titled "The Prophet of the Hebrews—the Prince of Peace—conducting the Jews to the Promised Land," pictured Brothers leading a crowd up a hill toward the gate of Jerusalem, while St. Paul's and the rest of London collapsed into a flaming pit. Brothers was portrayed with the face of an idiot, and his followers included several stereotyped Jews: shabbily dressed, swarthy, with hooked noses, the first carrying a box of trinkets he had been selling. A connection was also made between Brothers and Jacobinism. Brothers is dressed as a sans-culotte, and on his back in a bag are the leaders of the opposition, Fox, Sheridan, and Lord Stanhope.[48]

Brothers's sudden notoriety inspired at least one rival prophet to denounce him as the agent of Antichrist. In late 1794 and early 1795, Mrs. S. Eyre, of Cecil Street, had a series of long letters published in one of London's daily newspapers. Why the *Oracle*, which published very few letters, should have published four of Mrs. Eyre's rambling prophetic pronouncements is a mystery. The paper had been founded in 1789 by the bookseller John Bell and was devoted largely to gossip and theatrical news. Its politics were confusing. It received a sudsidy from the government, but its editors were closely associated with the opposition, particularly with Richard Brinsley Sheridan and Lord Lauderdale. It is only a guess, but the *Oracle* may have published Mrs. Eyre's letters because her attacks on Brothers consisted of a series of bizarre prophetic pronouncements that no reader of the *Oracle* would take seriously.

Mrs. Eyre made it very clear that the times foretold in the book of Revelation had come. France was the Beast, and Richard Brothers had been sent to lead England to her destruction. "Thou villain," she cried, "to persuade us to peace with that false beast, to our utter destruction. . . . What have you been doing, ye lazy churchmen, to leave this to a woman?" "I will give my life," she continued, "if things do not go well with us; for it is not I that speak, but the Spirit of God that directs me what to say."[49]

48. M. Dorothy George, *A Catalogue of Prints and Drawings in the British Museum: Division I, Political and Personal Satires*, 11 vols. (London: The Trustees, 1870-1954), 7: 161-62; James Gillray, *Works of James Gillray* (New York: Blom, 1968), no. 116.
49. *Oracle*, 18 November 1794, p. 4. On the *Oracle*, see Lucile Werkmeister, *A Newspaper History of England, 1792-1793* (Lincoln: University of Nebraska Press, 1967),

Joanna Southcott, twenty years later, was to announce that she was pregnant with Shiloh, the second Christ. Mother Ann Lee had been declared by her Shaker disciples to be herself the Christ. Sarah Flaxmer had known since 1779 that she would be the one chosen by God to "reveal Satan." Mrs. Eyre, too, saw herself as a woman divinely appointed to prepare the world for the millennium. She was called not only to warn England against the French and Richard Brothers but also to bring about among the women of England a complete reformation of morals. "I shall give my countrywomen a letter called Truth," she wrote, "for a woman and truth are beyond all things." English women "crucified" the Lord daily "by their wicked inventions of plays, balls, routs, cards, and all such devil's tricks. Women must banish every vice, every wickedness, as they are the authors of all wickedness."[50]

Mrs. Eyre had her own interpretation of the vials poured out by the angels in the Last Days. The "sore" which the first angel poured out upon men was surely the terrible yellow fever epidemic which had struck Philadelphia in 1794. America was "that unfortunate country acknowledged by the French," and her destruction had been carried further by the arrival of "that wretch Dr. Priestley, with his pestiferous breath denying the God-head of our blessed Saviour."[51]

It was a terrible time for England, with "devils" in the kingdom and the French "dragon" treatening destruction, but the troubles would end with the Second Coming of Jesus Christ and the inauguration of the millennium, when "butter and honey shall all eat that are left in the land . . . the day is at hand when none can work, the great Sabbath of the Most High God."[52]

On 4 March, the *Times,* a subsidized newspaper in which the government frequently "placed" stories, devoted a long column to "the Great Prophet of Paddington Street." It noted that "great political convulsions have always been accompanied by great moral revolutions." Just as the French Revolution had been preceded by the formation of subversive sects like the mesmerists and by individuals like Dom Gerle and Suzette Labrousse, so now there were in England men "who propose to employ the same means to attain their end." The *Times*'s account was hostile to Brothers, and its tone was ironic, but it showed some perception in suggesting that there was a direct

pp. 23, 117; and Stanley Morison, *John Bell, 1745–1831* (Cambridge: Printed for the author at the University Press, 1930), pp. 29–30.
50. *Oracle,* 31 March 1795, p. 2; and 2 April 1795, p. 2.
51. Ibid., 26 January 1795, p. 3.   52. Ibid., 2 April 1795, p. 2.

connection between Brothers's own experiences and his prophecies. Having failed to secure his navy pay on his own terms and having been sent to the workhouse, Brothers was told by God the next night that the Admiralty would be punished. Confined to Newgate and fed a penny loaf of bread, Brothers decided that London was a Babylon and must be destroyed. When the war caused Brothers's mind to be *"revolutionarily exalted,"* he wrote the king, the queen, and the ministers that France had been chosen to execute God's plan. Rebuffed, he now prophesied that "universal destruction" would begin on the first of the following June.[53]

No sooner did the *Times*'s account reach the streets than Brothers was arrested. On the basis of an Elizabethan statute, he was charged with "unlawfully, maliciously, and wickedly writing, printing, and publishing various fantastical prophecies, with intent to create dissensions, and other disturbances within this realm." The contemporary accounts agree that Brothers, an unusually large and powerful man, offered no resistance. He told the messengers who had come to arrest him that they must "oblige" him to get into the coach, "as then his prophecy would be fulfilled," and "when seated in the coach, he exclaimed with great energy, 'Now my prophecy is fulfilled,' after which he was silent and submissive."[54] The *European Magazine* reported further that the messengers had "much more danger to apprehend from the fury of the multitude, but even that, with some difficulty, they escaped." Taken before the Privy Council, "he comported himself with great dignity and coolness." He insisted that he "held an immediate communication with GOD, as asserted in his writings."[55]

On 27 March, upon the recommendation of two physicians, Brothers was declared insane and placed in a private madhouse located in a large mansion in Islington. There he remained until 1806.

On 31 March, Nathaniel Halhed made a speech in the House of Commons that Southey called "the most extraordinary perhaps that ever was delivered to a legislative assembly." The speech was given before a full house, which listened in respectful silence. Halhed again urged his colleagues to compare Brothers's statements with the Bible, on which the prophet claimed to base them, and he mocked, with elegant irony, the government's illogicality in arresting a man for treason and then confining him as a lunatic. Halhed emphasized the fact that very respectable persons visited Brothers—

53. *Times*, 4 March 1795, p. 3.   54. *European Magazine* 27 (1795): 217.
55. *Oracle*, 6 March 1795, p. 2.

persons who would never have gone to see him had they thought him a traitor. "His house, in the forenoon, was constantly filled by persons of quality and fortune, of both sexes, and the street crowded with their carriages."[56] If it was his books that had caused Brothers to be arrested, Halhed was surprised that they had been allowed to continue to circulate, especially since their sale had "most rapidly and inconceivably increased since the confinement of their author." Plenty of "scandalous" matter appeared daily in London in pamphlets, newspapers, and printed cartoons. Halhed remarked ironically that if he announced that he was going to fly over London to Westminster Abbey and demand that the king seat him on the throne and kiss his big toe, most people would consider him mad, but he certainly would "not dream of being apprehended for treason" for the performance. At issue were two miracles. The first was Richard Brothers's turning his rod into a serpent and then, accompanied by an angel in a "form of fire," going to George III to receive his crown. The second was the king's *handing* his crown and his authority to an obscure subject. Since these were miracles, the prophet's imprisonment was no obstacle to their fulfillment. Halhed was no "enthusiast," he said, but surely the Bible was correct that if "this work be of men, it will come to nought; but if it be of God, ye cannot overthrow it."

Halhed urged the members to give their leisure to *Revealed Knowledge*, as he had done. He offered his own copy, with copious notes, for the use of any member who wanted to examine it. He moved that Brothers's claims be examined by the House, but his motion found no seconder. Like the National Assembly when Dom Gerle had advanced Suzette Labrousse's claims in a similar fashion in 1790, the House of Commons moved to the Order of the Day.

In the months following Richard Brothers's arrest, the flood of pamphlets supporting or rejecting his claims continued unabated. The newspapers carried few news stories about the affair, but their columns nevertheless indicate that public interest in Brothers continued to run high. In the last of her letters to the *Oracle*, Mrs. Eyre criticized the archbishop of Canterbury for failing to see that Brothers was in fact the false prophet predicted in Revelation, come to prepare the world for the millennium: *"If you had one grain of faith, you would rejoice that this man was come to give you warning of our*

56. Robert Southey, *Letters from England*, ed. and intro. by Jack Simmons (London: Cresset, 1951), p. 432. Halhed's speech was quoted extensively in a number of London newspapers. It is printed in Cobbett, ed., *Parliamentary History of England*, 31: cols. 1414–21.

Lord and Saviour's approach, that you may prepare all people, to expect our *real* Lord and Saviour."[57]

The *Oracle* also advertised the publication of the first three numbers of a weekly periodical called *The World's Doom; or, Cabinet of Fate Unlocked*. It sounds very like Pierre Pontard's *Journal prophétique*; it was to be "an ample collection of all Ancient and Modern Prophecies which relate to the present and nearly approaching times . . . many of them from original Manuscripts now in the hands of the Editor." The periodical would be "embellished with elegant Portraits of Mr. Brothers, N. B. Halhed, Esq., &c. &c."[58] The publisher was the bookseller B. Crosby, at whose shop "the Whole of the late prophetic Pamphlets" could be had.[59]

The prophecies of Richard Brothers may have been a matter of profound significance for some; for others, they were a fashionable topic of the day. *Harrison's Lady's Pocket Magazine* announced that its current issue contained three portraits: the Prince of Wales, Richard Brothers, and the Italian Opera House in the Haymarket.[60] And in St. George's Fields, where Southey had seen the "Surprising Large Child," the Royal Circus offered a pantomime called "The Prophecy; or, Mountains in Labour": "The Crisis being arrived, and the event dreaded, causes a general consternation in the minds of the Pantomimic Group, till Mirth, with all-inspiring Magic, brings forth the fantastic Sprite, Harlequin, to avert the Prophet."[61]

Just as Suzette Labrousse's followers had circulated testimonies supporting her prophetic claims, so did Richard Brothers's, with the significant difference that the testimonies to Brothers were all printed pamphlets, openly sold in shops and bookstalls throughout England. John Wright became a bookseller, specializing in works by and about Brothers. George Riebau called himself "bookseller to the Prince of the Hebrews." In late April 1795, he listed fifteen testimonies in support of the prophet that were available at his shop.[62] The testimonies are too few and too diverse to make possible any generalizations about the kinds of people who became followers. Obviously, those who wrote the pamplets tended to be either the most zealous or the most literate of the converts. All the testimonies reflect a general acceptance of both the significance of signs and portents and

---

57. *Oracle*, 2 April 1795, p. 2.
58. Ibid., 4 April 1795, p. 1. I have been unable to locate any copies of the periodical.
59. *E. Johnson's British Gazette and Sunday Monitor*, 5 April 1795, p. 1.
60. Ibid.   61. *Oracle*, 10 April 1795, p. 1.
62. The list of publications is found on the back cover of William Wetherell, *An Additional Testimony in Favour of Richard Brothers* (London, 1795).

the literal fulfillment of scriptural prophecy. It would be tedious to deal in any detail with them, and a summary of some of their arguments will suffice. One follower testified that he had doubted the authenticity of the biblical prophets, but then "in one moment (*oh, happy*, though *alarming moment*)," God granted him understanding, and he then "knew the possibility of MR. BROTHERS bearing the divine mission of his God, and being spoken to by Angels." God had allowed Brothers to be imprisoned in order "to make room for his further succeeding mysteries."[63]

Another convert quoted a long passage from Jeremiah predicting that "evil" would "go forth from nation to nation." Surely, he argued, this was connected "with the present war—the horrible destruction of the human species within the tropics, and the recent and bloody massacres in Poland."[64] In general, however, the war was not given the same attention by Brothers's less distinguished followers that Halhed gave it.

Several testimonies concentrated on the argument that Brothers *might* be a prophet sent from God, and it would therefore be dangerous to ignore him. William Wetherell, for example, pointed out that Elias had promised that God would send someone in the Last Days to warn mankind and to collect the chosen people, "and *who* can prove that Mr. BROTHERS is *not* the man?"[65] An anonymous pamphlet titled *Look before You Leap* warned that England must beware the fate of the Jews who rejected Jesus. God's ways were "INSCRUTABLE TO MAN . . . and so, we should be very careful how we interfere with what may be his divine pleasure."[66] J. Crease of Bath argued that since Brothers's followers were "respectable characters" and men of "righteousness and sound integrity," the prophet might indeed be sent from God as he said he was.[67]

Another believer wrote that he had paid little attention to the Bible until he chanced upon a copy of Brothers's prophecies. He began to read the Bible, studies of the Apocalypse, and the sermons of Dr. Gill, "who foretold in a wonderful manner the revolution in France." Like Halhed, he was impressed with Brothers's manner. There was "*je ne sçai quoi*, something so striking in his dress, and so

63. William Sales, *Truth or Not Truth; or, Discourse on the Prophets* (London, 1795), pp. 14, 19.
64. Samuel Whitchurch, *Another Witness! or, A Further Testimony in Favour of Richard Brothers* (London, 1795), pp. 15–16.
65. Wetherell, *Additional Testimony*, p. 8.
66. *Look before You Leap* (London, 1795), pp. 4, 17.
67. J. Crease, *Prophecies Fulfilling; or, The Dawn of the Perfect Day* (London, 1795), pp. 1, 6.

awful in his countenance."[68] Brothers's former landlady, Mrs. Green, was also impressed. In her case, the prophet even appeared in her dreams. Some months after he had left the workhouse, she had dreamed of seeing him surrounded by a crowd. A voice said to her, "How do you know, but He is *John the Baptist*." She told of several other dreams in which a tall man whom she took to be Brothers figured prominently. After having read his *Revealed Knowledge*, she had prayed to God to "direct" her and had been rewarded with an "open vision" in which a "fine" man six feet tall appeared before her window in a sky the color of blood.[69] There is nothing in the extant literature of French popular religion of the period remotely like the testimonies of visions, dreams, and omens that were produced in support of Richard Brothers. Both they and the elaborate analyses of Scripture that Brothers and many of his supporters engaged in indicate that the 1790s revived most of the oddities that had characterized the excited millenarianism of the seventeenth-century sectarians.

Some of the individuals who wrote in opposition to Brothers's claims used arguments and language markedly similar to those of his followers. Among the most zealous antagonists was William Huntington, who called himself the Sinner Saved.[70] Illegitimate, barely educated, and a onetime coal-heaver, Huntington had for thirteen years been one of the most successful preachers in London, at Providence Chapel in Oxford Market. Himself a millenarian and prophet of sorts, he later predicted the downfall of Napoleon and the imminent triumph but ultimate downfall of popery. A strict Calvinist, Huntington was assured by Jesus that he was one of the elect. In 1795 he was also a convinced supporter of the king and the war. His sermons, like the letters of Mrs. Eyre, are an indication that the religious "public" was deeply divided on the issues of war and prophecy in the 1790s.

Huntington had first determined to speak and write against Brothers because of the wide credence that the latter's false prophecies were receiving. Apparently, some members of his own Providence Chapel had become followers of Brothers, for Huntington re-

68. Henry Francis Offley, *Richard Brothers, Neither a Madman Nor an Imposter* (London, 1795), pp. xxii, 6–7.
69. Green, *Letter to the Publisher*, pp. 5–6, 7–8.
70. *Dictionary of National Biography*, 1921–22 ed., s.v. "Huntington, William, S.S." by James McMullen Rigg; Southey, *Letters from England*, p. 330; William Hamilton Reid, *The Rise and Dissolution of the Infidel Societies of the Metropolis* (London, 1800), p. 46; and Thomas Wright, *The Life of William Huntington, S.S.* (London, 1909), pp. 105–9.

minded his congregation in 1797 that when "the devil sent forth one of his drummers to beat a march to the Holy Land," he had told them it was "a trick of the devil, which gave great offence to some, who soon after prepared for the journey; but they have been ashamed to show their heads since."[71] Huntington's objections were in part patriotic. Like the unspeakable Tom Paine, Brothers condemned the British monarchy and predicted its downfall, whereas, in Huntington's opinion, "the principal seat of the church of God in this day is Great Britain; . . . there is but very little of the power of godliness elsewhere; nor is there much of it here."[72] Later, in 1798, he rejoiced that "what with hanging, transporting, and going to America, God is causing the evil spirits to pass out of the land."[73]

Equally important, Huntington objected to Brothers's version of the millenium. It was not true that the time had come for the restoration of the Jews. The angel proclaiming the fall of Babylon and the angel bearing the "Everlasting Gospel" must first appear. Brothers held that the "new heavens and the new earth" (2 Peter) meant the regeneration of mankind, but the passage must be understood literally: the heavens would melt away and the earth be burnt up. It was not true, as Brothers claimed, that the thunder of January 1791 had been the voice of one of the angels of Revelation. This had been "only common, not mystical thunder; and common thunder is not the voice of angels, but the voice of God."[74]

Aside from Huntington and Mrs. Eyre, those who wrote against Brothers in 1795 do not tell us much about the state of popular religion in England. Most of the writings were either feeble attempts at humor at the prophet's expense or else tedious refutations of his theology. One effort which received wide praise in the literary reviews was signed with the name George Horne, the late bishop of Norwich and a noted religious controversialist. Having denied in detail and at great length the prophetic interpretations of Brothers and Halhed, it concluded: "God has already *revealed* his will, and it is impious to suppose that, *after his Son*, he would send such an humble prophet as—Brothers."[75]

71. William Huntington, *A Watchword and Warning from the Walls of Zion* (London, 1798), pp. 55–56. See also Huntington, *The Lying Prophet Examined, and His False Predictions Discovered* (London, 1795), preface; and Huntington, *Discoveries and Cautions from the Streets of Zion* (London, 1798), p. 10.
72. Huntington, *Watchword and Warning*, p. 65.
73. Huntington, *Discoveries and Cautions*, pp. 37–38.
74. Huntington, *Lying Prophet Examined*, pp. 8, 27, 45.
75. Walley C. Oulton, *Sound Argument Dictated by Common Sense* (Oxford, 1795), p. 52.

N. B. Halhed continued to write in support of Brothers, but his emphasis shifted from the truth of the prophecies to the injustice of the prophet's condemnation. On 21 April, Halhed again addressed the House. Once again, a large crowd heard him in respectful silence, and once again his motion failed to receive a second. This time Halhed wanted Parliament to examine the warrant for Brothers's arrest. He wished to know whether the man was a traitor or a madman, for he certainly could not be both at once. He pressed the same point in two pamphlets, denouncing "this heterogeneous amalgam of treason and lunacy, to form one indefinable crime."[76] The tone of Halhed's pamphlets was not entirely what one would expect of a scholarly politician. He concluded his *Letters to Lord Loughborough* by pointing out to the lord chancellor that Brothers had predicted in his books that God would destroy London if Brothers were harmed. God had recently desolated Lisbon and Calabria; surely it was not worth while to risk the safety of London "for the mere gratification of medical caprice." For, "if violence is done to Mr. Brothers, and an earthquake *should happen*, how will you persuade mankind, that it is a mere natural phenomenon? . . ."[77]

All the biographies of Brothers miss an important fact in connection with the events of 1795. Surprising though it may be, there clearly was widespread apprehension that Brothers's prophecies would come true and that London would be destroyed by earthquake on 4 June, the king's official birthday. The contemporary descriptions of the excitement are not numerous, but they exist. William Huntington wrote in 1795 that many wanted to flee London "that they might escape Mr. Brothers's predicted destruction of this city," and some in fact closed their businesses in preparation. The retired soldier John Stedman, a man utterly unconnected with the controversy over Brothers, noted in his private journal on 5 June, "London disloyal, superstitious, villainous, and infamous. An earthquake prophesied by Brothers. Many leave town."[78]

About a month earlier, that excellent observer Robert Southey had written to his brother from Bath: "Richard Brothers makes a strange outcry . . . some Mr. Charles Cotter has had a vision and he

---

76. Nathaniel Brassey Halhed, *Two Letters to the Right Honourable Lord Loughborough, Lord High Chancellor of England, on the Present Confinement of Richard Brothers in a Private Mad-House* (London, 1795), p. 8. See also Halhed, *Essay on the Slain Lamb* (London, 1795).
77. Halhed, *Two Letters to the Right Honorable Lord Loughborough*, pp. 9–10.
78. Thompson, *Making of the English Working Class*, p. 127; Timbs, *English Eccentrics*, pp. 191–93; Huntington, *Lying Prophet Examined*, p. v; and Stedman, *Journal*, p. 382.

declares that London will be destroyed by an earthquake next week. Many very many have left town on the strength of this wiseacres revelation."[79] The *Oracle*, in an article headlined "Another Imposter?" told the same story: "As the contents of the following handbill, industriously circulated, have operated so far on the public credulity that THOUSANDS ARE PREPARING TO LEAVE LONDON, we hope the Magistrates will adopt effectual measures to check the farther progress of these false alarms." The handbill consisted of two letters dated 15 and 19 April and signed "Christopher Cotter," the name of a seventeenth-century Bohemian prophet who had been included in one of the prophetic collections of the preceding year. The author stated that while he was walking home, a man had stopped him and said, "*Look, Look, Look,* for the Lord's wrath is on the land." He looked at the sky, then back toward the man, but he had disappeared. Then, around a star in the north, he saw nine angels with trumpets, and out of the star "came forth a man in purple robes with a white wand in his hand." The man told "Cotter" that there would be an earthquake in twenty-nine days; London would be "sunk;" and then the French would land in Wales and sweep across the island. Three days before the city fell, Satan would appear there, "as a wolf in sheep's clothing." He concluded the first letter: "I have taken the first opportunity to acquaint you of it, *that it may be published as a warning* to all citizens to prepare for that AWFUL DAY." The second letter concerned Richard Brothers, who had appeared to the author "and revealed the wonderful things that would come to pass, within these four weeks."[80]

Brothers himself also predicted an earthquake for 4 June. He had been anticipating disaster for some years but had interceded with God to spare London for the time being. By late 1794, he had reached the firm conviction that London's destruction would be the signal for him to assume his kingly role. In the last pages of *Revealed Knowledge*, he recorded that the Lord had told him on 25 October 1794 that between then and "the Beginning of the Month called June 1795," Brothers would perform the Mosaic miracle of changing his rod into a serpent, thus revealing himself to the Jews as their leader. Five of the Seals described in the book of Revelation had already been opened. The opening of the Sixth Seal would bring not only the restoration of the Jews to their homeland but also earthquakes, "Storms of Wind, Hail, and showers of Rain, with violent

79. Robert Southey, *New Letters*, ed. Kenneth Curry, 2 vols. (New York: Columbia University Press, 1965), 1: 95 (9 May 1795).
80. *Oracle*, 5 May 1795, pp. 2–3.

Thundering and Lightning."[81] On 5 March 1795, Brothers wrote a letter to the lord chancellor informing him that the Lord's kingdom would commence by the beginning of June.[82]

Several of the testimonies to Brothers warned that a terrible destruction awaited the English people if they did not heed the prophet. William Wetherell, for example, wrote at the end of April that "the time of his revelation must necessarily happen before another month is at an end, *perhaps* another fortnight, and then the world will be convinced, *too late I fear*."[83] George Riebau and John Wright launched yet another prophetic collection in late April, with the splendid title *God's Awful Warnings to a Giddy, Careless, Sinful World*. They invited their readers to contribute portents of which they had knowledge for inclusion in future installments: "The account of any authentic vision, meteors, signs, or remarkable judgments, communicated on a line directed to J. W., no. 48, Dorset-street Manchester square, or G. R., no. 439, Strand, (post paid), will be thankfully received." Only the first installment was published: a fairly unremarkable collection of visions, dreams, meteors, and the like, many of them dating from the seventeenth century. It did include, however, the testimony of Ann Ash, to whom an unusually tall man said on 4 March that thousands of unbelievers "would perish, *in this metropolis*" within three months.[84]

There is one more indication that Brothers's prophecy of an earthquake on the fourth of June was a matter of general knowledge. On that day, James Gillray, the most celebrated cartoonist of his day, published a cartoon titled "Presages of the Millennium, with the Destruction of the Faithful, as Revealed to R. Brothers."[85]

The only detailed account of the popular response on 4 June is to be found in the *Recollections* of John Binns. A radical printer in 1795 and one of the leaders of the London Corresponding Society, Binns wrote his memoirs sixty years later, after a long and successful political and business career in Pennsylvania. The distance in time from the events he was describing makes it hard to believe that Binns could recall in such detail the night of 4 June 1795. However, Binn's account of his political activities can be checked against other sources, and it is accurate, as are his recollections of Joseph Priest-

81. Brothers, *Revealed Knowledge*, 2: 86.
82. *Ninth Report of the Historical Manuscripts Commission, Part 2* (London, 1884), p. 486.
83. Wetherell, *Additional Testimony*, p. 10.
84. George Riebau and John Wright, eds., *God's Awful Warnings to a Giddy, Careless, Sinful World* (London, 1795), p. 1.
85. Gillray, *Works*, no. 127.

ley's last years, when Binns was printing the *History of Christianity* for him. And finally, Binn's account is consistent with the evidence that a state of millenarian excitement did exist in May and June 1795.

Binns wrote that when Brothers published his prophecy that London would be destroyed for its sins by earthquake on 4 June, "it would be difficult . . . to convey an adequate idea of the nature and extent of the fears and apprehensions to which this prediction gave birth." Binns was on his way to a meeting of the London Corresponding Society on that evening, when a terrible storm, with wind, rain, and lightning, erupted. He went into the barroom of a hotel for shelter and found fifty or sixty men and women there, with their children. "It seemed to me," he wrote, "that every one in the room knew something of Brothers's prophecy, and of the time at which it was to be fulfilled. . . . There was a general feeling and expression of alarm."[86]

Gentleman's Magazine confirms Binns's meteorological recollections. A violent thunderstorm began between seven and eight on that evening, accompanied by heavy rain and hail. There were also terrible storms in the north of England, "attended by the most awful lightning." The inhabitants were "overcome with terror and dismay." Two months later, a correspondent who signed himself "Anti-Bedlamite" remarked in the *Oracle* that on the day that the mad Richard Brothers had predicted an earthquake, there had indeed been a deluge.[87]

A few days after the storm, Binns wrote, he went to call on Brothers. Brothers assured him, "with all solemnity and placidity of manner, that the earthquake had, at his earnest and oft-repeated intercession, been, by the Almighty postponed, and the destruction of London averted." Binns continued to call on him for some months, "regarding him as insane on the one subject, sane on all others, and intelligent on many."[88] Was Binns, a stranger, permitted to visit a notorious madman in this fashion? It does not seem likely.

Yet Brothers was able to publish a number of letters and pamphlets while confined in Dr. Simmons's madhouse, and in *Exposition of the Trinity*, published by Riebau at the end of October, Brothers explained the events of 4 June in a manner very similar to Binns's reported conversation with him. The thunder on that evening was the voice of the angel mentioned in the fourteenth chapter of Revelation who preaches the Everlasting Gospel, saying, "Fear God, . . . for

86. John Binns, *Recollections* (Philadelphia: By the author, 1854), pp. 48–50.
87. *Gentleman's Magazine* 65 (1795); 517–18; *Oracle*, 8 August 1795, p. 2.
88. Binns, *Recollections*, p. 50.

the hour (meaning the *year*) of his judgement is come." The Sixth and Seventh Seals were now opened and "in this year, the consequences . . . will be feelingly known." Unless he were released from the madhouse, "death will take place on thousands; London falls, and the British empire sinks, never, never to rise any more."[89]

The unusual and violent weather persisted throughout 1795, as both *Gentleman's Magazine* and Mrs. Piozzi were careful to note. In November, there was even an earthquake, which Mrs. Piozzi believed had occurred on the day predicted by Brothers. Yet despite the weather, the continued economic and political crisis, and the continuing circulation of the writings of Brothers and his supporters, the *Analytical Review* was probably correct when it wrote in August that "Public curiosity, with respect to the *prophecies* of Mr. Brothers, is, we apprehend, by this time nearly exhausted."[90] In fact, the interest in prophecies in general seems to have abated for the time being, to rise again after 1800, when Napoleon and Joanna Southcott provided a combination even more heady than the Jacobins, the famine, and Richard Brothers.

89. Brothers, *Exposition of the Trinity*, pp. 36, 43–44.
90. Piozzi, *Thraliana* 2: 946; *Gentleman's Magazine* 65 (1795): 960–64; and *Analytical Review* 22 (1795): 201.

CHAPTER 9

Brothers, Southcott, and the "Chiliasm of Despair"

RICHARD Brothers lived for another thirty years after his arrest and confinement in 1795. He continued to call himself the Prince of the Hebrews and to make elaborate plans for the day when God would enable him to rule the world from Jerusalem. Gradually, his followers fell away as Brothers retreated into the world of his delusions. He continued to write on a variety of subjects, but his convictions became increasingly peculiar.

Brothers blamed William Pitt for most of his misfortune. He had described the prime minister in *Revealed Knowledge* as a hidden Jew specially marked by God to aid Brothers in his mission, but Pitt now became the villain whose persecution of the prophet fulfilled the prediction of St. John the Divine by making Brothers "the slain Lamb."[1]

In 1806, after Pitt had died, the lord chancellor removed the warrant for high treason and ordered Brothers's release from the asylum, but he refused to lift the lunacy judgment, possibly because of George III's hostility to the prophet. In the last decades of Brothers's life, his most zealous disciple was a Scottish lawyer named John Finlayson, with whom he lived until his death. Finlayson had first heard of Brothers from reading Halhed's first speech to Parliament in the newspapers in 1795. Finlayson obtained a copy of *Revealed Knowledge*, which was not then available in Scotland, read it, and was convinced. In 1797, he quit his legal practice in order to go to London and serve Richard Brothers.[2] He devoted the rest of his long life to arranging for the publication of the prophet's later works, several of

---

1. Richard Brothers, *A Description of Jerusalem: Its Houses and Streets* (London, 1801[1802]), p. 153.
2. John Finlayson, *An Admonition to the People of All Countries, That Our Saviour's Second Coming Is at Hand* (Edinburgh, 1797), pp. 47–49; John Finlayson, *The Last Trumpet and the Flying Angel* (London, 1849), pp. 15–17.

which were expensive volumes containing numerous colored illustrations of the palaces, uniforms, and flags of the New Jerusalem. He also conducted a lengthy litigation to force the government to grant him, with compound interest, the back pay he contended that the Royal Navy still owed to Brothers.

Finlayson named four others, including Captain Hanchett and George Riebau, as still connected with Brothers at the time of his death. Almost all the rest had fallen away, many to take up the cause of Joanna Southcott, the prophetess whose career in some respects parallels Catherine Théot's but whose fame in her own lifetime surpassed even that of Brothers.

Neither of the two "witnesses" who had given the first public testimony to belief in Brothers, John Wright and William Bryan, seems to have retained his convictions to the end. John Wright disappeared from sight. William Bryan became the "herbal doctor of Hoddesdon;" it is not known whether he remained a millenarian, but it would be surprising if a man of his intense religiosity had abandoned his beliefs very readily. As to the few others whose names are known, they recall the Midwestern cult, so well described in *When Prophecy Fails*,[3] that successfully weathered "disconfirmation" when a flying saucer did not arrive to save them from the imminent destruction of the earth. Similarly, the committed core of Brothers's followers remained believers despite God's failure to destroy London by earthquake and despite Brothers's incarceration in a madhouse. They remained loyal to him for several years, then left him for a prophetess whose conception of the millennium they found more congenial in the changed political climate after 1800.

What follows does not pretend to give the full story of Joanna Southcott and the welter of Southcottian sects that based themselves on her prophecies. G. M. Balleine has narrated the story of Joanna and her successors capably, and a social history of the Southcottians would require a thorough exploration of provincial libraries and archives, particularly in Yorkshire and the West Country.

Having in the previous chapters examined the kinds of traditions, popular beliefs, and religious undercurrents that for a brief period focused on the person of Richard Brothers, I now want to describe, at least tentatively, the reasons for the Brothers's almost total isolation ten years later. It is not enough to say that he was a prophet who "failed." For the committed believers, this was nearly irrelevant.

3. Lionel Festinger, Henry W. Reichen, and Stanley Schlachter, *When Prophecy Fails* (Minneapolis: University of Minnesota Press, 1956), pp. 192–205, 231–33. A similar episode is described at the end of Alison Lurie's novel, *Imaginary Friends* (New York: Coward, McCann, 1967).

Several disciples, in the years after 1795, wrote pamphlets that claimed that some of Brothers's prophecies had already come true and that the rest would soon be fulfilled. For example, in 1799, Thomas Holcroft, during a visit from William Sharp, teased the engraver about Brothers. "I asked him," Holcroft wrote, "why the earthquake did not happen at the time positively appointed by Brothers; and he said, that unless I were one of the inspired, it was a thing he could not explain."[4]

One would expect Napoleon to have inspired, after 1799, the same sorts of millenarian hopes and fears in people like Sharp that the Jacobins had aroused in 1794, but this does not seem to have been the case. There were plenty of people, however, who took Napoleon to be Antichrist. Mrs. Piozzi noted that many were saying that he was "the Devil Incarnate, the Appolyon mentioned in Scripture."[5] She believed that his name in the Corsican dialect was N'Apollione, "the Destroyer," and "he does come forwards followed by a Cloud of Locusts from ye bottomless Pit."[6] She learned from the ladies of her village in Wales that Napoleon's titles, translated into Roman numerals, totaled 666.[7] Earlier, in 1798, Mrs. Piozzi and many others had looked for the fulfillment of prophecy in Napoleon's conquest of Rome and in deposition of the Pope. Mrs. Piozzi had wondered if perhaps Napoleon would in addition be "ye Instrument of Jewish Restoration."

With the Pope deposed and governments destroyed, "it goes like a Wheel down Hill . . . ; we shall have no Kings in Europe at all I suppose soon. All over!" Mrs. Piozzi wrote in 1799 that the prophetic three years and a half had elapsed since Collot d'Herbois had defiled the Christian religion during his suppression of the rebellion at Lyons. She had thought that the teachings of the Bible would have revived by now. ". . . but either I am mistaken,—or blinded like the Men who walked to Emmaus. . . . I verily *did* once believe the Jews would have been called by *now*: but perhaps the Turkish Empire must end first."[8]

Thus, like Joseph Priestley, whose doctrines she so deplored, Mrs. Piozzi at the end of the century was disappointed, puzzled, but not yet

4. Thomas Holcroft, *The Life of Thomas Holcroft,* ed. Elbridge Colby, 2 vols. (London: Constable, 1925), 2: 246.
5. Hester Thrale Piozzi, *Thraliana: The Diary of Mrs. Hester Lynch Thrale, 1776–1809,* ed. Katherine C. Balderston, 2d ed., 2 vols. (Oxford: Clarendon Press, 1951), 2: 1003.
6. Hester Thrale Piozzi, *Retrospection; or, A Review of the Most Important Events, Characters, Situations, and Their Consequences Which the Last Eighteen Hundred Years Have Presented to the View of Mankind,* 2 vols. (London, 1801), 2: 523.
7. Hester Thrale Piozzi, *Piozzi Marginalia, Comprising Some Extracts from Manuscripts of Hester Lynch Piozzi and Annotations from Her Books* (Cambridge: Harvard University Press, 1925), pp. 118, 408–09.
8. Piozzi, *Thraliana,* 2: 988, 990, 995–96.

despairing in her hopes that the millennium was at hand. Like Priestley, she tried to fit Napoleon into the prophetic scheme, but without much success. All she could do was await the restoration of the Jews or one of the other prophetic events. Perhaps the lost tribes would turn up in Afghanistan, or Mungo Park would find them during his explorations in Africa.[9]

The interpretation of current events in the light of scripture continued to be a popular activity for the faithful. The *New Annual Register* in 1806 devoted a whole section in its book reviews to the topic. But while there were a few new wrinkles, the political interpretation of prophecy followed the general lines already set down in the early 1790s.

In 1800, Francis Dobbs announced in the Irish Parliament that Christ was coming very soon—to Ireland. In 1806, Bishop Samuel Horsley, one of Priestley's most tenacious antagonists, wrote his brother that Napoleon was going to conquer Europe, settle the Jews in Palestine, and set himself up as a false Messiah until the Jews turned on him and destroyed him.[10] Both William Blake and Richard Brothers were examining the possibility that the Druids of England had been the chosen people. In 1813, a London stationer named Ralph Wedgwood declared that Napoleon was the Beast of Revelation, whose destruction would be accomplished by Alexander of Russia, the conqueror come out of the North, and by "British Israel," the kingdom that had "worshipped the true god" and been "the peculiar possession of the Messiah since the time of the Druids."[11]

E. P. Thompson has described the Southcottian movement as the "chiliasm of despair," a product of the terrible conditions of life during the early Industrial Revolution.[12] The phrase is a good one, but the sense in which Thompson uses it is wrong. The "despair" that is reflected in the writings of Southcott and his disciples was that the earthly millennium envisaged in the 1790s by Jacobins, English radicals, and millenarians alike would never be achieved. It

9. Piozzi, *Retrospection*, 2: 538; Piozzi, *Thraliana*, 2: 1000.
10. *New Annual Register* (1806), pp. 291–93; Richard Soloway, *Prelates and People: Ecclesiastical Social Thought in England, 1783–1852* (London: Routledge & Kegan Paul, 1969), p. 40.
11. Ralph Wedgwood, *The Book of Remembrance* (London, 1814), pp. xiv, xvii, 38, 77.
12. E. P. Thompson, *The Making of the English Working Class*, rev. ed. (Harmondsworth: Penguin Books, 1968), pp. 420–28, 878–83. Thompson's statement that most Southcottians were poor is denied by John Evans, a one-time believer, in his very informative *Sketch of the Various Denominations of the Christian World*, corrected and brought down to the present day by J. H. Bransby, 18th ed. (London: Longman & Co., 1842), pp. 284–85; and by John F. C. Harrison, *Quest for the New Moral World: Robert Owen and the Owenites in Britain and America* (New York: Charles Scribner's Sons, 1969), p. 111.

was not prophecy that had failed; it was the Revolution. One result was the abandonment by Joanna and her followers of the sort of politicoreligious analysis of events that had occupied men as dissimilar as Pierre Pontard, Joseph Priestley, and Richard Brothers. Southcott's ideas were perhaps closer than theirs to the principal thread of the tradition that extended back to Joachim of Fiore. The "Long-wished-for Revolution," she explained in 1806, would come when Satan's power had been destroyed and men sinned no more. The French Revolution was not that revolution: "What happiness hath it caused to mankind[?] Only deluged Europe with blood."[13] That same year, the Lord assured Joanna that Brothers's followers would become hers, as they turned "from what they thought [was] an earthly prince endowed with all power—but now begin to see it must be a heavenly one to complete their happiness."[14]

Even William Sharp, so eager for the triumph of the Jacobins and seeing in Napoleon's victories in 1799 the hand of God, could write only four years later that sin was the source of all the world's evil, which would be overcome only "by the second coming of Christ in spirit."[15]

Even Richard Brothers had abandoned some of his earlier political convictions in 1800. He no longer warned the rulers of England of the terrible fate that awaited them if they failed to assist God's agents, the French. All governments were good and should be loyally supported by their subjects. He singled out for praise the same Catherine the Great whom six years earlier he had described as one of the four Beasts of the book of Daniel.[16]

Brothers wrote the king who had placed him in the asylum, asking for money with which to buy seed and ploughs for the New Jerusalem:

> Your majesty, I hope, will remain my friend,
> To assist me forward to my journey's end.
> For which, your Majesty I'll love most true,
> And all good men that will assist the Jew.[17]

13. Joanna Southcott, *The Long-wished-for Revolution Announced to Be at Hand . . .* (London, 1806), pp. 3, 9.

14. Joanna Southcott, *Communication in Answer to Mr. Brothers's Book and a Vision He Had of Two Suns* (Bradford, 1859), p. 9; dated 3 May 1806 and originally published in that year.

15. William Sharp, introduction to Joanna Southcott, *Divine and Spiritual Communications* (London, 1803), p. vi; dated 25 December 1803.

16. Richard Brothers, *Wisdom and Duty* (London, 1805), pp. 3, 22; dated 3 January 1801.

17. Richard Brothers, *A Letter to His Majesty, and One to Her Majesty. Also a Poem, with a Dissertation on the Fall of Eve and an Address to Five Eminent Councillors* (London, 1802), p. 21.

He compiled lists of the supplies he would requisition for his Jews from all countries of the earth, not forgetting the kingdoms of Azem, Aracan, Ava, Siam, Cambodia, and Cochinchina. Among his more novel proposals was the dismantling of the pyramids so that the stones could be used to build Jerusalem.[18] He planned in detail every aspect of his kingdom, in a kind of mad anticipation of the communitarian projects of the Owenites and Fourierists of the next decades.

Brothers also launched an attack upon the teachings of Copernicus and Newton. The notion that the earth revolved around the sun was "the most erroneous, wild, and unnatural, that ever entered the imagination." He had first reached that conclusion many years before while serving in the Royal Navy, for if the earth moved, "the sea being a loose moveable body, with a ship and convoy sailing on it, would be quickly shook off the earth." Genesis was literally true: the story of creation "was, as God himself has informed me, communicated by himself to Adam."[19] The knowledge was passed from generation to generation until Noah eventually wrote it down.

What does not seem to have concerned Richard Brothers very much in the years after 1795 was his mission as the chosen Prince of the Hebrews, who would lead the Jews back to the Holy Land. He became absorbed instead in such things as listing the crops to be grown there: parsnips, carrots, potatoes, cabbage, and cauliflower. "I am particular in enumerating all these things, as I know what I write will be universally read, universally regarded."[20]

The volume in which this pathetic statement was made is signed, "God's Anointed King, and Shiloh of the Hebrews." Brothers had explained earlier that he was "denominated the Shiloh, or Collector of the Jews in the latter time of the world."[21] This is probably where Joanna Southcott got the idea for the mission that concluded her own prophetic career, when in 1814 she announced that she was miraculously pregnant. She would give birth to Shiloh, the second Messiah, who would lead the Jews back to Palestine. The idea that Shiloh was a person, let alone Richard Brothers or the divine son of Joanna Southcott, rested on a peculiar reading of Genesis 49:10 in the

18. Richard Brothers, *Letter from Mr. Brothers to Miss Cott . . . with an Address to the Members of His Brittanic Majesty's Council and through Them to All the Governments and People on Earth* (London, 1798), pp. 89–126. See also Brothers, *Description of Jerusalem*, pp. 1–77; and Brothers, *The New Covenant between God and His People* (London, 1830) [written in 1806], p. 21.

19. Brothers, *Description of Jerusalem*, pp. 82, 108, 137.

20. Brothers, *Address to the Members of His Brittanic Majesty's Council*, p. 83.

21. Ibid., pp. 53, 200; Brothers, *Wisdom and Duty*, p. 9.

Authorized Version. The verse said that sword would not pass away from Judah "until Shiloh come."

The question of who or what was meant by Shiloh was not asked by the two prophets only. Joseph Priestley, among others, had discussed whether Shiloh was a person or a place in the pages of the *Theological Repository* in the 1780s. The Baptist preacher John Gill, whose prophetic sermons were reprinted in the excitement of 1794, had used the title Shiloh to refer to the Messiah who would come again and restore the Jews to their kingdom. Mrs. Piozzi thought Napoleon had appropriated the title for himself. She wrote that Napoleon had called the Jews together and promised to restore them to Palestine in the year 1800. He had struck off many portraits of himself with *Shiloh* printed under them. A friend of hers had bought one in London, and, added Mrs. Piozzi: "she has it in Possession *now*."[22]

With the possible exception of Shiloh, there is no evidence that the ideas that Richard Brothers put forward during his last years influenced any but his handful of followers. These few never constituted a sect, and it is impossible to say how many there were. Brothers himself described the arrest of seven or eight individuals in Yorkshire in 1800, "to whom God gave by revelation a knowledge of myself as restorer of the Hebrews."[23] The less committed of his followers must have drifted away after the prophet's arrest and the "disconfirmation" of 4 June. A combination of factors—more stringent police measures, increasing public support for the government's anti-French policy, and lessened social and economic tensions—combined to make Brothers's message of revolutionary millenarianism less attractive after the summer of 1795 than it had been before. The flurry of interest in the fulfillment of prophecy in contemporary political events also declined; there were many fewer pamphlets and sermons on the themes that had engaged so much interest in 1794 and 1795.

The inner core of supporters remained faithful to the Revealed Prince of the Hebrews. The two "witnesses," William Bryan and John Wright, seem to have fallen away, but Halhed, Riebau, Sharp, and Captain Hanchett continued to believe in Brothers and to agitate for his release from the madhouse. Brothers even acquired

---

22. Piozzi, *Marginalia*, p. 115; John Gill, *The Sure Performance of Prophecy* (London, 1794), p. 30; delivered 1 January 1755. See also Joseph Priestley, *The Theological and Miscellaneous Works of Joseph Priestley*, ed. John Towill Rutt, 25 vols. (London: Smallfield, 1817-32), 7; 537-38.
23. Brothers, *Description of Jerusalem*, p. 165.

some new followers, who wrote testimonies in his behalf. These included John Finlayson, a young clerk named Basil Bruce, and an eccentric Leeds merchant named George Turner. Like the prophet himself, Turner received messages directly from God, which he wrote down and published.[24] Between 1795 and 1801, the messages were concerned mainly with demands for Brothers's release, in order that he might accomplish his mission. Gradually, after 1801, Turner and a number of other prominent disciples took up the rather different prophetic message promulgated by a domestic servant in the West Country, Joanna Southcott. It is the same pattern we saw in the drift of Suzette Labrousse's supporters into the very different orbit of Catherine Théot. Neither did the Midwestern sect described in *When Prophecy Fails* abandon its faith in miracles and wonders; instead, its adherents drifted variously into dianetics, spiritualism, and the reincarnationist teachings of the Edgar Cayce Foundation.[25] In the case of Brothers's followers, the intention was not initially to break with the prophet. Rather, they were attracted by Joanna Southcott's renewed assurances that the millennium was indeed at hand. Brothers's communications were by this time limited to mad proclamations of his kingly role addressed to his fellow monarchs and potentates. Southcott's utterances were very different. They were produced by a kind of automatic writing, usually directed by God himself, often in the form of inelegant, but rather charming, doggerel verse. Instead of Brothers's rather wearing message of doom and political upheaval, Southcott provided a more soothing combination of English patriotism and Methodistical piety.

It was in the spring of 1801 that word of a prophetess in Exeter first reached London. Joanna Southcott had been receiving and transcribing divine messages since 1792, when she was forty-two years old. She now began corresponding with interested individuals throughout England, and a delegation of seven persons, six of whom had been followers of Brothers, went to Exeter to interview her. They became convinced. William Sharp, one of the seven, had a large box made to hold the prophecies she had been accumulating since 1792. In May 1802, she and the box came to London. Like Richard Brothers

---

24. George Turner, *A Testimony to the Prophetical Mission of Richard Brothers* (1795; reprint ed., Leeds, 1798); Turner, *Communications of the Holy Spirit of God* (Leeds, 1798); Turner, *A Call to All Worlds* (Leeds, 1800); Turner, *A Vindication of Richard Brothers' Prophecies, for the Honour of God* (Leeds, 1801); and Basil Bruce, *An Exhortation to All People to Forsake the Sin of Swearing Oaths* (London, 1798).
25. Festinger et al., *When Prophecy Fails*, pp. 192–98, 230–33.

before her, Joanna lived in Paddington, received visitors, and had great quantities of her writings published as cheap pamphlets, which were sold throughout England. The Quaker physician Dr. Lettsom wrote a friend that he had seen in the City of London a sign on which was printed in gold letters, " 'To be had here, the Prophecies of Joanna Southcott.' " He stopped, bought one of the thirty or so titles for sale, and found it "unintelligible."[26]

Gradually, Southcott supplanted Brothers in the loyalties of his followers. Initially, however, she was perfectly content with prophetic coexistence. Only in 1806—the year, perhaps not coincidentally, that Brothers was released from the asylum—did she repudiate him and his prophetic claims. Brothers *had* been a prophet, but his inflated pretensions for himself and his complaints that God had treated him harshly showed that he was one no longer. Brothers's prophecies of 1791-92, Joanna wrote, had come "perfectly true." He must therefore have had "some visitation from the Lord, or he could not have foretold the things he did." According to what some of his former disciples had told her, his believers at first had been drawn to him "from the truth that followed concerning the war, and left to time the things they did not understand though they said that many things in his writings stumbled them; but they were afraid to draw too hasty a judgment."[27]

Southcott wrote this in 1806, but her letters of 1801, written to men who were still loyal to Brothers, took much the same position. She also maintained a certain distance from him and declined an offer from one of his followers to send her copies of Brothers's prophecies, explaining: "I never read any book at all; but write by the spirit as I am directed. . . . All I know of Mr. Brothers is, what was explained to me from my dream."[28] The dream, she wrote to William Sharp in another letter, was of horses and wagons that passed close by her and signified "the Spirit of the Lord in the hearts of men to press her forward." When her own writings were proven to have been from God, "if they do not clear our friend Brothers they will bring all the judgments pronounced on themselves."[29]

26. John Lettsom, *Memoirs of the Life and Writings of the Late John Coakley Lettsom . . . with a Selection from His Correspondence*, ed. Thomas Joseph Pettigrew, 3 vols. (London, 1817), 2: 145.
27. Joanna Southcott, *Answer to Mr. Brothers's Book, Published in September 1806, and Observations on His Former Writings* (London, 1806), pp. 16–17.
28. Joanna Southcott, *Divine and Spiritual Letters of Prophecies, Sent to Reverend Divines and Other Spiritual Good Men* (London, 1801), p. 11. Because of a divine command that this book be exactly 48 pages long, the title is on p. 48.
29. Ibid., p. 22.

Joanna developed the significance of the dream more fully in a book she published the next year. God told her that the wagon represented Brothers himself:

> I said that Brothers broke the ground all through;
> The heavy-loaded Waggons so did go.

Thus he had cleared the road for those who would follow him doing the Lord's work. But now, God said, Brothers's mind was "heavy laden." In prison, "the Powers of Darkness" were tempting him to pride and to envy of Joanna, for he feared he would not be "worshiped above all men on Earth," if her prophecies were believed. God continued:

> But now I tell thee I will free the Man,
> If he'll confess he wrote by SATAN'S Hand;
> And every Word therein he now will Blame,
> I'll free the Man and Satan put to Shame.[30]

Thus Southcott's prophetic mission did not simply supplant Brothers's; it encompassed and transcended it. She absolutely denied that he was to rule as a king over anybody. A letter included a query from God: "Then whom will you crown in my stead? Will ye trust in a man that cannot deliver himself? That hath no name given him above another name? For ye are all my brothers." "The name of Mr. Brothers stumbles himself and all men,"[31] Southcott wrote in another letter. Brothers had suffered imprisonment, but so had she: "There is a great mystery in his having been in prison near seven years; and I have suffered imprisonment in mind and heart, in temptation and persecution, in sorrows more than pen can paint or heart conceive, for near ten years."[32] As these passages clearly suggest, the contest between the two prophets was an unequal one. Without calling into question the genuineness of Southcott's belief in the divine origin of her messages, they did have a way of subtly, not blatantly, wooing Brothers's followers away from him. Her claims for herself, at least until the Shiloh fiasco a decade later, were more modest and vague than Brothers's. His pretensions and his inflexibility made him an easy target.

---

30. Joanna Southcott, *A Communication Given to Joanna, in Answer to Mr. Brothers's Last Book, Published the End of This Year, 1802* (n.p., 1802), pp. 8, 11, 16.
31. Southcott, *Divine and Spiritual Letters*, p. 45.
32. Joanna Southcott, *The Second Part of the Continuation of Joanna Southcott's Prophecies* (London, 1802; reprint ed., 1813), p. 68; this letter, addressed to "a London Gentleman," is dated 20 October 1801.

William Sharp and George Turner became followers of Southcott in 1801, but they did not abandon Brothers until 1806. There is some evidence that Brothers and a few of his disciples forced the choice between Southcott and himself. A letter from Joanna to the Reverend Stanhope Bruce indicates that George Riebau was one of those who had received a copy of some of her prophecies in 1801, and he is listed as a seller of one of her first publications. Beginning in 1802, however, his name ceases to appear in her pamphlets as a distributor.[33] Also in 1802, Southcott told of a visit that friends of Brothers, including one man of property (Hanchett?), had paid to the widow of Basil Bruce, Stanhope Bruce's son and one of the first of the Brothers circle to become interested in Southcott. Basil Bruce died suddenly on the eve of the trip to Exeter to see the prophetess. The "man of property" told his widow that Bruce's death had been the judgment of God "on account of his belief in these writings." Other disciples had written letters to Mrs. Bruce and had also "conveyed lies to Mr. Brothers himself, to cause *him* to attack her if possible."[34]

Brother's attack on Southcott is in the *Dissertation on the Fall of Eve*, published late in 1802. He never referred to her by name, but those who were familiar with the situation would surely have known that she was intended. Brothers wrote that the woman clothed with the sun mentioned in the twelfth chapter of Revelation was none other than his own future bride, "the Queen of a Man that is metaphorically represented as the Sun—the Restorer of the Hebrews."[35] When she fled into the wilderness, she would simply accompany her husband to Jerusalem when he ascended his throne there. He disposed of Southcott's claim to be the woman who would free the world from sin by arguing at great length that the snake in Genesis 3 was simply a snake and not Satan at all.

The prophetess responded immediately. Like many of her prophecies, this one took the form of rhymed verses communicated to her by the Lord. God was furious that Brothers had made him the author of Eve's temptations:

> And if that way the Prophet do appear,
> I tell you soon he'll feel the furious Bear:
> For that's the way he never shall turn back,

33. Eugene Patrick Wright, comp., *A Catalog of the Joanna Southcott Collection at the University of Texas* (Austin: Humanities Research Center, 1968), p. 12.
34. Joanna Southcott, *The Answer of the Lord to the Powers of Darkness* (London, 1802), p. 24 n.
35. Brothers, *Letter to His Majesty, . . . with a Dissertation, on the Fall of Eve*, pp. 60–61.

The Bear shall meet him, and his Bones shall break;
And he shall never see the Promis'd Land!
The Woman's seed must every Bliss command.[36]

It was at this point also that Southcott appropriated to her followers the identity with the Jews on which Brothers had based some of his own claims:

To *Circumcision* next I'll come,
A thing I ordered to be done
For Man his Wisdom he must lost
When I begin to pay the cost;
And his foreknowledge take away,
In Circumcision all will lay.

One could quibble with God's grammar in these lines, but we must remember that he was very angry with Brothers. The prophet, all alone in his prison, had succumbed to the temptations of Satan, and

Deep are the Sorrows he would bring on man,
Had I not sav'd them by the Woman's hand.

"I shall not bring in My Kingdom," the Lord continued, "to raise one to a prince, and the rest to be his subjects."[37]

The twelfth chapter of Revelation, around which part of the dispute between the prophets centered, also contains the Beast with seven heads and ten horns that Priestley, Halhed, and Brothers himself had so eagerly identified with the "kings *now*" of the Revolutionary era. It is significant that there is no indication in the controversy of 1802 that the political interpretation of prophecy had importance any longer.

The same indifference to the political situation is found in William Sharp's introduction to Southcott's *Divine and Spiritual Communications* of 1803. Her book, he wrote, proved that Christ's Second Coming must be "in Spirit," that men might be freed from the power of evil. A woman, Eve, had brought the knowledge of evil into the world, so a woman must also bring the knowledge of good. Sharp's earlier radicalism had been transformed. The light of spiritual love must spread through the world. Human learning must disappear, unless it promoted the love of God and of mankind. Ministers of the Church of England would disseminate the "divine knowledge" that God revealed through Joanna. Eventually the whole

36. Southcott, *Communication Given to Joanna*, p. 4.   37. Ibid., pp. 6, 10, 11.

world would be saved, "but the English nation will be the first redeemed."[38]

William Wetherell, who had testified to his belief in the mission of Richard Brothers in 1795, wrote a testimony to Joanna after he had become a Southcottian. God "has sent his Son in Spirit to a Woman, as predicted in Scripture," in order to reconcile all religious differences and to bring the whole world under one faith. "This grand work must commence in One Country first, and England is that happy Land."[39]

The process of redemption consisted of the "sealing" of the faithful through the issuing of squares of paper on which were written, "the Sealed of the Lord, . . . to be made Heirs of God and Joint Heirs with Jesus Christ."[40] They were signed by Joanna Southcott and by the believer, then folded like an envelope, closed with wax, and sealed with a seal that the prophetess had picked up some years before at divine command. The scriptural inspiration was the third verse of the seventh chapter of Revelation—the same verse that led Catherine Théot to initiate ceremonies of kisses: "Hurt not the earth . . . till we have sealed the servants of our God in their foreheads."

At this point in her career, Southcott's conception of her divinely ordained role was very similar to what Catherine Théot's had been. Joanna was the woman promised in Revelation to free the world from the burden of sin and to give the faithful the assurance that they would be preserved after the Second Coming. Southcott spent much of 1803 traveling through western and northern England issuing the sealed letters. One effect must have been to isolate Brothers still further from what was by now the dominant current in millenarian popular religion in England.

The sealing, along with other issues and controversies, occupied Southcott for the next several years. In 1806, the year that Brothers regained his freedom, she began to attack him again. God told her that "every date has passed, and none of these things fulfilled which he said was spoken by ME to be accomplished at the time he mentioned." Brothers had fallen because he had ascribed to himself "the honour and power" that was God's alone.[41]

38. William Sharp, intro. to Joanna Southcott, *Divine and Spiritual Communications*, pp. v–vii, ix–x.
39. William Wetherell, *A Testimony of Joanna Southcott* (London, 1804), p. 10.
40. Quoted in George R. Balleine, *Past Finding Out: The Tragic Story of Joanna Southcott and Her Successors* (New York: Macmillan Co., 1956), pp. 40–43.
41. Southcott, *Communication in Answer to Mr. Brothers's Book*, pp. 1, 11.

This *Communication* shows that three of Brothers's most prominent followers remained loyal to him until 1806 but thereafter began to fall away. One was William Sharp, who had written Brothers not long before, but the letter had been returned unopened. Another was Nathaniel Brassey Halhed. He had quarreled with Brothers, Southcott said, because Brothers "persists it is the Lord who has deceived him." The third was George Turner of Leeds. He too had tried to remain faithful to both Brothers and Southcott. Now he conceded that he had been deceived. Fifteen years later, after he, like Brothers, had been confined in a madhouse, Turner was planning to go to Jerusalem (as soon as Shiloh came) and rule there in splendor. He pronounced anathema on the teachings of his former leader, declaring that God had told him: "Of R——B——'s visions, or any pretended teachings that he may have, I give him my command, the Lord, that he gives no more visions or teachings in my name."[42]

In one of the notebooks of unpublished communications now in the Southcott Collection at the University of Texas, there is the report of a visit that Southcott, Sharp, and two other followers paid to Halhed at his home in Pall Mall on Saturday, 11 October 1806, after attending Charles James Fox's funeral. The occasion indicates that the political battles of a decade before had not been totally forgotten. The communication is particularly interesting in two respects. In the first place, it shows that Halhed had retained his millenarian convictions. Like Joseph Priestley, he had simply postponed the glorious epoch beyond the lifetime of his own generation. They might not see the millennium, but their children would. In the second place, it is clear that Southcott used substantially the same arguments with him that she had used in her published writings. Satan had deceived men like him into following Brothers along the wrong path. Like him, they had expected some earthly glory when instead they should have been honoring God and longing for his coming, even if they could not expect to be alive when it occurred. Their reward would come in heaven.[43] Joanna Southcott had not in fact strayed very far from the Methodist and Church of England preachers she had heard in Exeter when she was young.

The legacy of French Revolutionary millenarianism and of Richard Brothers survived into the nineteenth century in the prophecies of

42. George Turner, *Wonderful Prophecies by George Turner, the Servant of God, Being a Call to the Jews to Return*, 2 vols. (London, 1818–20), 2: 63.
43. Joanna Southcott, "Answer to Halhed," Southcott Collection, University of Texas, Austin, ss. 23–26.

Joanna Southcott, but the tradition underwent some profound changes. When Southcott wrote of politics, it was often in such lines as

> To France the ruin it will come,
> If to the Gospel they don't instant turn.[44]

When she wrote of "signs of the times," it was in vague and hackneyed terms: "And now discern from the earthquakes abroad, and the falling of the mountain, and all the wars and tumults going on, and see how my Gospel is fulfilling . . . but as this nation hath been warned, and hath been invited, and sees the stroke abroad, I tell thee, when it cometh upon this land it will come suddenly . . . in a way and manner not expected.[45]

Not long after her death, a former disciple wrote of Joanna Southcott, "Bold as were her claims, . . . she generally contrived to elude us in an impenetrable cloud."[46] Her message was that the French Revolution was the work of God, but not in the sense that Suzette Labrousse, Richard Brothers, and even Catherine Théot had conceived of it. The Lord had visited the nations surrounding England with calamities for fifteen years "as a warning to *this* land." England would be the first nation to be redeemed, and then England would awaken the rest of the world that the Beast might be destroyed. But the Beast was not the papacy or monarchy any more than it was Jacobinism or religious dissent. The Beast was sin. Thus Joanna Southcott belongs as securely in the "onslaught of respectability" of the pre-Victorian decades as Mrs. Trimmer or Hannah More. She expressed this most clearly in her writings of 1801–6, before the excitement that surrounded Shiloh's birth diverted her attention and that of her disciples from the very conventional and traditional import of her prophecies. The "Long-wished-for Revolution," she wrote in 1806, was not one of nations and kings, for "sin and sorrow went on the same." The French had destroyed their king, and all they got was a more powerful monarch in his place. Micah had promised that swords would be beaten into plowshares and universal peace would reign, but this prophecy could not be fulfilled *"by any revolution of man against kings, emperors, popes, or whatever heathens may be, that the nations may revolt against."*[47]

---

44. Southcott, *Divine and Spiritual Letters*, p. 44.
45. Southcott, *Answer to Mr. Brothers's Book*, p. 21.
46. Evans, *Sketch of the Various Denominations*, pp. 282–84.
47. Southcott, *The Long-wished-for Revolution*, p. 3.

Conclusion

IN BOTH France and England, popular revolutionism had to find expression initially in the values and conceptions of traditional culture. The language and imagery of millenarianism may have served as a medium for the reception of what we can recognize today as a modern revolutionary consciousness. In one sense, millenarians gave expression to convictions and doctrines that had changed remarkably little over the centuries. They could pray for the new heavens and new earth that Peter's epistle had promised, they could discuss the identity of the Beast and the Whore whose destruction would precede the Second Coming, or they could await the miraculous deliverer, whether Jesus or Elias. They could work for the conversion of the Jews and the reunion of all men in "one sheepfold under one shepherd." Yet it has been the peculiarity of millenarianism that it is concerned with the transformation of this world. The conviction that the literal millennium was at hand might be set aside—both Pierre Pontard and Joseph Priestley seem to have done so—but the deeper sense of a regeneration that would be both spiritual and social was not abandoned. It was a very similar quality of religious urgency that gave to the whole of the French Revolution its exceptionally compelling power to arouse hopes and fears. In the 1790s, the millenarian literature produced in France and England was only one facet of a far more generally held conviction that the world was in process of being transformed, for better or worse.

We have seen that millenarianism in the eighteenth century was one of a number of cultural currents that articulated the sense that changes of cosmic significance were in the offing. The coming of the French Revolution had the effect of giving awesome reality to what had before been only speculation. The surge of interest in prophecy of all kinds was one indication of the need to fit what was new and unprecedented into categories that were old and familiar. As a result, the vague pronouncements of Suzette Labrousse could enjoy, for a brief period, considerable prominence. Her prophecies contained ideals that had been part of popular religion for many centuries. The church would be restored to its original purity and would embrace the entire world; France would assume her moral primacy over all nations; "the great" would be brought down and "the lowly" raised up. She thus provided a comforting message in the anxious first year of the Revolution. Her discourses and pamphlets, rambling, disjointed, and credulous as they are, attempt with some success to translate the developments of political revolution into the language of popular religion. One can dismiss her obsession with her "mission" as fantasy and agree with Pontard that her pilgrimage to Rome was "respectable folly." What cannot be ignored is the way in which her prophetic declarations could articulate and give Christian form to the revolutionary consciousness of 1790.

For her small circle of believers, Catherine Théot provided the same kind of comfortable words in the Paris of the Terror. In its essentials, she preached the same combination of piety and patriotism as Labrousse. God would restore a religion "entirely pure," and France's armies would bring peace and equality to the whole world. Once again, the metaphors and imagery of traditional piety could make the experience of revolution comprehensible.

In England, the intermingling of religion and politics in the revolutionary crisis was far more evident than in France. Millenarian ideas were more respectable, and the free circulation of popular literature meant that they could be readily disseminated. As in France, millenarianism was simply one of several cultural currents that expressed the sense that changes of cosmic significance were imminent. The popular fascination with earthquakes was one expression of this notion, and it was a simple transposition to see the Revolution as the greatest of "earthquakes." They were divine warnings, but at the same time they provided assurance that Providence was at work in human history.

One of the more surprising features of the popular culture of the revolutionary period was the remarkable surge of interest in old prophecies. In England, where they had been collected and printed for two centuries, prophecies became a topic of intense popular interest in the 1790s. Applying the prophecies to the French Revolution required selection and interpretation, and here complications developed. Instead of communicating a comforting sense of divine precognition, the prophetic literature forced difficult choices. Events had placed Protestant England on the side of Catholic Europe, against Revolutionary France. Where, then, was the Beast? As war was followed by economic hardship and social and political discontent, the religious justifications for the government's foreign policy, which the government itself had generated through propaganda and national days of prayer, came more and more into question. It is in this context that Richard Brothers's significance is to be found. His ideas, his rhetoric, and his prophetic style were very different from those of the French prophetesses; but, like them, he was responding to the wholly unfamiliar events of the Revolution by employing the modalities of traditional religion. And like Labrousse and Théot, Brothers owed his prominence far less to his own abilities than to pronouncements that transmitted a new political consciousness in familiar religious imagery.

The more peculiar features of Brothers's revelation all had their base in English popular religion. His claim to be Prince of the Hebrews, come to lead the hidden Jews to their homeland, derived from an identification of England and Israel that predated the Commonwealth. The meticulous attention to biblical chronology was at least as old, and the fascination with natural disasters as omens from on high was immemorial. Despite his discovery of Jewry among the English, Brothers's attacks on royal policy and his predictions of national disaster denied to his prophetic stance the sanction of patriotism that both Labrousse and Théot could claim. When Southcott and her disciples restored England to divine favor in the very different political climate of the Napoleonic wars, they were only returning to the norm in popular millenarianism.

Brothers, Pontard, Count Grabianka, and Joseph Priestley had all described a perfected society that did not necessarily have to await divine action. Revolution and millennium both affirmed the possibility that heaven could be built on earth. For millenarians, the New Jerusalem was to be accomplished finally by God's intervention, but equally basic was the idea that an earthly millennium was indeed possible and that men could help to bring it about. And since the preparation for the millennium was to take place within history, among the nations of men, it was neither inconceivable nor inconsistent (at least in their eyes) that some millenarians should devote their energies to accomplishing the political revolution and thus in a sense participate in divine Providence. Dom Gerle's and Pierre Pontard's political and journalistic activities in the National and Legislative Assemblies are examples of the sort of activism that a religiously-inspired revolutionism could catalyze; quite possibly, Gerle's retreat into mysticism was the result of the frustration of his ecclesiastical and political career. What is important to emphasize is that he was neither more nor less a millenarian after 1792; the messages of Labrousse and Théot continued to provide a comprehensible explanation of what had happened to him and to France. The same might be said of men like William Sharp, Joseph Priestley,

Nathaniel Halhed, and if we knew more of his revolutionary activities, Count Grabianka. In every case, millenarianism offered a coherent and compelling ideology with which they could justify their political efforts. One could say essentially the same of Karl Marx's career: having discovered that revolution was inevitable, Marx devoted his life to accomplishing the inevitable.

While we cannot say with any certainty how or why it should have happened, it is a striking feature of the socialisms of the 1830s and 1840s that they were characterized by the same mixture of religious imagery and secular activism that we have seen in the millenarianism of the French Revolutionary period.[1] The same combination of the political and the spiritual and the same mood of imminence and urgency are evident in the pronouncements of Robert Owen and Etienne Cabet as in those of Joseph Priestley and Pierre Pontard. Owen was no Christian, let alone a millenarian, yet John Harrison has argued that the continued prevalence of what Harrison calls "a 'culture' of prophecy and eschatology" in post-Napoleonic England led Owen to present his message of social reform in language and imagery redolent of millenarianism.[2]

As for Cabet, whom Engels in 1847 described as the leading representative of the French working class, he, too, found it effective to communicate his conception of democratic communism in religious language, although he was no more a Christian than was Owen. He might call his New Jerusalem Icaria, but like Owen's "New Moral World," the vision and the ruling metaphor were essentially millenarian. They reflected a social and political consciousness that was new, but which could be communicated only in the familiar language of traditional religion and popular culture. "Materialism and belief in the class struggle were largely foreign to this culture," Christopher Johnson has written. "Christianity was not, and neither, thanks to the French Revolution, were such Jacobin concepts as dedication, virtue, and dignity."[3] It was surely no coincidence that one of the centers of Cabetian communism was Lyons, where Convulsionaries

1. Henri Desroches, "Messianismes et utopies: Note sur les origines du socialisme occidentale," *Archives de sociologie religieuse*, no. 8 (1959), pp. 31–46; Jean-Baptiste Duroselle, *Les débuts du catholicisme sociale en France* (1822–70) (Paris: Presses universitaires de France, 1951), pp. 127–53; and D. G. Charlton, *Secular Religions in France* (London: Oxford University Press, 1963), chap. 4.
2. John F. C. Harrison, *Quest for the New Moral World: Robert Owen and the Owenites in Britain and America* (New York: Charles Scribner's Sons, 1969), pp. 100, 133.
3. Christopher Johnson, "Communism and the Working Class before Marx: The Icarian Experience," *American Historical Review* 76 (1971): 688.

and Masonic millenarians had found a haven in the eighteenth century.

By pointing out the unique capacity of millenarian doctrines to carry a message of political revolutionism, Marxist historians have provided an invaluable insight. The traditions of biblical prophecy and popular religion provided a whole vocabulary for transmitting a new sociopolitical consciousness born of eighteenth-century thought and the experience of the French Revolution. Rather than call these millenarians prepolitical, it might be better to say that they expressed in an archaic and transitory fashion an advocacy of political revolution that was both concrete and potentially activist.

There was an additional dimension to the varieties of millenarianism that the era of the French Revolution engendered. They demonstrate what the sociologist Yonina Talmon, in her comparative study of millenarian movements, called "the potency and partial independence of the religious factor."[4] Historians are coming to recognize that the eighteenth century was in certain respects a period of religious revival. A number of religious movements emerged that reemphasized emotionalism and the experience of spiritual regeneration, among them Methodism, Pietism, Hasidism, and Convulsionism. The century also saw, among Protestants, Catholics, and Jews, a search for spiritual experience in the traditions of mysticism.

In the teachings of Swedenborg and among the various bodies of mystical Masons, mysticism merged with other sources of spiritual enlightenment—animal magnetism, mesmerist séances, occultism, and cabalism—to provide the new revelations of the divine that eighteenth-century "men of desire" so earnestly sought. For them, the pieties of orthodox religion and deism were equally unsatisfying. Millenarianism was one more current in the religious revival of the later eighteenth century. To some, it offered one more demonstration that the world could confidently expect profound changes that would involve not only the reorganization of society and politics but spiritual revival, too. As we have seen, those who adopted millenarianism frequently continued to seek further revelations through séances or the occult, or they might continue their spiritual pilgrimages through sects and movements in which millenarian doctrines were not present or where (as in the case of Swedenborgians) they differed profoundly from the traditional notion of the millennium.

4. Yonina Talmon, "Millenarian Movements," *European Journal of Sociology* 7 (1966): 190.

The Revolution gave urgency and tangible reality to millenarian convictions, but in the cases of most of the individuals whose careers we have traced, it did not *make* them millenarians. Suzette Labrousse, Catherine Théot, Count Grabianka, and William Bryan were all convinced well before the outbreak of the French Revolution that they were bearers of divine revelations, called to aid in the spiritual redemption of mankind. They all welcomed the Revolution as, in effect, the confirmation of their own missions. In the case of Joseph Priestley, it was his distinctive combination of piety, rationalism, and biblical literalism that led him in the 1780s to believe in the imminence of the millennium. It is true that Priestley always associated that event with political revolution, but so had the prophet Daniel. And we should remember that for Priestley, the "revolution" he envisioned was first and foremost the restoration of primitive Christianity through the destruction of the false and corrupting alliance of church and state. Pierre Pontard may have been led to millenarianism in a similar fashion. Like Dom Gerle, he found in the pronouncements of Labrousse the vision of a spiritualized and universal Christianity superior to the church he himself had served with some distinction. Only after his own career had gone sour did Pontard come to emphasize the political implications of the millennium.

For all these individuals, the need to believe in the millennium was essentially a religious need, related to the facts of social and political experience, shaped by them, but not arising out of them.

In French Revolutionary millenarianism, we have one dimension of what Pierre Goubert has called "the slow death of the old regime" in the century after 1750.[5] Just as traditional social and political structures underwent a gradual but decisive process of transformation into those of industrial capitalism and mass democracy, so did systems of belief move toward a divergence between the secular and the religious. In the transitional era of the French Revolution, a new mental universe of revolutionary political action merged with ancient piety and religious belief in a combination that was transitory, unstable, and ultimately, doomed.

---

5. Quoted in Gerald J. Cavenaugh, "The Present State of French Revolutionary Historiography: Alfred Cobban and Beyond," *French Historical Studies* 7 (1972): 606.

Index

THE JOHNS HOPKINS UNIVERSITY PRESS

This book was composed in Baskerville text and Weiss Roman display type by Jones Composition Company from a design by Susan Bishop. It was printed and bound by Universal Lithographers, Inc.

Library of Congress Cataloging in Publication Data

Garrett, Clarke, 1935–
    Respectable folly.

    Includes bibliographical references and index.
    1. Millennialism—France. 2. Millennialism—England.
3. France—History—Revolution. I. Title.
BR845.G36   209'.44   74-24378

ISBN 0-8018-1618-1